CAPITALISM AND DESIRE

CAPITALISM AND DESIRE

The Psychic Cost of Free Markets

Todd McGowan

COLUMBIA UNIVERSITY PRESS

NEW YORK

Columbia University Press
Publishers Since 1893
New York   Chichester, West Sussex
cup.columbia.edu
Copyright © 2016 Columbia University Press
All rights reserved
Library of Congress Cataloging-in-Publication Data

Names: McGowan, Todd, author.
Title: Capitalism and desire: the psychic cost of free markets / Todd McGowan.
Description: New York: Columbia University Press, 2016. | Includes bibliographical
references and index.
Identifiers: LCCN 2016005309| ISBN 9780231178723 (cloth: alk. paper) | ISBN
9780231542210 (e-book)
Subjects: LCSH: Capitalism—Psychological aspects. | Capitalism—Social aspects. |
Psychoanalysis—Philosophy.
Classification: LCC HB501 .M55347 2016 | DDC 330.12/2019—dc23
LC record available at https://lccn.loc.gov/2016005309

♾

COVER DESIGN: Mary Ann Smith

References to websites (URLs) were accurate at the time of writing. Neither the author nor
Columbia University Press is responsible for URLs that may have expired or changed since
the manuscript was prepared.

For Bea Bookchin
the only anticapitalist I've ever met

Contents

Acknowledgments

Chapters 2 and 3 contain work revised from earlier publications. Thanks to Ashgate Publishing for permission to reprint "Driven Into the Public: The Psychic Constitution of Space," in *Architecture Post Mortem: The Diastolic Architecture of Decline, Dystopia, and Death*, eds. Charles David Bertolini, Simone Brott, and Donald Kunze (London: Ashgate, 2013), 15–30. Thanks also to Wayne State University Press for permission to reprint "The Capitalist Gaze," *Discourse: Journal for Theoretical Studies in Media and Culture* 35, no. 1: 3–23, copyright © 2013 Wayne State University Press.

More than anyone else, Wendy Lochner at Columbia University Press was the engine for the publication of this book. She is an incredibly thoughtful and conscientious editor, and her efforts to sustain the publication of theoretical works today are unequalled.

I also appreciate the work that Christine Dunbar at Columbia University Press did in order to help this book to appear.

Thanks to Dashiell and Theo Neroni for their constant insights into how capitalism insinuates itself into the structure of our desire.

The students at the University of Vermont played a decisive role in helping me to think through the psychic appeal of capitalism. Ryan Engley has been especially influential on my thinking, especially concerning the theoretical underpinnings of the banal.

My film studies colleagues at the University of Vermont—Deb Ellis, Dave Jenemann, Hilary Neroni, Sarah Nilsen, and Hyon Joo Yoo—have created a stimulating environment in which to teach and write.

The Theory Reading Group—Joseph Acquisto, Bea Bookchin, Hilary Neroni, John Waldron, and Hyon Joo Yoo—have made the University of Vermont a place of respite from the demand for success.

Quentin Martin has helped to direct my thinking about capitalism through his trenchant critiques of it and has always been available to provide equally trenchant critiques of various chapters.

I appreciate Jean Wyatt's careful readings of the first chapters of the book. Without Jean's help, they would be twice as long and half as legible.

Thanks to Danny Cho, Joan Copjec, Anna Kornbluh, Donald Kunze, Juan Pablo Luccheli, Hugh Manon, Jonathan Mulrooney, Ken Reinhard, Frances Restuccia, Rob Rushing, Russell Sbriglia, Fabio Vighi, and Louis-Paul Willis, who have provided a theoretical milieu in which no one is content but everyone is satisfied.

Jennifer Friedlander and Henry Krips have continually nudged me to think in directions that I hadn't foreseen, while at the same time giving me credit for the new turn.

Thanks also to Slavoj Žižek for his obscenely generous help in finding the appropriate place for this book to come out.

I would like to also thank Richard Boothby, whom I encountered while in the middle of this project. After that encounter, which I experienced as a miracle, everything was different for me because there was someone else, cut from precisely the same cloth, who could interrupt my dogmatic slumbers.

Mari Ruti provided the most thorough and thoughtful reading that anyone has ever given me. The book took a great leap forward thanks to her contribution.

Sheila Kunkle has supported this project in innumerable ways. It would be unthinkable without her existence in the world, and she remains my fundamental co-conspirator.

I owe the greatest debt to the three people who guide my thinking: Walter Davis, Paul Eisenstein, and Hilary Neroni. They are in the capitalist world but not of it.

CAPITALISM AND DESIRE

Introduction

After Injustice and Repression

PSYCHOANALYSIS OF CAPITALISM

Can we psychoanalyze capitalism? Freud himself would probably have had his doubts. Toward the end of *Civilization and Its Discontents*, he questions whether or not one can psychoanalyze an entire society and concludes that one cannot. The problem is not a practical one. Even though one cannot submit an entire society or an economic system to a series of psychoanalytic sessions, every social order and every economic system speaks through articulations that betray its psychic resonances, and we can analyze these articulations from the perspective of psychoanalytic theory. For Freud, the barrier to psychoanalyzing a society is a theoretical one. The psychoanalyst can't condemn an entire society as neurotic, for instance, because this diagnosis depends on a standard of normalcy with which to contrast the neurosis. But the irony of this conclusion coming in a book that psychoanalyzes social order as such must have escaped Freud. He is able to perform this act because no social order is complete and perfectly self-identical. Rather than being self-contained and thus impervious to critical analysis, every society opens up a space outside itself from which one can analyze it and make a judgment on it. The same holds for capitalism as a socioeconomic structure. The space for the psychoanalysis of capitalism exists within the incompletion of the capitalist system.

If we accept the verdict that we cannot psychoanalyze capitalism as a socioeconomic system, then we implicitly accede to the arguments of the apologists for capitalism. Defenders of the system claim that capitalism is a function of human nature—that there is a perfect overlap between capitalism and human nature—and thus that there exists no space from which one might criticize it. From this perspective, any foundational critique is inherently fanciful and utopian. But much more than other socioeconomic systems, capitalism necessarily relies on its incompleteness and on its opening to the outside in order to function. One can psychoanalyze capitalism though the very gaps the system itself produces and through its reliance on what exceeds it. It is the case, however, that the practice of psychoanalysis has not always been equal to this task.

Many critics of capitalism associate psychoanalysis with capitalism. It functions, according to this critique, as one of capitalism's ideological handmaidens. It has the effect of shoring up potential dissidents and transforming rebellious subjects into more quiescent ones. This tendentious understanding of psychoanalysis is not wholly unjustified. In its practice (especially in regions of the world most fervently committed to capitalism, like the United States), psychoanalysis has certainly played a role in enhancing the docility of its patients rather than unleashing their revolutionary passion. But the verdict on psychoanalytic practice is decidedly mixed. Psychoanalytic theory has played a key role in the critique of the capitalist system, though it has never played the decisive role.

Most of the attempts to understand how capitalism works have focused on its economic structure or on the social effects that it produces. While important, these approaches necessarily miss the primary source of capitalism's staying power. The resilience of capitalism as an economic or social form derives from its relationship to the psyche and to how subjects relate to their own satisfaction. This is why psychoanalysis is requisite for making sense of capitalism's appeal. Psychoanalysis probes the satisfaction of subjects and tries to understand why this satisfaction takes the forms that it does. It does not transform dissatisfaction into satisfaction, but analyzes why certain structures provide satisfaction despite appearances. In this sense, it represents a new way of approaching capitalism and of understanding its staying power.

To psychoanalyze a system is inherently to criticize it. But previous efforts at marshaling psychoanalysis for the critique of capitalism have consistently placed psychoanalysis in a secondary position. Critique has been primary, and critics have deployed psychoanalysis to serve the critique. In the chapters that follow, I will do the reverse: the psychoanalysis of capitalism will remain the motor for the analysis, and if a critique of capitalism emerges from this psychoanalysis, it will never become the driving force of the analysis. Of course, no one is a neutral analyst of capitalism. But it is my contention that immersing oneself within its structure and within its psychic appeal must function as the prelude to any effective critique or defense of the system.

THE INJUSTICE OF EQUALITY

When the critique of capitalism began in earnest in the nineteenth century, the focus was on the injustice of the system. Capitalism may have unleashed society's productive forces to a hitherto unforeseeable extent, but this expansion of productivity brought with it vast differences in wealth. It was a system in which the material benefits did not enrich those who directly made them possible. The mere investment of capital received an almost infinitely greater reward than the hours of toil that produced this reward. The setup itself appeared unjust and gave rise to a range of possible remedies for this injustice—from radically egalitarian communal retreats to the total transformation of the society.

But as defenders of capitalism have noted, the mere fact of this critique is itself a testament to the justice of the system. It is only after the introduction of the capitalist economy that one can recognize the injustice perpetuated by unequal relations. In this sense, capitalism has only itself to blame for the critiques leveled against it. The idea of equivalence inheres within capitalist relations of production: any commodity can be traded for any other, and even time, the one resource that we cannot replenish or replace, acquires a price and thereby becomes a factor of equivalence. The worker trades labor time for wages and thereby makes clear that time relates to the general commodity form just like any other commodity. The fact that everything can be made equal reveals that everything isn't, and this makes possible the critical response.

Prior to the capitalist epoch, inequality inheres in economic systems themselves, not in their failure to realize the equality that they already promulgate (as is the case with capitalism). In a society where slaves perform the labor, there is no sense of even a disguised equality between the laborer and the master who benefits from this labor. The same inequality continues in feudalism, where the feudal lord offers serfs livelihood in exchange for their labor. The inegalitarian nature of this exchange is admitted from the beginning. The lord holds all the cards, and the serfs can only try to make themselves useful for the lord. In any system involving masters and servants or citizens and slaves, revolt is possible—Spartacus, for instance, is not unthinkable—but its chances of success are limited because it challenges not just the system's structural arrangement but also its philosophical basis. To grant freedom to Spartacus would amount to an admission of equality that would have undermined the entire Roman world.

With capitalism, the economic relation ceases to be inherently unjust, which is why the blatant persistence of injustice gives rise to critical voices only after the birth of capitalism. The idea that the greatest philosopher of his time, like Aristotle, would not only countenance but justify slavery becomes impossible to imagine within the capitalist epoch.[1] Even though the critique of injustice is most often a critique of capitalism, it is to capitalism itself that we owe the emergence of this critique. It is not by chance that Karl Marx educated himself by reading the first theorists and defenders of capitalism. They help to make possible the critique of the system they set out to justify. Though capitalism doesn't invent the concept of equality, it is the first economic system to include this concept within its mechanism of production.

From the beginning to the end of his analysis, Marx takes the injustice of the capitalist system as his point of departure. In the early *Economic and Philosophic Manuscripts*, he laments the impossible bind that confronts the worker, for whom no amount of labor will pay off. He writes, "The worker becomes all the poorer the more wealth he produces, the more his production increases in power and size. The worker becomes an ever cheaper commodity the more commodities he creates."[2] The system is rigged against the worker: it rewards the capitalist, not the worker, for the extra productivity that the latter achieves. The theorization of this injustice becomes the foundation of Marx's fully developed analysis of capitalism.

In his mature work, Marx specifies more clearly the site of the injustice—the appropriation of surplus value. The exchange between the capitalist and the worker is equal as far as it goes. The capitalist provides a wage in exchange for the worker's labor time. But the injustice comes from the creative power of labor itself. In the act of laboring, workers don't just produce enough to sustain themselves but rather an excess, and the capitalist capitalizes on this excess in the form of surplus value, which translates into profit. Without the excessive productivity of labor that falls outside the realm of an equal exchange, the capitalist would be left without any profit. As Marx comes to recognize, profit is theft. That is the acme of the egalitarian critique of capitalism, and this critique predominates into the beginning of the twentieth century.

According to this critique, capitalism is an unjust economic system because it deprives those who produce value of the value they produce. It reduces the working class—that is, the productive class—to bare reproduction. Workers receive a necessary wage, a wage necessary for their reproduction as productive laborers, not a wage necessary for the enjoyment of life. Marx believes that the capitalist will not pay workers more than this necessary wage, and thus they cannot enjoy the surplus value that they themselves produce. This excess belongs instead to the capitalist, who organizes production but doesn't herself or himself generate value. A system such as this cannot be just.

From the standpoint of this egalitarian critique, capitalism works out well for the capitalists and poorly for the workers. The incentive to change it rests wholly with the workers, whose interests are dramatically opposed to those of the capitalists. Marx never thinks to address his critique to the capitalists because they find the system, as he sees it, perfectly satisfying. Though they are on the wrong side of history, they want to preserve capitalist relations of production intact and fight to keep them so. In the twentieth century, however, this understanding of the capitalist undergoes a radical transformation as the fundamental critique of capitalism shifts to a new territory.

THE REPRESSIVE ECONOMIC APPARATUS

It is difficult to overestimate Freud's impact on the critique of capitalism. But mobilizing his thought for emancipatory politics meant finding the possibility for hope amid the bleakest despair. As Michel Onfray rightly notes in his scathing account of Freud, he created "a viscerally pessimistic philosophy in virtue of which the worst is always certain."[3] Despite Freud's conviction that the worst is certain, that we will never be able to overcome repression and realize our desires, his understanding of repression allowed for the development of the leftist critique of capitalism in a wholly unanticipated direction. No anticapitalist thinker of the nineteenth century thought to criticize the repressive nature of the capitalist system, but in the twentieth century, thanks to Freud and the critics who took up his mantle, it became almost impossible to avoid it.[4]

The critique of capitalism for most of the twentieth century was a critique of capitalism's repressiveness, though of course the critique of inequality never disappeared. The turn from equality as the primary ground of contestation to repression resulted in an expansion of the challenge to the system. Capitalism became a problem not just for workers toiling without just remuneration for their labor but also for the exploiters themselves. Even the capitalist enjoying the profits deriving from the appropriation of surplus value remains caught within the spell of repression. The factory owners who can buy whatever they want nonetheless suffer under a system that prohibits any proper satisfaction of desire. The problem with capitalist success is not so much the inequality it produces as its intractable emptiness. This development of the critique required the revolution to do more heavy lifting: it would promise not only equity but also deliverance from repression.

The turn from the critique of inequality to the critique of repression manifests itself most clearly in the case of the Frankfurt School. Whereas Marx takes capitalist inequality as the fundamental problem confronting the critic of capitalism, the Frankfurt School, in a stunning turnaround, sees the equality that capitalism produces as its chief danger. Rather than failing to engender equality, the capitalist form of injustice is a forced equality. Capitalism's repressiveness functions through the elimination of all genuine difference, and thus even the communist attack on capitalism falls into its trap by leveling all difference through enforced economic and social equality.

The Frankfurt School's critique of capitalist equality reaches its apex in Theodor Adorno's *Minima Moralia*. Here Adorno offers a revelatory statement that incorporates both an unremitting indictment of capitalism's elimination of difference and one of his few positive proclamations about an anticapitalist alternative. He begins, "That all men are alike is exactly what society would like to hear. It considers actual or imagined differences as stigmas indicating that not enough has yet been done; that something has still been left outside its machinery, not quite determined by its totality."[5] As Adorno sees it, capitalism's victory does not consist in leaving the proletariat outside, but in their inclusion within a repressive system in which nothing unique or singular can persist. This is a line of thought that one could not imagine from Karl Marx, even though Adorno clearly situates himself in the Marxist tradition, as do the other members of the Frankfurt School. But their Marxism has encountered the thought of Sigmund Freud.

Adorno goes on to offer a vision of emancipation that also veers away from that of Marx. It is not a society in which the workers appropriate the value that they themselves produce but one in which singularity could remain intact. Adorno continues, "An emancipated society, on the other hand, would not be a unitary state, but the realization of universality in the reconciliation of differences."[6] This idea of emancipated society takes as its starting point as much Freud's analysis of repression as Marx's of capitalism. Repression, according to the Frankfurt School, is the forgetting of what fails to fit within the capitalist system, and the critical task becomes one of drawing attention to this repressed material. This repression is not, however, always sexual repression, as it would be for other theorists attempting to bring Marx and Freud together.

Several anticapitalist theorists following in Freud's wake equated the destruction of capitalism with the complete elimination of sexual repression. They either worked to bring about sexual liberation with the belief that this would portend the end of capitalism, or they worked to combat capitalism with the belief that this would free repressed sexuality. Otto Gross and Wilhelm Reich were the key exponents of this position, but it gained popular support in the student movements of the 1960s, in which the idea that political and sexual revolution were intertwined became an accepted dogma. Both Gross and Reich believed that political and sexual revolution would be mutually reinforcing. If one produced sexual revolution, that would lead to political revolution, and vice versa. Hence, they often theorized about how changes in either the political or sexual arena might lead to the elimination of repression in both.

One can see this intertwining of the political and the sexual in much of Gross's late work. The title of his essay "Zur funktionellen

Geistesbildung des Revolutionärs" (On the Functional Intellectual Formation of the Revolutionary) makes evident his political aspirations. There the link between these aspirations and his investment in psychoanalysis comes to the fore. Toward the end of the essay, he says, "As a precondition of each moral and spiritual renewal of humanity is the necessity for a total freeing of the coming generation from the violence of the bourgeois family—and even the patriarchal proletarian family is bourgeois!"[7] Contra Freud, Gross sees neurosis as the result not of the fundamental antagonisms of human sexuality but of the repressive force of the bourgeois family and the restrictions that it places on the free expression of sexuality. Gross conceives of free sexuality—the slogan of the 1960s—as the basic human desire. The proletarian revolution would not only free workers from their chains but also sexuality from bourgeois repression.[8]

In the years after Gross's premature death at the age of forty-two in 1920, Wilhelm Reich took up the mantle of the revolutionary psychoanalyst. Like Gross, Reich links neurosis to social repressiveness, and, also like Gross, he believes that political revolution is inextricable from sexual revolution. His attack on the repressiveness of capitalist society finds its most cogent expression in *The Sexual Revolution*, a work that attacks bourgeois marriage and restrictions on forms of abnormal sexuality.[9] Whereas Gross largely faded into history, Reich became a theoretical point of reference for the countercultural revolution of the 1960s.[10] The relative success of the sexual revolution and the failure of the political revolution had the effect of quieting the dream that we might overcome repression completely. There are few followers of Reich today.

For the most part, critics of capitalism accepted Freud's contention that no society could do without some degree of repressiveness. But they added a codicil to this contention that renders it less politically stultifying. The prevailing idea among leftist critics of capitalism has been that the system demands too much repression. If every society requires some repression in order to function, capitalism requires what Herbert Marcuse in *Eros and Civilization* calls "surplus repression." Whereas Marx targets surplus value as the embodiment of the problem with capitalism, Marcuse places surplus repression in this role. This turn tells us everything we need to know about the transformation of the critique of capitalism. Now, we can demand a socialist alternative on the grounds of this additional repression in capitalism that a socialist society would eliminate. The problem isn't the inequality involved with the appropriation of surplus value, but the unnecessary demand for surplus repression that creates a society of one-dimensional equals.[11]

Even when capitalist society seems to allow for the fulfillment of desire, the repressive regime continues to function. Happiness under capitalism is not an index of a break from repression. As Marcuse puts it, "the individual lives his repression 'freely' as his own life: he desires what he is supposed to desire; his gratifications are profitable to him and others; he is reasonably and often exuberantly happy."[12] As long as desire remains within the channels that capitalism provides for it, there is no possibility for satisfaction, just a false happiness that serves as the form of appearance for profound dissatisfaction. Desire directed toward commodities is inherently repressed desire. Satisfaction requires breaking from the logic of the commodity altogether, and this becomes the hope for revolution.

Once the idea of repression enters into the critique of capitalism, the idea of revolution itself undergoes a complete revolution. Marx invests revolution with the promise of equality: it would create a world in which everyone had access to the fruits of her or his own labor and in which no one would be excluded. After Freud, however, equality is no longer enough; revolution must do more. A communist revolution would free desire from the trap of repression. There would be equality, but there would also be an elimination of the surplus repression the exchange economy demands. This does not necessarily imply complete sexual liberation, as Gross and Reich would contend. Instead, the revolution would inaugurate a society where sublimation took the place of repression or where repression was no longer omnipresent.[13] This image of revolution depends on the identification of the capitalist economy with a form of repression that goes beyond what is necessary. But perhaps it is time to revisit this long-standing identification and question whether the essence of capitalism lies in its repressiveness.

Of course, the putting into question of the link between capitalism and repression has already been accomplished. In the first volume of the *History of Sexuality* and in some of his lecture series at the Collège de France, Michel Foucault challenges the repressive hypothesis and even names Reich as a specific target for critique. He begins the first volume of his *History of Sexuality* with a direct riposte to the identification of capitalism with repression. He claims, "By placing the advent of the age of repression in the seventeenth century, after hundreds of years of open spaces and free expression, one adjusts it to coincide with the development of capitalism: it becomes an integral part of the bourgeois order."[14] For Foucault, power in the capitalist system doesn't function through repression, not through negation or prohibition, but in a positive way. Power produces desire rather than just restricting it. Foucault's redefinition of power and categorical rejection of the repressive hypothesis attempt to point toward a third version of the critique of capitalism—beyond injustice and beyond repression.

But even as Foucault mocks the association of capitalism with the repression of sex, his critique takes the same angle as that of the Freudian Marxists from whom he distances himself. That is to say, Foucault abandons the idea that capitalism demands the repression of desire, but he clings to a belief that capitalism blocks or damns up what would otherwise flow freely. His vitalism—his insistence on the spontaneous power of life itself—leaves him incapable of fully abandoning the image of capitalism as a system of constraint. Though capitalism doesn't constrain desire, its discursive regime of sexuality that forces sex to speak and that forces bodies to become sexualized acts as a barrier to the flow of bodies and pleasures. Foucault's politics consists in unleashing this flow, which is why he would feel so comfortable writing a preface to *Anti-Oedipus*, Gilles Deleuze and Félix Guattari's panegyric to decoded bodily flows.

Ironic though it may be, the critique leveled by Foucault is just another version of the attack on repression. Despite what Foucault himself says, the model for the freeing of bodies and pleasures—the ethic he pronounces at the end of the first volume of the *History of Sexuality*—is the liberation of desire that one finds clearly articulated in the thought of Gross and Reich. Bodies and pleasures do not suffer from repression, according to Foucault, but power does stifle them. This is the key point: power doesn't permit the free movement of bodies and deprives them of the pleasure that they are capable of experiencing. Critique or revolution then fights against this restriction. Though Foucault rejects the terms *repression* and *desire,* his replacements—*power* and *bodies*—perform precisely the same roles. In this sense, he does not mark a new epoch in the history of the critique of capitalism.

Foucault's diagnosis of what transpires with capitalism clearly differs from the traditional Freudian Marxists, but his response is homologous. He is a Freudian Marxist—he is Otto Gross—in disguise. Life must be disentangled from power in order to discover the pleasure that capitalism blocks. Despite his vehement disdain for the counterproductivity of the repressive hypothesis, Foucault remains within the vision of emancipation proffered by its champions.

FINDING SATISFACTION UNSATISFYING

Both Marx's critique of capitalism's injustice and the pseudo-Freudian critique of capitalism's repressiveness focus on what the economic system denies to its adherents rather than what it provides for them. This focus unites Marx, Reich, and Foucault. It has been primarily the apologists for capitalism, as one might expect, who have focused on what the system does offer. But we can examine what capitalism provides from the perspective of critique. Capitalism has the effect of sustaining subjects in a constant state of desire. As subjects of capitalism, we are constantly on the edge of having our desire realized, but never reach the point of realization. This has the effect of producing a satisfaction that we don't recognize as such. That is, capitalist subjects experience satisfaction itself as dissatisfying, which enables them to simultaneously enjoy themselves and believe wholeheartedly that a more complete satisfaction exists just around the corner, embodied in the newest commodity.

In this light, this book represents a third direction in the critique of capitalism. Rather than taking inequality or repression as the starting point, it begins with the satisfaction that capitalism provides. The problem, I contend, is not that capitalism fails to satisfy but that it doesn't enable its subjects to recognize where their own satisfaction lies. The capitalist regime produces subjects who cling feverishly to the image of their own dissatisfaction and to thus to the promise, constantly made explicit in capitalist society, of a way to escape this dissatisfaction through either the accumulation of capital or the acquisition of the commodity.

The fundamental gesture of capitalism is the promise, and the promise functions as the basis for capitalist ideology. One invests money with the promise of future returns; one starts a job with the promise of a higher salary; one takes a cruise with the promise of untold pleasure in the tropics; one buys the newest piece of electronics with the promise of easier access to what one wants. In every case the future embodies a type of satisfaction foreclosed to the present and dependent on one's investment in the capitalist system. The promise ensures a sense of dissatisfaction with the present in relation to the future.

One of the constant complaints from critics of capitalism is that the capitalist system has the ability to incorporate every attack by integrating the attack into the system. The accuracy of this truism is readily apparent in the way that commodification works. Capitalism seizes apparently revolutionary practices or figures and transforms them into commodities. An acquaintance with a Che Guevara T-shirt or a Karl Marx coffee mug, let alone the sight of sex toys in a shopping mall or eco-friendly cars at the neighborhood dealership, seems to bespeak its truth. But the secret of capitalism's integration of critique lies not in the process of commodification, no matter how self-evident it appears. The secret is in the promise. If one invests oneself in the promise of the future, through this gesture one accepts the basic rules of the capitalist game.

The promise of the better future is the foundation of the capitalist structure, the basis for all three economic areas—production, distribution, and consumption. If we examine only the field of consumption, universal commodification seems to hold the key, whereas if we confine ourselves to the field of production, the imperative to accumulate appears foundational. In the field of distribution, it is the idea of speed: one must move commodities to market in the least amount of time possible. If we look at what these three fields have in common, however, the answer is the promise of the future. One buys the commodity to discover a potentially satisfying pleasure, one accumulates more capital to some day have enough, and one speeds up the distribution process to increase one's future profit.[15] Any sense of satisfaction with one's present condition would have a paralyzing effect on each of these regions of the capitalist economy.

This is the problem with the insistence on revolutionary hope: it partakes of the logic that it tries to contest. Revolutionary hope represents an investment in the structure of the promise that defines capitalism. As a result, it is never as revolutionary as it believes itself to be. Though obviously the act of promising precedes the onset of a capitalist economy, once this economy emerges, the promise enters completely into the capitalist logic. To take solace in the promise of tomorrow is to accept the sense of dissatisfaction that capitalism sells more vehemently than it sells any commodity. As long as one remains invested in the promise as such, one has already succumbed to the fundamental logic of capitalism.

From the early Charles Fourier and Robert Owen to Fredric Jameson and Antonio Negri, the idea of a better future has driven the Left in its critique of capitalism. In his discussion of Marx, Jacques Derrida exemplifies this type of investment, as he emphasizes the emancipatory promise at the heart of his deconstructive politics. He notes, "Whether the promise promises this or that, whether it be fulfilled or not, or whether it be unfulfillable, there is necessarily some promise and therefore some historicity as future-to-come."[16] While every other concept is subject to deconstruction, this promise of "justice-to-come" functions as the condition of possibility for deconstruction and thus cannot be deconstructed. Deconstruction does not encapsulate the entirety of anticapitalist politics today in any sense, but Derrida's investment in the promise is representative. But it is just this investment in the promise that must be abandoned, along with the sense of dissatisfaction inherent in it. As long as radical politics operates with the belief that revolution will remove some of the prevailing repression, it accepts the ruling idea of capitalism and buys into the fundamental capitalist fantasy. No revolution can transform dissatisfaction into satisfaction, but this is how revolution has been conceived throughout the entirety of the capitalist epoch. The revolutionary act has to be thought differently. The revolutionary act is simply the recognition that capitalism already produces the satisfaction that it promises.

And yet, this revolutionary act is far more difficult than storming the Bastille or the Winter Palace. In the latter instances, all that is required is sufficient political force. But the break from the promise of a better future seems theoretically untenable alongside a position of critique. Critique appears to imply a future ideal from which one launches the attack on the capitalist present. The task is thus that of freeing critique from the promise of a better future. Why would one be critical at all without such a promise? What could be the possible ground for the critique?

This work attempts to answer these questions by situating the future not as a possibility on the horizon but as the implicit structure of the present. There is, in other words, no future to realize except to accede to the exigencies that are already written into the ruling capitalist system. The point of critique is not promissory, not futural, but wholly immanent.

Obviously, a critique that is not futural still points toward a future that is better in some sense of the term. One cannot avoid implicitly positing some version of a better future when one analyzes the present— otherwise one would simply accept the present rather than analyzing it. But the point is that one must not imagine a future that would produce a level of satisfaction history has hitherto denied to us. There is no deeper or more authentic satisfaction that will overcome the antagonisms of society or the failures of subjectivity, despite what anticapitalist revolutionaries have traditionally promised. We do not need the belief in a future replete with a deeper satisfaction in order to reject capitalism, if that is what we decide to do.

The alternative to capitalism inheres within capitalism, and the revolutionary act is one of recognizing capitalism's internal and present future. The measuring stick for critique is not the promise of a better future but capitalism's underlying structure. The identification or recognition of this structure provides the key to the emergence of an alternative. Capitalism's hold over us depends on our failure to recognize the nature of its power.

Capitalism functions as effectively as it does because it provides satisfaction for its subjects while at the same time hiding the awareness of this satisfaction from them. If we recognized that we obtained satisfaction from the failure to obtain the perfect commodity rather than from a wholly successful purchase, we would be freed from the psychic appeal of capitalism. That is not to say that we would never buy another commodity, but just that we would do so without a psychic investment in the promise of the commodity, which is already, in some sense, a revolution. This change would eliminate the barrier to structural changes to our socioeconomic system and would create a different system. Problems of political organization and struggle are difficult, but they pale in comparison to the problem of capitalism's psychic appeal. Understanding the importance of the psychic investment in the capitalist economy and the need to break from it is Freud's legacy for the contemporary critique of capitalism.

The great task for twentieth-century critical thought was that of bring-ing Marx and Freud together, of thinking through the analysis of capi-talism in light of Freud's discovery of the unconscious. In order to carry out this task, thinkers alit on the role that capitalism played in repres-sion. But repression was not Freud's last word on the unconscious. It be-came increasingly less important as his thought changed toward the end of his life. This change in the significance of repression occurred as the structure of Freud's system underwent an overhaul. Whereas the early Freud associated repression with unacceptable sexual desires, the later Freud linked it the subject's intractable attachment to loss.

With Freud's 1920 discovery of the subject's tendency to repeat loss and failure, the edifice of psychoanalysis underwent a profound readjust-ment. Rather than targeting sexual repression, Freud turned his focus to the satisfaction that the subject derives from repeating experiences that don't provide pleasure. This forces Freud to distinguish between pleasure and satisfaction, and he concludes that satisfaction trumps pleasure. Repetition comes to define subjectivity for Freud: the unconscious doesn't just hide disturbing sexual ideas from the subject's consciousness, but impels the subject to act in ways that subvert its own interests, and the subject finds satisfaction in these acts because they produce a lost object for the subject to desire and enjoy. The subject's satisfaction is inex-tricable from self-destructive loss, and even though it represses its self-destructiveness, lifting this repression would provide no relief. After 1920, Freud discovers a subject that incessantly undermines itself, and this undermining extends to all attempts at a cure.

As Freud sees it, the fundamental proof of an attachment to loss and failure is the refusal to be cured that patients display. Freud labels this refusal the "negative therapeutic reaction," and its emergence suggests that subjects find satisfaction in their suffering. If therapy threatens to relieve this suffering, patients often respond by finding ways to make themselves worse again. Freud doesn't dismiss this behavior as a function of neurosis but sees in it a verdict on the subject as such. It manifests itself most clearly in the inability of any subject to live out a harmoni-ous existence. Freud concludes that the satisfaction of subjects depends on a disturbance to their psychic equilibrium, on the absence of what they desire rather than its presence. The presence of an object reveals its inadequacy, while its absence allows the subject to find it satisfying. This creates a world in which subjects subvert their own happiness in order to sustain their satisfaction.

Freud himself has difficulty formulating the implications of the new theory of subjectivity and integrating it into his existing theory, and yet it represents the most radical moment of Freud's thought because it enables us to understand why subjects so often fail to act in ways that would obviously benefit them. That said, many refused to follow Freud in this discovery, and those who tried to combine Marx and Freud often adhered to the early Freud, the Freud of repressed sexuality. This makes sense for the revolutionary: Freud's early model provides a clearer target for emancipatory politics than his later model, which seems difficult to reconcile with any form of politics other than complete conservatism. The later Freud is a far more politically pessimistic thinker.

According to the first model, we repress a possibility that we hope to realize. According to the second, we repress an act that we are perpetually accomplishing. Though Freud locates at all times the source of neurotic illness in the past—*"Hysterics suffer mainly from reminiscences,"* as Freud and Josef Breuer put it in the opening work of psychoanalysis—the emphasis moves from a past desire for a different future to the repetition of a past trauma in the present.[17] Freud emphasizes repression less in his later thinking because it provides no barrier at all to the effectiveness of repetition.

In a certain sense, we might think of the early Freud, the Freud focused on sexual repression, as a thinker still invested in the capitalist ideology of the promise. Even if he refused to believe in the possibility of fully overcoming repression, he nonetheless viewed psychoanalysis as a solution that promised a better future. The shift that the patient could undergo is palpable. After writing *Beyond the Pleasure Principle*, however, Freud recognizes that the repetition would act as a constant barrier to a better future, and he becomes increasingly skeptical about fundamental change in individuals and in society. The attitude that Freud takes to the subject's repetition becomes less futural because the possibility of overcoming repression ceased to play a central role.

The repression of sexual desires appears to work: though subjects may manifest these desires through obsessional rituals or hysterical pains, they are not actually having the illicit sex of their unconscious fantasies.

Repeatedly adjusting one's batting gloves (as many baseball players do) may in fact be a wholly sexual act, but not everyone will readily recognize it as such. One can do it in public without violating laws against public indecency, whereas one could not openly masturbate in the same situation without risking arrest. Similarly, no one interprets the silence of the hysteric who cannot speak as a public performance of fellatio. Repressed sexuality manifests itself in symptoms—like adjusting one's batting gloves—that don't themselves appear sexual. Repression not only brings suffering to the subject but also shelters this subject from the obvious manifestations of its repressed sexuality. This is not the case with the compulsion to repeat. Though Freud believes that the subject represses the idea of its repetition, the satisfaction that the repetition of loss produces occurs without abatement or obstruction.

Repression becomes a less important category in Freud's later thought because he comes to accept that the repression provides no barrier at all to the satisfaction the subject derives from repetition. As long as repression concerned just sexuality, Freud could believe in the transformative effect of lifting it. Psychoanalysis, according to this early conception, might enable the patient to pass from dissatisfaction to satisfaction by uncovering the repressed. This offers a tidy link between psychoanalysis and revolutionary politics, between Otto Gross and Rosa Luxemburg.

Once the idea of a satisfying repetition takes hold, however, this image of psychoanalysis ceases to be tenable. There is no clear political gain from lifting the repression associated with repetition. All that psychoanalysis can do—the extent of its intervention—is to assist the patient in recognizing its mode of repeating and the satisfaction that this repetition provides. The dream of freeing patients from dissatisfaction dies with the discovery that patients resist the psychoanalytic cure precisely because they already have the satisfaction that psychoanalysis promises them.

The thinkers who have brought Freud to bear on the analysis of capitalism have turned to psychoanalysis to prove that capitalism is even more dissatisfying than earlier critics thought it was. The problem is not just inequality for the working class but repression for all. For someone like Adorno, this is apparent in the widespread investment in astrology among capitalist subjects. While it appears as a harmless enough interest, astrology infects the social order, especially the middle class (and not necessarily the economically oppressed), with a false satisfaction. In his essay "The Stars Down to Earth," Adorno notes, "It is as though astrology has to provide gratifications to aggressive urges on the level of the imaginary, but is not allowed to interfere too obviously with the 'normal' functioning of the individual in reality."[18] The popularity of astrology columns in newspapers, even if one reads them just for fun, signals the existence and repression of desires that the system cannot gratify. The victims of capitalism in Adorno's eyes are not just the working class but everyone subjected to the repressiveness inherent in the mode of subjectivity that capitalism demands.

This broadening of the analysis of capitalism has led to stunning insights into just how expansive the problem of capitalism is, but at the same time, this new critique buys the capitalist dream with its insistence on dissatisfaction. It could do this only insofar as it stuck to Freud's early theory of the psyche and refused to integrate his later thought. This later Freud has had no place in the critique of capitalism as it was developed by traditional Freudian Marxism in the twentiethth century. As a result, the task of bringing Marx and Freud together remains for us today. If the real Freud is the Freud of the subject's self-destructiveness, then this is no easy task. The fit between this Freud and Marx is not a comfortable one.

The aim of this book is not to provide another catalogue of capitalism's horrors or its defects. That is the province of other works. Instead, it tries to understand why so much satisfaction accompanies capitalism and thus what constitutes its hold on those living within its structure. The starting point of this power is capitalism's relationship to desiring subjectivity, which the first chapter investigates. The next chapters that make up the core of the book explore how capitalism protects us—from the encounter with the public, from our gaze, from sacrifice, from the absence of guarantees, from infinitude, from our nonproductivity, from love, and even from abundance. But it does enable us to experience the sublime in everyday life, as the concluding chapter shows. The book ends with capitalism's sublimity, but this is also where it starts. The staying power of capitalism, its resistance to critique, is inextricable from its production of sublimity, which gives it the power to satisfy. Capitalist subjects cling tightly to their dissatisfaction, and this dissatisfaction is the main thing holding them to capitalism. No matter how attractive it appears, there is no commodity that holds the appeal of a lasting dissatisfaction.

[1]

The Subject of Desire and the Subject of Capitalism

MOSES AND THE PROPHETS

The difficulties that capitalism engenders begin with its definition. The problem stems from the incredible historical and spatial breadth of the capitalism system. This system ranges from the burgeoning markets of early European modernity to the unbridled laissez-faire societies of nineteenth-century Britain and the United States to the authoritarian society of the formerly communist China of the early twenty-first century. As both proponents and critics acknowledge, capitalism has a remarkable elasticity that appears to defy any strict pronunciations concerning its essence. It is almost impossible to identify the points at which capitalism begins and where it ends.

For most defenders of the capitalist economy, its capacity for the inclusion of difference is its crowning virtue. In fact, capitalism is such a variable system that we cannot speak of a single system. There is not one capitalist system, but many capitalist systems.[1] According to capitalism's critics, this variability distinguishes capitalism from all other economic systems and highlights its nefariousness. As Guy Debord sees it, the commodity form developed within capitalism colonizes every other social form, and this process reaches its endpoint in what he calls the society of spectacle. He claims that "the spectacle corresponds to the historical moment at which the commodity completes its colonization of social life. It is not just that the relationship to commodities is now plain to see—commodities are now *all* that there is to see; the world that we see is the world of the commodity."[2] The spectacle is not qualitatively different than earlier forms of capitalism: capitalism doesn't just accommodate differences, but violently integrates them into a logic that eliminates them. But the key lies in understanding what this logic is.

Both adherents and opponents of the capitalist system agree that it places the law of the market—buying and selling what people themselves choose to buy and sell—at the center of the social organization. Even if the state intervenes in the market by injecting money, stabilizing prices, or supporting certain industries, the system remains capitalist, according to most theorists, as long as the free market plays the determinative role. In a capitalist economy, the state can play a supportive role and can even act as a brake on untrammeled capitalist development, but the market must ultimately have the last word. This definition is compelling and accurate as far as it goes, but it fails to capture capitalism's specific relationship to the psyche of those invested in it. It is on the psychic level that one discovers how capitalism functions.

To understand the psychic benefits that capitalism metes out, it is important to distinguish it from culture. Though capitalism includes within itself vast cultural differences, it is not itself a culture, and thus one should never speak of the culture of capitalism. From the perspective of capitalism itself, it is a matter of indifference which culture germinated it and which culture nourishes it. If Europe receives the credit or the blame for capitalism's emergence, this is a matter of pure historical contingency when one considers how capitalism works. It is not a Eurocentric phenomenon, but a universal one that remains fundamentally the same even when it transforms itself to include cultural differences.

Capitalism transcends culture and offers its subjects psychic rewards that are radically different from those that cultures provide. As a member of a culture, I gain a stable symbolic identity associated with a structure that extends beyond my own subjectivity. This stability is the primary weapon with which culture lures its adherents, and it contrasts entirely with the weapons that capitalism employs. Culture gives the subject a sense of belonging that capitalism does not.

The capitalist subject constantly experiences its failure to belong, which is why the recurring fantasy within capitalism is that of attaining some degree of authentic belonging (in a romantic relationship, in a group of friends, in the nation, and so on). Though capitalism spawns this type of fantasy, it constantly militates against the fantasy's realization. Capitalism offers the promise of belonging with every commodity and with the commodity as such, but the subject can never buy the perfect commodity, or enough of them, to unlock the secret of belonging. Unlike the subject of a particular culture, the capitalist subject does not have a place that offers a sense of identity. There is only a lack of place that spawns the search for place through the process of constant enrichment, a process that serves only to augment the subject's lack of place and identity. The only identity the capitalist subject has lies in its absence of any identity.

The essence of capitalism is accumulation. The capitalist subject is a subject who never has enough and continually seeks more and more. But this project of endless accumulation is built, ironically, on the idea of its end. Capitalist accumulation envisions obtaining the object that would provide the ultimate satisfaction for the desiring subject, the object that would quench the subject's desire and allow it to put an end to the relentless yearning to accumulate. In this sense, an image of the end of capitalism is implicit in its structure, and the key to capitalism's staying power lies in the fact that this ultimately satisfying object doesn't exist. Capitalism commands accumulation as an end that the subject can never reach, and this command holds in all aspects of the capitalist system—production, distribution, and consumption. The producer must produce more in order to earn more money, the distributor must distribute more in order to maximize profit, and the consumer must consume more in order to find the truly satisfying object. In each case, the failure to accumulate enough is inscribed in the system and is the source of the satisfaction that the system offers.

There is thus a radical difference between the image capitalism presents to its subjects and the real satisfaction they find in it. The capitalist system requires that subjects invest themselves in the idea of accumulation and the promise of an ultimate satisfaction that accompanies the idea. There is no capitalist subject—and thus no capitalist system—without this idea. With all the variety that we find in the capitalist universe, the one constant is a commandment to accumulate that operates in the psyche of every capitalist subject. Any struggle against the capitalist system must begin with the psychic investment in the promise of accumulation that it necessitates. This investment is much more difficult to avoid than any financial investment because it infects even those who believe that they have opted out of the system and live off the grid. The psychic reach of capitalism far outstrips its socioeconomic reach.

Capitalism commands accumulation and promises a satisfaction that it cannot deliver. This failure has its origins in the structure of the subject's psyche and the way that the subject finds satisfaction. The psyche satisfies itself through the failure to realize its desire, and capitalism allows the subject to perpetuate this failure, all the while believing in the idea that it pursues success. The link between capitalism and the psyche provides the key to understanding the appeal of capitalism. It is a system that enables us to envision the possibility of a satisfaction that is structurally unattainable for us while, at the same time, it allows the real traumatic source of our satisfaction to remain unconscious. This double deception creates a system with an inordinate staying power, a system that appears to be written into our genetic makeup.

THE DIVISION OF THE OBJECT

Despite appearances, capitalism is not the result of human nature. The system's apologists who insist on this point do so in order to sustain an aura of inevitability around it. But nonetheless, beyond the bare socioeconomic agenda of its proponents, we can understand why this association arises. Associating capitalism with human nature is an ideological gesture, but the feeling that capitalism fits our mode of desiring is not wholly ideological. Capitalism's emergence and its psychic appeal are related to the nature of human subjectivity, though this subjectivity is itself unnatural, a function not of natural processes but of a disjunction from the natural world. Capitalism succeeds as it does by playing into the alienation from nature that occurs through signification. Though the development of capitalism was not necessary—one can imagine a world in which it didn't emerge—one can nonetheless understand its rise and staying power in terms of the structure of the psyche.[3] We are, one might say, psychically disposed to invest ourselves in the capitalist system. Capitalism succeeds because it capitalizes on our status as unnatural beings.

If humans were simply instinctual animals, capitalism would neither develop nor take a psychic hold on us. It is not just by accident that there is no capitalist system flourishing in the animal world. In this sense, the claim of a link between capitalism and human nature should be rejected out of hand. Capitalism's appeal is inextricable from the emergence of the signifier and the transformation that this emergence effects on speaking beings. The passion that subjects exhibit for capitalism derives from the break from nature that occurs when subjects begin to speak. Through this break, natural human needs undergo a complete transformation and become susceptible to the allure of accumulation and of the commodity that capitalism will bring to the fore. We aren't capitalists because we are animalistic but because we are fundamentally removed from our animality. The commodity does not fulfill a natural need but a desire distorted by the signifier, a desire that emerges through the signifier's distortion of animality. There are thus no prototypical capitalist structures in the animal world. It is language that gives birth to the possibility of this economic form. The exploration of capitalism must first and foremost be an exploration of what occurs with the introduction of the signifier.

Signification makes capitalism possible because it alienates the individual from its environment by introducing a layer of mediation into all of the individual's interactions.[4] Rather than simply feeling hunger and eating the nearest apple in the manner of a human animal, the subject will seek a satisfaction that transcends the apple through the apple. For the subject of the signifier, unlike for the human animal, an apple is never enough. Once the world of signification exists, the apple's noncoincidence with itself becomes apparent, and the empirical apple ceases to prove satisfying. As an object of need, the apple is just an apple and can satisfy the need. But after the introduction of the signifier, the apple's self-division enables it to signify something beyond itself. A supplement attaches itself to the apple in the form of the signifier, and this excess remains irreducible to the object. The subject in the world of signification can never just eat an apple but eats instead what "keeps the doctor away," what is juicy and delicious, or what connotes original sin. The apple will embody something more as a result of the division introduced by signification, and this excess attached to the apple produces a satisfaction for the subject that an apple by itself—an apple that isn't an "apple"— can never provide for an animal that eats it.[5]

We tend to miss the apple's self-division not just because apples, before they are eaten, appear to be whole but primarily because the signifier carries with it the illusion of transparency. In fact, signifiers hide their opacity through the guise of transparency. The signifier seems simply to provide an identity for an object that already exists without changing that object: there are objects hanging on trees, and someone decides to assign the name "apples" to them. Signifiers don't appear to alter what they signify, and, as a result, we don't recognize the mediation that shapes our world. The world appears as an immediate set of elements laid out for us to perceive as we will. But the signifier is nonetheless opaque. This means that it distorts what we perceive and changes the elements with which it interacts.

The signifier causes us to see "apples" rather than apples. Every object takes on the hue given to it by the system of signification and loses its image of self-identity. The object of need becomes an object of desire.[6] The distorting power of the signifier does not occur in addition to our perception—like a pair of colored glasses that we might wear—but rather is our perception. We perceive through and as a result of the distortion. Grasping the effects of this distortion looms as a key problem in modern thought, and it also offers an initial key to understanding capitalism's appeal to us as subjects of the signifier.

Because the subject confronts divided objects, it can never obtain an object that would enable it to realize its desire. No object is whole or fulfilling for the subject. Though it can't make objects whole, capitalism transforms the image of objects. As commodities, objects appear whole and present opportunities for the subject to achieve fulfillment. Capitalism doesn't eliminate the division in the world reflected in signification, but it does present this division as a contingent rather than as a necessary obstacle. It maps itself onto signification in order to hide signification's inherently traumatic structure.

The signifier produces a divided world. Ferdinand de Saussure famously describes the divide as one between the signifier and the signified, though other linguists have used different terminology. What is instructive is that the signifier introduces the conception of a split, so that the world of appearance becomes simply apparent and not all that there is.[7] This split creates the possibility of sense. If we relate to an undivided reality, nothing can have any signification whatsoever. Objects do not constitute a significant whole that awaits us to discover its sense. As Saussure notes, we don't begin with significations that await signifiers to pin them down.

He claims instead, "Without language, thought is a vague, uncharted nebula. There are no pre-existing ideas, and nothing is distinct before the appearance of language."[8] Language creates a significant world to which we can relate, but it also makes evident the division of this world from itself. The signifier is not identical with the signified. Isolated instances that suggest an equivalence, such as onomatopoeia, are not primary but rather secondary attempts to bridge a fundamental chasm.[9]

The division between the signifier and signified indicates the presence of absence within the world. There is a gap between the word and what it signifies, between the name and the idea of the object or action, and no amount of precision can ever fill this lacuna. Capitalism, in contrast to signification, relies on the belief that the proper commodity will eliminate this absence and produce an enduring presence. But this presence never actually comes about within the capitalist economy. Capitalism presents itself as structured differently than signification, but it leads to the same failures that arrive with the signifier.

We produce or consume additional commodities in order to realize our desire definitively, but we never achieve this realization. In the same way, we use other signifiers to define a signifier, but they can never do so authoritatively. There is always more to say because the search for the signified is unending, just like the process of production and consumption is unending. One meaning always leads to another, and one commodity always leads to another. This is evident in the case of signification but hidden in that of capitalism.

The signifier indicates a signified that is not present and that will never become present. Every attempt to discover the signified—through, say, looking a word up in the dictionary—will only lead to other signifiers that will attempt to approximate it. No dictionary in existence could provide direct access to the signified because the signified is nothing but the absence of the subsequent signifier that would define the first. Sense, which seems to reside on the side of the signified, actually remains on the side of the signifier insofar as we must use signifiers to define signifiers and explain what we mean. There is thus no end to the search for sense and a blank space where we expect an answer. The perfect commodity, in contrast, promises an end to the search.

When the subject encounters the world of signification, it encounters an intractable absence. It always seeks something and yet finds nothing.

The initial signifier points to another that would complete it but never does. The world of signification promises an answer it never delivers, and this is how it installs an absence at the heart of the desiring subject. There is no ultimate resolution for the subject's desire, just as there is no ultimate resolution to signification itself. Once the signifier emerges, absence inhabits every moment of subjectivity and establishes the structure of desire.[10]

This constant confrontation with absence orients the subject around loss. As a human animal, the instinctual being can discover objects that will fulfill its needs. The satisfaction that comes from obtaining an object is always a possibility, though never a certainty, for this being. A lion can feel hungry and find satisfaction in eating a gazelle. But for the subject of the signifier, no such object exists. There are no satisfying gazelles on the subject's table, even for meat eaters. No object is identical to itself, and the subject cannot find the object that would provide satisfaction because this object transcends the subject's field of possible experience. The distance that separates the signifier from the signified also separates the subject from the satisfying object.

With the onset of capitalism, the speaking being enters a system that promises relief from the absence that inheres within the basic structure of signification. Other systems have integrated loss into social life in various ways—through ritual sacrifice, through ceremonies that consume great resources, and so on. But capitalism represents an epochal change. Loss becomes contingent rather than necessary, and the commodity provides an answer to this traumatic contingency.

LOSING WHAT WAS ALREADY GONE

The status of the object within capitalism changes along with the subject's relationship to loss. Just as loss comes to seem contingent in the capitalist epoch, the lost object that haunts all speaking beings ceases to be constitutively lost. Jacques Lacan identifies the lost object (which he calls the *objet a*) as what orients the subject's desire even though the subject has never had it. But in capitalism the lost object acquires a substantial status it doesn't actually have. It appears as something substantial that the subject has lost through a traumatic event insofar as it appears accessible in the form of the commodity.

Though absence must inhere within being itself, signification redoubles this absence and installs it at the center of the signifying system. Thus, to exist within signification is to accept loss as constitutive, a situation that psychoanalysis calls lack. Signification retroactively creates a lost object that was lost with the entrance into signification and that would have provided complete satisfaction if it had actually existed. Even though this object has no substantial status and can never acquire any concrete form, it shapes the contours of subjectivity. All of the subject's multifarious activity within the world of signification centers around the attempt to rediscover this object that it never possessed.

One of the fundamental errors of psychoanalysis consists in granting the lost object a substantial status.[11] This is often visible in object relations psychoanalysis, which understands the subject as first and foremost relational rather than traversed by loss. This form of psychoanalysis makes the same error that capitalism does concerning the object. At first glance, a relational understanding of subjectivity makes tremendous sense: it seems impossible to understand subjects in isolation from each other or the development of sexuality apart from other subjects. And yet, this form of psychoanalysis ironically represents a flight from Freud's own understanding of the power of mediation over subjectivity. That is to say, it constructs a myth of an original relation to the object unaffected by the travails of mediation. Even if the subject suffers from encounters with bad objects, these objects remain fully present for the subject in object relations theory and thus lack the constitutive absence that all objects have for the subject of the signifier.

This error becomes evident in the theorizing of even the most sophisticated object relations psychoanalysts such as W. R. D. Fairbairn. Fairbairn imagines a direct experience of the object from the period of infancy. In "Object Relationships and Dynamic Structure," he describes the infant's relation to objects as one in which the object itself might provide satisfaction without loss or mediation. He writes, "The real libidinal aim is the establishment of satisfactory relationships with objects; and it is, accordingly, the object that constitutes the true libidinal goal. At the same time, the form assumed by the libidinal approach is determined by the nature of the object. Thus it is owing to the nature of the breast that the infant's inherent incorporative tendency assumes the form of sucking with the mouth."[12] Here the infant aims at an attainable satisfaction embodied in the object, and nothing bars access to this object. Though the adult might lose this original relationship with the object, it does exist, for Fairbairn, prior to its loss.

Object relations psychoanalysis and its many derivations do attempt to account for the power that loss has over the subject. But they do not conceive of loss as constitutive, which is why their conception of the object parallels that of capitalism. Loss, for someone like Fairbairn, is an empirical rather than an ontological fact. There is an immediacy of presence prior to the mediation of absence. Loss may very well occur in every case, but it is always the loss of something. The breast is a paradise lost, whereas for Freud paradise exists—to the extent that it does—only in the act of losing. Paradise lost is the speculative equivalent to paradise regained. That is to say, loss doesn't represent a disruption of the subject's initial satisfaction but the emergence of the possibility for satisfaction. To regard loss as the loss of something is to fail to recognize loss as constitutive of subjectivity. But this is a conception of loss that escapes object relations psychoanalysis in the same way that it escapes the capitalist subject.[13]

When he writes *Beyond the Pleasure Principle* in 1920, Freud begins to define the subject through its constitutive loss. From this point on in his thinking, he conceives of the subject as completely determined by loss, as driven toward its own destruction—a process that he misleadingly labels "death drive." Though there are hints of this breakthrough in earlier works, the radicality of the 1920 revolution should not be understated. In fact, even Freud himself did not fully grasp its radicality, as evidenced by his failed attempt to reduce the subject's repetition of failure and loss to a tendency to return to an inorganic state. Death drive connotes a desire to die, which is why it leads readers of Freud (and even Freud himself) astray. What he is really onto with this concept is that the subject finds satisfaction in repeating loss, that the subject's satisfaction is inextricable from failure.

No one sets out consciously to fail, and, even if one did, the act of making failure a goal would immediately transform it into a different form of success. Within consciousness the subject cannot give failure primacy. Consciousness is oriented around projects in which the subject aims at succeeding, and the failures of these projects, from the perspective of consciousness, are only contingent failures the subject can attempt to remedy by trying again or trying harder. Unconsciously, however, the subject depends on failure to satisfy itself. Failure and loss produce the object as absent, and it is only the absence of the object that renders it satisfying. Absence animates the subject, driving it to act, in a way that presence cannot. If we think about who marches in the street, it is those who lack, not those who have, and when those who have do march, it is because the threat of loss manifests itself. Even though they march for the elimination of this lack, it is absence that motivates them to march in the first place. It is also absence or the threat of it that enables us to get out of bed in the morning and go to work. The subject that had no absence in its existence would be unable to act and would lack the impetus even to kill itself. After seeing numerous patients display their attachment to absence and loss, Freud concludes that it holds the key to the subject's form of satisfaction.

We can see this play out in sports fandom. Though we consciously root for our favorite team to win, we find more unconscious satisfaction in the persistent struggles of the sports team that we root for than in its unqualified successes. The close game is infinitely more interesting than the blowout because it enables the fan to experience loss while not having loss enter into consciousness. No one wants to root for a team that wins all its games, and if fans flock to the games of teams that win all the time, they go to see the loss (or potential loss) that will disrupt the winning, just like auto racing fans go to see cars crashing (or potentially crashing), though this desire remains unconscious. Even when our favorite team wins a championship, we begin almost immediately to consider how they might fare the next year. This is a way of leaving the terrain of success for that of potential failure. When we achieve the pinnacle of success, we seek out a way to return loss into our existence by imagining a new challenge or embarking on a new project.

Loss injects value into the subject's existence and gives it an object that provides satisfaction. Freud's conception of the priority of loss and its repetition troubles other psychoanalysts (like Fairbairn, for instance) because it highlights the impossibility of any satisfaction associated with obtaining the object. After this point, for Freud, one simply cannot have the satisfying object. Any notion of success becomes unthinkable, and one must reconceive satisfaction in terms of how one fails. Failure becomes the only option.

On the basis of privileging failure, Freud reimagines the object in a way that challenges both much of the history of philosophy and the psychic demands of capitalism. The object is not an object that the subject hopes to obtain but a limit that the subject encounters. The subject cannot overcome the limit but constitutes itself and its satisfaction through the limit. That is to say, the object that thwarts the subject's efforts at obtaining it retroactively creates the subject around the recalcitrance. The subject seeks out what it cannot obtain and latches itself onto these objects. Its failure with regard to them provides a satisfaction that completely defies the capitalist image of reality.

Freud's conception of the object enables us to rethink the famous slogan from May 1968 in France. The mantra of this movement—*jouir sans entraves* (enjoy without hindrances)—expresses the critique of capitalism's repressiveness, the critique that dominated much of the twentieth century. The problem with this slogan is that eliminating the barriers to enjoyment would eliminate the source of enjoyment. By slightly changing it to *jouir les entraves* (enjoy the hindrances), we capture the constitutive importance of the obstacle. Satisfaction exists in the obstacle that the object erects in the face of the subject's efforts to obtain it rather than in the eradication of all obstacles. But this is what the capitalist imperative to accumulate enables us to avoid confronting.

The speaking subject satisfies itself through its process of failing to obtain its object, even if this goes unrecognized by the subject itself. The relationship between subjectivity and loss leads the subject to flee this recognition and find asylum in the framework of capitalist accumulation. The subject repeats a constitutive loss because loss is the only way that the speaking subject has to relate to objects, even though capitalism provides the image of an alternative. The signifier confronts the subject with an absence that forms subjectivity and that the subject can never overcome. But the loss that haunts the subject also constitutes the subject, which is why it seeks to repeat this loss.

The signifier creates the subject through the act of removing what is most essential for the subject, even though this essential object doesn't exist prior to its removal. From this point on, the subject will remain unable to divorce satisfaction from loss. One might say that through the signifier the subject loses the object into existence. Loss generates the object at the same time that it marks its disappearance, which has a determinative effect on how the subject satisfies itself. The subject may find fleeting pleasure in success and achievement, but its only satisfaction will take the form of the repetition of loss. Subjects undermine themselves and self-sabotage not because they are stubborn or stupid but because this is their path to satisfaction. For the speaking subject, winning is only a detour on the way to losing.[14] Even the winners in the world of the signifier are ultimately on the side of defeat, but just take a longer time to get there than others.

When we understand the difference between instinctual beings and speaking subjects, the appeal of thinking about ourselves in terms of instinct rather than subjectivity becomes self-evident. Instinctual beings have the capacity to overcome loss and obtain satisfaction through the object they seek. Instinctual beings can become winners that suffer only contingent failures rather than remaining ensconced in perpetual failure. Instinct holds within it the promise of a satisfaction untainted by loss, a full satiation that, even if it soon disappears, can often be replicated. The being envisions a goal that would provide satisfaction and then either attains the goal or not. Success may be difficult and may not endure, but it's not impossible.

But the subject attains satisfaction through the repetition of its inability to obtain its object. Failure is the subject's mode of success. Lacan describes this in one of his most lucid explanations of the structure of subjectivity. In *Seminar XI*, he separates the subject's goal from its aim and uses a metaphor to explain the aim. He claims, "When you entrust someone with a mission, the *aim* is not what he brings back, but the itinerary he must take. The *aim* is the way taken."[15] The satisfaction of the subject derives from the path that it takes. But what Lacan fails to add here is that this path necessarily involves an encounter with loss: rather than seeking out its object, the subject finds ways to miss it and to ensure that it remains lost. The lost object is constitutively lost, and the satisfaction that it offers depends on it remaining so. The subject has no hope that it might attain its lost object, which is why psychoanalysis must refrain from describing the infant's satisfying relationship with the mother's breast prohibited by the father. It is only in retrospect (or from the perspective of an observer) that this relationship appears perfectly satisfying.

Freud first conceives of the appeal of loss in response to his observation of self-destructive actions that appear to violate the pleasure principle. It is the penchant for self-sabotage and self-destruction that leads Freud to speculate about the existence of a death drive that aims at a return to an inorganic state. But we don't have to indulge in this type of hypothesis if we recognize the constitutive role that loss plays in the subject's satisfaction. Without the lost object, the subject would lose what animates it and the source of its enjoyment. The act of self-sabotage, even though it detracts from the subject's pleasure, enables the subject to continue to satisfy itself. In *Beyond the Pleasure Principle*, Freud theorizes that the negative therapeutic reaction that subverts the psychoanalytic cure is not just the product of resistances. The subject does not want to be cured because it associates healing with the loss of its foundational loss, a prospect much more horrifying that the pain of the neurosis. With the recognition of the constitutive role of loss in the psychic economy, psychoanalysis must alter its conception of the cure. Rather than simply ending repression or even overcoming loss, the cure has to involve changing the subject's relation to its lost object, experiencing the intimate connection between loss and satisfaction.

THE ALLURE OF BUYING A BUNCH OF THINGS

Every subject of the signifier endures loss. This is the primary fact of subjectivity. But the tragic nature of subjectivity leads the subject to misrecognize how it obtains satisfaction. The subject's devotion to loss remains necessarily unconscious as it consciously strives to win. Though the subject attains its satisfaction from the absence of the object, it nonetheless consciously associates satisfaction with the object's presence. For this reason, the subject fails to recognize its own satisfaction and believes itself dissatisfied, but this dissatisfaction feeds on hope for a future success. Though the disappointments pile up, the subject who fantasizes about ultimately obtaining its object continues to look toward the next object as potentially being the one. The subject can keep up its hopefulness only by forgetting the series of disappointments that its previous acquisitions of the object have produced.

The subject moves from object to object in order to avoid confronting the fact that it misses the same lost object again and again. The perpetual movement of desire obscures its rootedness in missing the object rather than obtaining it. The subject fails to see that the object is satisfying as an object and not as a possible possession. When the subject invests itself in the fantasy of obtaining the object, it avoids the monotony of the subject's form of satisfaction. One has dissatisfaction, but one also has a variety of objects that one desires with the promise of a future satisfaction. This future satisfaction never comes, and obtaining objects brings with it an inevitable disappointment. One thought that one was obtaining the impossible lost object, but one ends up with just an ordinary empirical object that pales in comparison. I believed that the piece of chocolate cake that I just ate embodied the lost object itself before I ate it, but after having done so I realize its underwhelming ordinariness.

Perhaps it is because cinema enthusiasts recognize how the film almost perfectly lays out the relationship between the lost object and its inadequate replacements that most acknowledge Orson Welles's *Citizen Kane* (1941) as the greatest film of all time.[16] After an exterior traveling shot of the gate to his mansion, the film begins with Charles Foster Kane (Orson Welles) uttering his dying word, "Rosebud." This word occasions an investigation by newspaper reporter Jerry Thompson (William Alland) in which the story of Kane's life, related by those who knew him, is told through a series of flashbacks. Thompson begins with the idea that the object signified by *Rosebud* will reveal the truth of Kane's desire, though after failing to find this object he concludes that no such object could possibly exist. The final shot of the film, however, belies his concluding remarks by showing Kane's childhood sled with the name *Rosebud* adorning it.

The point is not, as one might expect, that Kane would find fulfillment if he obtained the lost sled representing his abbreviated childhood and the attachment to his mother, but that the sled embodies loss itself. As such, it animates Kane's entire existence. He is a subject insofar as he has endured a constitutive loss. But he consciously seeks out, as the film shows in the interval between the utterance of "Rosebud" and the revelation of the object, a series of expensive objects that cease to provide satisfaction the moment Kane obtains them. The sled metaphorizes loss: it substitutes for what is not there, representing loss as such. In contrast, the objects that Kane collects—statues, paintings, exotic animals, and so on—reveal the metonymy of Kane's desire. He moves from object to object in search of one that might satisfy him, but none does.[17]

While Kane is caught up in the logic of success, he actually follows the path of the failure—and this is true of all seeming winners in the world. His continual failure to find a satisfying object through striving for success produces the unconscious satisfaction of failure. Kane satisfies himself unconsciously through the serial quest for a missing satisfaction. Though he seeks success, he perpetuates failure, and the repetition of failure is the logic of subjectivity. While Kane enacts this process, the spectator undergoes the same dynamic. The film presents a series of flashbacks that promise to reveal the ultimate truth of Kane, but each time the film comes to the end of a flashback, the mystery remains. The spectator's satisfaction in viewing the film doesn't derive from the final revelation but from the repetition of the failed revelations that the final revelation of the lost object punctuates. As a result, the spectator can recognize where to locate her or his satisfaction in a way that Kane cannot.[18]

The final revelation of the truth of the signifier *Rosebud* does not represent a realization of desire for the spectator but a confrontation with the fundamental nothingness of the lost object. This is why the disappointed reaction, "It's just a sled," is entirely appropriate. The sled reveals that, even when there really is an object to be rediscovered, the object embodies nothing and thus cannot offer the ultimate satisfaction. Desire avoids this encounter with the nothingness of the lost object by turning to accumulation, and *Citizen Kane* makes the failure of this path evident. The relative failure at the box office of the film on its highly anticipated release suggests that audiences wanted to cling to the logic of accumulation rather than confront its inevitable failure.

The fact that *Citizen Kane* associates the turn away from the failure of subjectivity with Kane's acquisition of wealth is not coincidental. Capitalist accumulation and consumption, which proceed through the refusal of constitutive loss, operate with the hope of ultimately obtaining the object. One continues to accumulate more capital and more objects, but no amount of accumulation can bring satisfaction. Kane reveals this through the complete indifference that he displays toward the objects he has purchased. Welles also demands that we as spectators share in this indifference. At the end of the film, we see workers simply throwing many of these objects into a fire. The failure of accumulation—and the fantasy that motivates it—becomes fully explicit. But, paradoxically, it is this failure, not future success, that provides the only possible satisfaction. No matter what tack the subject takes, it cannot help but feed the repetitive failure it endeavors to escape.

Nonetheless, failing to grasp the necessity of failure distorts the subject's relation to the Other (the figure or figures of social authority). The subject that fails to grasp the necessity of loss looks for the secret key to the object in the Other. The Other appears to know something that the subject itself does not. For the subject caught up in the logic of success, the Other is captivating because it appears to escape the loss that damages the subject itself. The subject invested in success remains dissatisfied because it fails to register the constitutive nature of loss and seeks satisfaction in an object that the Other desires.

The capitalist subject constantly wonders which object is the most desirable or the most desired by other subjects. For instance, a subject buys a car hoping to find just the right model and color to speak to what other subjects desire. The subject will search for—and never find—the car that perfectly embodies what Jacques Lacan calls the desire of the Other. This is the desire that the subject associates with the other or others that the subject itself desires (and supposes to know the secret of desire). We desire what we assume the Other desires because the Other desires it and because we want to attract the desire of the Other. It is in these two senses that our desire is always the desire of the Other.

The mystery of the desire of the Other lures the subject through its irreducibility to signification. The desire of the Other escapes the signifier—it is what can't be said—but it appears to be attainable through a hermeneutic effort. If we study what the Other wants, it seems as if we could divine the desire that the signifier obscures. But this is a loser's game: there is no substantial Other whose desire we might interpret. Like the subject itself, the Other is divided from its own desire and looks elsewhere to find out what it wants. The desire of the Other appears as a puzzle that one might solve, but this is its great lure. The fantasy of obtaining the object that the Other desires works to convince the subject that it can find satisfying objects. But the crucial insight of psychoanalysis is that the subject's satisfaction is located in how it desires and not what it obtains. With this insight, it provides an important clue for understanding how capitalism works.

BARRIERS WITHOUT BOUNDARIES

The genius of capitalism consists in the way that it manipulates the relationship between the subject and its own satisfaction. Capitalism enables subjects to avoid the trauma of their self-destructive satisfaction and to immerse themselves in the promise of the future. It blinds us to the necessity of loss and immerses us in the logic of success, even though success is nothing but a path on the way to loss. The structures of capitalist production and consumption demand that the subjects involved in them think in terms of success rather than failure, or else these structures would cease to function. The fantasy of successfully obtaining the lost object is essential to the perpetuation of capitalism.

Capitalists must believe that they can acquire the lost object through their investment in the capitalist system. This is most evident in the case of the consumption of the commodity: consumers purchase each new commodity with the hope that this object will be the object that will provide the ultimate satisfaction. But they inevitably find, after some initial pleasure, only more dissatisfaction, which inspires them to purchase another new commodity holding the same illusory promise. Many people buy new cars not so much because the old one no longer works but because they hope to find a satisfaction in the new one that the old one failed to provide. If the old commodity did provide this satisfaction, capitalism would not function, and consumers would not feel obliged to seek out new commodities that they didn't need. What Marx calls capitalism's production of needs treats consumers as subjects that believe in the possibility of the truly satisfying object.[19] Capitalism leads the consumer from one commodity to the next according to the metonymy of desire.

The problem is that the closer the subject comes to the object, the more the object loses what makes it desirable and becomes just an image that cannot provide the promised satisfaction. There is a strict opposition between the image of the object and some other dimension of the object—the object as a remainder that doesn't fit within the world of representation and that renders it desirable. Proximity has a deleterious effect on both the subject's desire and the object's desirability.

The same problem infects capitalist production as well. Capitalists want to increase the productivity of the production process in order to realize greater and greater profits, but increased productivity has the effect of lowering the rate of profit. In short, the very effort to maximize profit becomes a barrier to profit. Marx notices this irony in his perspicacious analysis of capitalism's contradictory processes. He says, "The profit rate does not fall because labour becomes less productive but rather because it becomes more productive. The rise in the rate of surplus-value and the fall in the rate of profit are similarly particular forms that express the growing productivity of labour in capitalist terms."[20] Marx's point here holds whether one accepts the theory of surplus value or not. Capitalists constantly work to increase the productivity of labor in a particular industry, but this increased productivity leads to a lesser rate of profit. More efficient labor enables capitalists to sell for less, and this damages the amount of profit that the capitalist produces. The effort to generate a greater rate of profit within the capitalist system paradoxically lowers the rate of profit.

Capitalists demand increasing productivity in search of the object of their desire—ever growing profit—and they end losing up what they sought. Similarly, crises develop within capitalism not, as one would expect, from a lack of production, but from a surplus. The capitalist crisis is a crisis of too much production or of too many objects. When the production increases and the capitalist economy booms, the economy eventually reaches a point at which consumers no longer have enough money to buy the products, and a crisis results. It is a crisis of too much, not a crisis of not enough, which parallels the crisis that perpetually haunts desire. Like capitalism in crisis, desire has an infinite quantity of objects, but none provide the satisfaction that it seeks. In the arenas of both consumption and production, capitalism remains within the logic and limitations of the fantasy that the satisfying object exists. It adheres to this fantasy and attempts to distance itself at all times from the trauma of subjectivity's inherent failure.

The engine for capitalist production is the accumulation of capital. The capitalist invests in order to accumulate more, and more capital functions as a constantly reappearing object of desire. When I have successfully accumulated a quantity of capital that I anticipate will be satisfying, I experience the dissatisfaction that always accompanies obtaining the object of desire and seek out an additional quantity that I associate with the satisfaction that I have just missed. For the capitalist producer, this process of desire and fulfillment has no temporal or spatial barrier. It can go on infinitely, and the series of disappointments involved has the effect of increasing the subject's investment in the capitalist system. Today's failure energizes the promise of tomorrow.

This holds not just for the capitalist as a subject but also for capital itself. It reproduces itself and augments itself as capital through the attempt to transcend its own quantity. In the *Grundrisse*, Marx provides a precise description of this process that captures the psychic resonance of capitalist production. He says, "as representative of the general form of wealth—money—capital is the endless and limitless drive to go beyond its limiting barrier. Every boundary [*Grenze*] is and has to be a barrier [*Schranke*] for it. Else it would cease to be capital—money as self-reproductive."[21] The transformation of a *Grenze* into a *Schranke*, a boundary into a barrier, is a necessary condition for the self-reproduction of capitalism. If capital acted as if the boundary were a genuine boundary and not a barrier to transcend, it would not be capital—and we would be within a different system, one based on the structure of subjectivity rather than its obfuscation.[22]

The situation is almost exactly the same for the capitalist consumer. Instead of seeking the accumulation of capital, the consumer searches for the commodity that will provide the ultimate satisfaction associated with the lost object. Each new commodity arrives on the market bearing the promise of this satisfaction. I purchase the newest phone, video game, dress, or car with the hope that this commodity will offer the satisfaction that the last one failed to provide, and each time I will be necessarily disappointed. I may feel a few moments of pleasure when I acquire the new commodity, but soon its distance from the impossible lost object will become apparent. I will sink back into the desire for another commodity that hasn't yet failed to deliver.

One can witness the dynamic of the appearance and almost instantaneous disappearance of the lost object manifest itself clearly in the case of children in contemporary capitalism. The child will beg for an object as if this object embodied all possible enjoyment, but even seconds after obtaining the object, the child will cast it aside as completely devoid of the satisfaction that it promised only a very short time earlier. It is difficult to believe that anyone witnessing this commonplace experience would resist the psychoanalytic explanation of the lost object and its role in the subject's desire. Just like the capitalist producer, the consumer's repeated failures do not dampen the investment in the process of consumption but rather enhance it. This is because, while operating wholly according to logic of success, capitalism manages to satisfy the subject's unconscious drive to fail.

Though capitalist subjects experience continuing dissatisfaction when they attain each new and disappointing object, they find satisfaction through the repetition triggered by the perpetual search for the next commodity. This dynamic is crucial to capitalism's staying power. If it just offered dissatisfaction with the promise of future satisfaction, subjects would not tolerate the capitalist system for as long as they have. But capitalism does provide authentic satisfaction—the satisfaction of loss—in the guise of dissatisfaction. What appears as a dissatisfying movement forward from commodity to commodity is actually a satisfying repetition of the loss of the object. The fantasy of acquisition offers the promise of escaping from the trauma of subjectivity while leaving the subject wholly ensconced within it. By offering satisfaction in the form of dissatisfaction, capitalism gives us respite from the trauma of subjectivity without obviating the satisfaction it delivers. This is the genius of the system.

In order to see how dissatisfaction and satisfaction interrelate in the functioning of capitalism, one must refuse the temptation to dissociate them from each other. It is as if each concept represents a different way of looking at the same structure but doesn't itself indicate a distinct structure. Constant dissatisfaction and hope for the future are just a form of appearance that the subject's satisfaction adopts, a form of appearance that renders it amenable to consciousness and to the capitalist system. But this appearance itself doesn't detract from the subject's self-satisfaction, a satisfaction that persists under capitalism's regime of success. The subject under capitalism is satisfied but cannot avow this satisfaction while remaining invested in the capitalist system.

Capitalism's adherence to the fantasy of success at the expense of the necessity of failure is essential to its functioning. Subjects who do not accept this fantasy are not continually seeking new objects of desire and thus are not good consumers or producers, and they inevitably put a wrench in the functioning of the capitalist system. They content themselves with outmoded objects and recognize the satisfaction embodied in the object's failure to realize their desire. Such subjects don't simply settle for less than satisfying objects (as if they were proponents of the reality principle) but instead see their satisfaction in the object's inadequacy. For this type of subject, the fact that the car has a dent in the fender and hesitates going up hills becomes the source of the satisfaction that it provides.

This is a step that the great heroes of American literature—Captain Ahab, Huck Finn, Lily Bart, Jay Gatsby, and the narrator of *Invisible Man*—never make. At the end of each novel in which these characters appear, they continue to seek an adequate object, even if they take up an oppositional position relative to the social order. Huck Finn decides to leave civilization, but he does so in order to find an object that would realize his desire. In this sense, he remains, along with the others, entrapped within the logic of success that capitalism proffers. Even though these heroes expose the vacuity of the American fantasy, they do so from the perspective of the existence of a truly satisfying object and, in this sense, they remain exemplars of capitalist subjectivity.

When one recognizes that no object will provide the ultimate satisfaction, one can divest psychically from the capitalist system. One can reject a role in the incessant reproduction of the capitalist system, a rejection that coincides with a rejection of the logic of success as well. This rejection alone does not topple capitalism, but it is the necessary condition for revolutionary politics. Capitalism induces subjects into investing themselves in the system's reproduction by capturing them at the level of their desires, but this is precisely the level at which the subject can abandon the capitalist system. The logic of subjectivity is itself ultimately incompatible with capitalism and therefore provides the path to an alternative that envisions production and consumption in other ways.

The subject's self-satisfaction derails capitalism's need for perpetually dissatisfied subjects. The difficulty within the capitalist system lies with recognizing this self-satisfaction, since capitalist ideology constantly works to create a sense of dissatisfaction in subjects. The creation of dissatisfaction is almost the sole aim of the advertisement, which shows images of apparently delicious pizza in order to convince viewers that whatever they already have will not provide the same enjoyment as the pizza or which plays the sounds of a new song that promises to outstrip the enjoyment delivered by any older ones. The self-satisfied consumer is no longer a consumer, which is why the very term *customer satisfaction* is inherently misleading. Companies may want some degree of customer satisfaction, but their goal is ultimately enough dissatisfaction to keep customers returning for a new commodity. Such dissatisfaction is what the subject that recognizes its constitutive loss avoids. The production strategy of planned obsolescence, which is integral to the constant expansion of capitalism, depends on the existence of subjects who believe in the promise of the new commodity and thereby miss the satisfaction that exists in the failed commodity—the satisfaction in failure that capitalist subjects experience and yet don't recognize.

THE END OF THE OTHER

Psychoanalysis emerges in response to this unavowed satisfaction and attempts to assist subjects in coming to terms with it. It attempts, in other words, to move subjects from illusory dissatisfaction to a new way of relating to their satisfaction. The path of psychoanalysis, at least after Freud's theoretical revolution in 1920, is not one leading from dissatisfaction to satisfaction but from one form of satisfaction to another. The space in which psychoanalysis can act here is very limited. The cure could only involve allowing the subject to recognize where its satisfaction lies and how it already has what it's looking for. This type of intervention begins with the subject's relation to the Other.

The capitalist subject mistakes satisfaction for dissatisfaction because it fails to recognize the status of the Other. Social existence involves the encounter with others, but beyond these others the subject sees the Other, a figure of social authority that represents the social order as a whole and makes demands on the subject.[23] The subject's subjection to this authority stems from the belief in it, but the Other does not exist. There are figures of social authority (parents, athletes, film stars, presidents), but there is no social authority as such. No one, in other words, knows the secret of social order or how one might fully belong to it.[24] The in-crowd of whatever sort is populated by people who are themselves actually outsiders acting as if they belong. Through an illusion of perspective, the subject doesn't see this. It fantasizes an Other into existence in order to believe that someone knows the impossible secret of true belonging. But this illusion is necessary. The image of the desiring Other kick-starts the desire of the subject. The subject emerges out of the defiles of the desire of the Other that doesn't exist.

The problem of the desire of the Other exists wherever there is signification. But capitalism creates a singular focus on the desire of the Other in a way that no prior socioeconomic system has. This focus on the desire of the Other creates subjects who dedicate themselves to the interpretation of this desire. They spend their time reading fashion magazines, learning about the lives of Hollywood stars, or following the movements of famous sports figures. All of these activities that capitalist society fosters have as the goal interpreting the desire of the Other so that the subjects engaged in this interpretative process can solve the problem of desire. Capitalism brings possible solutions to the desire of the Other to the fore, and it insists that this desire actually exists.

But capitalism does not invent the desire of the Other. The system of signification depends on the gaps in its structure where desire can emerge, but subjects do not immediately desire on their own. Rather than forming organically out of physiological need, desire requires a stimulus, and this is what the desire of the Other provides. In this sense, the desire of the Other is a necessary illusion. The subject confronts the Other in the form of either a group of others or a single individual imbued with authority. From the Other, the subject seeks guidance as to what it should desire and—which is to say the same thing—as to how it might capture the desire of the Other.

There are no desires belonging to the subject itself that it gives up for the sake of the Other. The subject does not simply settle for the desire of the Other or betray its own desire by adopting that of the Other. To the contrary, the subject's own desire derives from its interpretation of the desire of the Other. I begin unconsciously to desire something when I interpret the Other as initially desiring it. This desire becomes my desire—and I believe it is fully genuine—but its origin lies outside my subjectivity. This initial alienation of the subject in the Other is not, however, the final barrier. The true problem is the existential status of the Other. Though the subject believes in the Other, the Other qua figure of authority that has a desire does not exist.

To say that the Other does not exist is not to accept the solipsistic verdict that the subject can know only itself. Instead, it means that there is no authority to guide the subject in its search for what it should desire. While the subject interprets the desire of the Other in order to discover its own desire, the Other itself simultaneously interprets some other desire in order to discover its desire. Desire arises out of this chain of interpretation that has no endpoint. There is no desire that is not the interpretation of a missing desire. If the desire were present and obvious, it would no longer be a desire. We would question what real desire was hidden beneath the manifest one and thus engage again in the act of interpretation.

The absence of a starting point for desire manifests itself in popular fashions. No one person initially decided, for instance, that not taking the tags off new clothes was a cool thing to do. This strange fashion trend began not with one subject's desire but with the interpretation of the desire of the Other.[25] That is to say, subjects adopt this style because they believe that it's already cool. The misinterpretation of the Other's desire retroactively creates an Other who originated the fashion. The subject who believes in an originator of fashion relies on a dangerous and paranoid misinterpretation. A correct interpretation would reveal that there is nothing existing to be interpreted.

FANTASIZING THE END

Since the desire of the Other can provide no concrete guidance for the subject in its search for what to desire, it must have recourse to fantasy. Here capitalism again comes to the subject's aid by providing innumerable fantasies that direct the subject's desire both toward the proper work and toward the proper commodity. Fantasy provides the subject guidance about what the Other desires and thus constitutes this desire as knowable. Without this guidance, there would be no way of approaching this desire or beginning to make sense of it. In some sense, the subject fantasizes this desire into existence: the fantasy gives coherence to the Other's desire by creating an imaginary scenario surrounding the Other. Lacan offers an enigmatic definition of fantasy in his seminar on *The Logic of Fantasy*. He says, "in the final accounting the fantasy is a sentence with a grammatical structure."[26] That is to say, fantasy gives the desire of the Other a concrete form that it otherwise lacks. Even if fantasy imagines a traumatic desire—the Other wants to destroy us—it nonetheless provides the security of an existing Other that can guide our desire.

We can see this dynamic in the way that the fantasy of the terrorist functions for American society. Of course, there are actual terrorists who want to kill Americans, but the power of the terrorist fantasy far outstrips the danger that these actual terrorists represent. Very few people fear driving in a car, and yet one is exponentially more likely to die in this mode of transportation than from a terrorist blowing up an airplane. The latter event occasions dread because it touches on our fantasy space, whereas death in a car—except as envisioned in David Cronenberg's *Crash* (1996), an exploration of auto-eroticism—remains largely fantasy-free. The fantasy of horrible death from terrorism is hardly a comforting one, but it does give American society a concrete image of the Islamic believer. The fantasy brings this believer into existence and renders his— almost always his in the fantasy—desire knowable. The threat to American society constitutes American identity as besieged and, at the same time, envied, which is why, after the terrorist attacks of September 11, 2001, George W. Bush proclaimed that American freedom itself was an overriding motive for the attacks. Even the most traumatic fantasy offers assurance.

The subject's subjection to the social order becomes complete through the acceptance of the fundamental fantasy underlying that order. Confronted with the impossibility of the Other's desire, the subject faces its failure to belong. The respite of fantasy is an image of belonging to an order that seems to bar the subject's entry. It is the password to a secret society. Even the subject who doesn't belong to Skull and Bones at Yale effectively does belong to a larger version insofar as it accepts the society's fundamental fantasy.[27] But the subject can never exist wholly in the world that fantasy constructs. The status of the fantasy must always be tenuous in order for it to work as a source of social cohesion. Capitalism utilizes fantasy to a remarkable extent, but it also sustains fantasy's tenuousness.

Under capitalism, the desire of the Other both remains fundamentally unknowable and appears accessible through fantasy. The subject never knows exactly what commodity to produce or consume, and yet the commodity itself provides a fantasmatic answer to this mystery. The commodity presents itself at once as the unknown desire of the Other and the fantasized solution to that desire. The fact that it maintains these two contradictory positions gives capitalism great power in the psyche. It rouses us by showing the Other as mysterious while comforting us with the idea that we might solve this purported enigma of the Other. If capitalism just offered the mystery of the Other or the fantasized solution of this mystery, it would fail to gain a psychic foothold. The two positions must constantly play off each other, or else the subject's disappointment—either in the irresolvable mystery or the ultimately inadequate solution—will break the commitment to the capitalist system. The fantasy constantly presents the possibility of full belonging to the subject, but, at the same time, the fantasy must remain an unrealized fantasy. The capitalist subject can never experience a sense of belonging while remaining a capitalist subject.

Of all previously existing economic systems, capitalism offers the most evident fantasmatic solution to the problem of the desire of the Other. That is to say, it offers the clearest path to social acceptance and belonging. When we imagine societies with clear marriage rules or entrance rituals, this claim seems clearly wrong. Their solution to the problem of desire appears superior to that of capitalism.[28] Traditional societies don't have the desire of the Other hidden in fashion trends or the production of electronics, but clearly spell it out in social regulations. But the psychic power of the commodity outstrips the most rigid societal structure in its capacity for illuminating the subject's path. The commodity form has the effect of clarifying the desire of the Other by making it manifest in a concrete object. If I doubt what the Other wants me to do, I need only follow the money. It will provide a clear fantasized solution to the desire of the Other. Traditional society, in contrast, offers regulations whose explicit status prevents a complete psychic investment. Capitalism forces the subject to interpret its way into the social order and in this way attaches itself firmly to the subject's desire. At the same time, it guides this interpretation through the commodity form and gives the subject a sense of security in the path of its desire.

When I feel as if I must have a new product, at that moment I fully immerse myself in the fantasy of what the Other desires. Often new products fail—many times more products enter the market each year than find a niche—because they do not manage to locate themselves within consumers' fantasy space. The inventors of failed commodities such as Pepsi Clear did not adequately carve out an appealing fantasmatic position. The success of any product is inextricable from its capacity to lodge itself within this space and to appear as if it completely solves the question of the Other's desire. Even products that endure, like Coke or Apple electronics, must constantly renew themselves in order to remain within the prevailing fantasy. Once they become old, once they are associated with an object that the consumer has already acquired and has discovered to be lacking, they will lose their fantasmatic power. This is why even successful brands have to continue to develop new selling points and to advertise this newness. Apple must produce a new version of the iPhone or the iPad or else consumers will abandon Apple entirely. The company will find itself in the situation of Zenith, a former leader in technological appliances and now a nonentity. We know that the old object does not respond to the desire of the Other, but the new object allows us to keep this fantasy alive.

The value of money depends on the fantasy of the Other that subtends it. I accept money from someone in exchange for a commodity because I have faith that the Other believes in the value of this money.[29] Faith in money is faith in a fantasy about the desire of the Other and its constancy. This is the basis for sociologist Georg Simmel's famous account of money in *The Philosophy of Money*. As Simmel puts it, "money transactions would collapse without trust."[30] If everyone suddenly lost faith in gold as a source of value, the metal would become valueless. This is even more apparent with paper money: we see its loss of value during periods of rampant inflation when people must use wheelbarrows to bring money just to buy groceries. The faith in the Other that informs every financial transaction is a fantasy that the Other actually exists and that everyone else will continue to believe in the existence of this figure.

The capitalist economy makes the fantasy of money its basis and then extends this fantasy into all aspects of economic and social life. The economy functions through speculation about fantasy. Traders on the stock market do not trade based on how they anticipate a company will perform (which might be informed prediction rather than fantasy). Such traders would quickly bankrupt themselves. Instead, they speculate based on their fantasy of fantasies about the Other's desire. They imagine how others who don't really know will envision what companies will produce products that people will want. The stock market is a vast world of fantasy taken to the nth power. But it succeeds because money serves as the royal road to the Other's desire.

FREED FROM THE OTHER'S DESIRE

The principal argument proffered by defenders of capitalism is that the economic freedom inherent in this system is the prerequisite for political freedom.[31] As someone like Milton Friedman has it, any abridgement of economic freedom leads to an abridgement of political freedom, which is why a socialist or communist planned economy must necessarily be totalitarian. The defining characteristic of government, for capitalist theorists, is not its structure or aims but the amount of control it exerts over citizens. From this starting point, there is no difference between a socialist government and a fascist one, since both involve controlling the economic sector and thus limiting (or eliminating) freedom. But this conception of freedom is not as absolute as it claims to be. They do not want freedom in the face of the Other's desire, and this is, not coincidentally, the type of freedom from which capitalism rescues us.

True freedom is freedom in the face of the Other's desire—or, more properly, freedom from the Other's desire. Freedom is an indifference toward the desire of the Other that the subject has when it finds itself fully immersed in its own satisfaction. The free subject ceases to concern itself with the question of the desire of the Other and pursues its own satisfaction regardless of its relationship to the Other. It neither tries to follow the desire of the Other nor deviate from this desire. But capitalism has a profound allergy to this type of freedom and does all it can to ensure a preoccupation with the desire of the Other.

Capitalist society encourages subjects not to decide freely on their work but to flock to where the jobs are. Demand for employment in a certain sector enables subjects to fantasize that this is what the Other wants from them, and they can undergo training to prepare themselves to live out this fantasy. The job market itself is a vast fantasy space where subjects can find the fantasmatic guidelines for how they should desire. A need for welders tells me that I should undergo training as a welder, and a glut of philosophy professors enables me to realize that the Other is telling me not to philosophize. But these various fantasies have nothing to do with the subject's own satisfaction and work actively to deprive the capitalist subject of its freedom.

The capitalist fantasy works not just with finding a job but also—and even more—with deciding what to purchase. With every purchase of a commodity (even an banana or a pastry), one also buys into a fantasy. I purchase what I fantasize that the Other wants from me, and the capitalist structure provides numerous forms of this fantasy from which I can choose. Advertising campaigns are vast explanations of what the Other wants and, by extension, dictates to the subject about what it should want. Advertisers proffer fantasies that the subject can accept in order to escape the burden of the Other's desire. The commodity itself, without any accompanying advertisement, also functions as a fantasy. Its very availability on the market tells me that this might be what the Other wants. Success on the market is the great capitalist fantasy. I must have the new commodity that everyone else must have simply because it is what everyone else must have: this commodity promises a successful answer to the Other's desire. It embodies the promise of fantasy itself.

Capitalism has a parasitic relationship to signification. It mirrors the effects that language has on the speaking being, while cementing the psychic dependence that the speaking being has on the illusory desire of the Other that emerges through signification. Capitalism remolds the subject in its own image and protects the subject from confronting its own traumatic satisfaction. It is, of course, possible to break this hold, to which the bare fact of recognizing it attests. But doing so requires discovering the extent and power of its reach.

Many critics of capitalism have failed to see that desire itself—specifically, the belief that we might realize our desire—is the problem rather than the solution. In an oft-cited statement from *Anti-Oedipus* (their treatise attacking both psychoanalysis and capitalism as they function together), Gilles Deleuze and Félix Guattari claim, "Desire can never be deceived. Interests can be deceived, unrecognized, or betrayed, but not desire."[32] Though Deleuze and Guattari recognize how capitalism appropriates desire—for them, in a manner of speaking, it is nothing but the appropriation of desire—they do not see how desire, though it might not be deceived, can itself be a deception. *Anti-Oedipus* is a panegyric to desire. Capitalism may function through desire, but in the end, it puts the brakes on desire and doesn't take desire far enough. What we need, according to Deleuze and Guattari, is more desire, more refusals of restrictions on desire.

Given the identification that I see at work between capitalism and the fantasy of unrestricted desire, what I am proposing here is an anti-*Anti-Oedipus*. Deleuze and Guattari attack capitalism and psychoanalysis for the obstacles they erect toward the expansion of desire. But the problem isn't the obstacles capitalism creates; it is that capitalism's contingent obstacles obscure the necessity of the obstacle. Capitalism's deception consists in convincing us, as it convinces Deleuze and Guattari, that desire can transcend its failures and overcome all barriers. We don't need more desire, but rather the recognition that the barrier is what we desire. It is this recognition that provides the key for divesting ourselves from the appeal of capitalism.

Even though capitalism's incessant self-reproduction seems to mimic the structure of subjectivity—constant repetition for its own sake—this movement, as manifested in the capitalist system, always has a goal to realize. The capitalism system must promise a better and wealthier future. Neither individual capitalists nor the system as a whole can function without the goal of future enrichment, whereas the subject always operates without the possibility of a more satisfying future. What separates the apparently repetitive circulation of capital from the subject's repetition is accumulation. The subject seeks loss, not successful accumulation, which means that any attempt to link capitalism to subjectivity involves a category error. The subject's satisfaction does not require, and in fact disdains, the illusion of gain that sustains the capitalist system.

The capitalist subject oscillates between dissatisfaction and pleasure, between absence and presence, and it cannot recognize the satisfaction that underlies this oscillation. This subject remains, however, a subject animated by a lost object. As such, it derives its satisfaction from the series of failures to arrive at the pleasure it seeks. Late in *Beyond the Pleasure Principle*, Freud suggests what was for him at the time a disturbing hypothesis. He says tentatively, "The pleasure principle seems actually to serve the death instincts."[33] If we understand "death instincts" here as the subject's attachment to loss, this brief sentence at the conclusion of Freud's brief book provides the most thoroughgoing critique of capitalism that anyone has ever written. The recognition that we are not really pursuing pleasure frees us from the chains of capitalism more completely than any other revolutionary gesture.

The Psychic Constitution
of Private Space

PURSES RATHER THAN PERSONS

Concerns about capitalism's tendency to discourage the constitution of a public world and simultaneously to encourage a retreat into privacy emerge almost as soon as capitalism becomes the dominant socioeconomic system in the world. In *The Social Contract* (which he wrote in 1762), Jean-Jacques Rousseau laments the destructive effect of the turn away from public service. Though he doesn't associate this effect directly with capitalism, he does lay out the alternative to participation in the public world in pecuniary terms. He notes, "As soon as public service ceases to be the Citizens' principal business, and they prefer to serve with their purse rather than with their person, the State is already close to ruin."[1] As capitalism has developed since Rousseau's epoch, this tendency toward privatization has grown exponentially and today threatens the very existence of public space or of a commons.

The increasing privatization that has occurred after capitalism's emergence is a direct product of the logic of capitalism. The more subjects become subjects of capitalism, the more they turn away from public space and seek refuge in their private worlds. Even when capitalism requires that subjects interact with each other in relations of production, distribution, and consumption, it demands that they do so as private beings. The philosophical proponents of capitalism inevitably tout this as a great benefit of the system. Rather than relying on a concern for the public world, it produces a society that succeeds solely on the basis of individuals pursuing their private interest.

What distinguishes the public world from private worlds is the absence of constraint on who can enter into it. Public spaces do not have fences to keep people out, and public forums do not bar anyone from participating. We create private worlds through the act of exclusion: private property is available only to its owners; private clubs are reserved only for members; and private discussions occur among an isolated few. Capitalism doesn't create privacy, but the development of capitalism necessarily coincides with an increasing turn to private worlds. The system has its basis in private property, and the public world implicitly calls this basis into question.[2]

The absence of public space is not simply a problem for the lower classes that cannot afford entry into amusement parks where their children can play or gated neighborhoods where they take a stroll without worrying about violence. The privatization of the commons also represents a retreat from subjectivity itself and from the way the subject satisfies itself. The subject is inherently a public being: its subjectivity forms through its interaction with the desire of the Other. Without this interaction, there would be no subject at all. But capitalism obscures the role the Other has in forming the subject and works to convince the subject that it exists first and foremost as a private being and that public interactions occur only on the basis of this privacy.

In other words, capitalism reverses the actual chronological relationship of public and private. The subject first comes into existence as a public being and subsequently establishes a private world in which it shields itself from the public and fantasizes its isolation from others. The public world gives the subject its desire and forms the subject through subjecting it to the signifier. There is no subject prior to the human animal's interaction with the public world, and the purely private subject is nothing but a capitalist fantasy.

Though Ludwig Wittgenstein did not imagine himself an anticapitalist philosopher, his critique of the idea of a private language in the *Philosophical Investigations* is actually an attack on this capitalist fantasy. Wittgenstein's aim with his discussion of language in this work is to show that language itself is inherently public, that we don't use language as a vehicle for expressing private thoughts that exist prior to or outside of language. Instead, public language provides the basis for the private thoughts that seem to exist independently of it. There can be no private language, Wittgenstin argues, because language depends on rules, and rules make sense only as a public phenomenon.

Wittgenstein contends that the fact that we view people as following rules when they use a language proves that we view them as public beings and language as a public structure. One cannot imagine someone following a rule privately: there would be no way to distinguish whether the person was following the rule or not since there would be no other arbiter of rule-following than the person herself or himself. In his analysis of Wittgenstein's private language argument, Saul Kripke points out, "if one person is considered in isolation, the notion of a rule as guiding the person who adopts it can have *no* substantive content."[3] Language depends on rules, and rules always imply a public. Thus, the speaking subject begins as a public subject, which is why we can judge whether or not this subject correctly follows the rules of the language it uses. If the subject were first a private being and only secondarily a public one, we could not judge the subject's relationship to the rules of language. The fact that we do reveals that we view the subject as a public being even as capitalism tries to convince us of its private status.

What's more, the satisfaction of the subject depends on its exposure to the public. The public world disturbs the psychic equilibrium of the subject, but this disturbance is the source of the subject's satisfaction. It inaugurates subjectivity by installing an obstacle for the subject that begins its desiring. The subject experiences the obstacle as a barrier to its desire, but it is this obstacle that constitutes the desiring subject. The subject depends on the public world for the obstacle that enables it to desire, even though this obstacle at the same time makes the subject's desire impossible to realize.

It seems counterintuitive to say that our satisfaction depends on the obstacle to our desire. But the counterintuitive status of this claim testifies to the extent of our investment in the priority of privacy. When we imagine ourselves as essentially private beings, we view the public world as a threat to the realization of our desire. This view leads one to safeguard one's privacy. But if we view the object as a necessary obstacle that provides us satisfaction only as long as it remains as obstacle, we will commit ourselves to the public world and the encounter with the other qua obstacle that occurs in that world.

We ensconce ourselves in privacy in order to ensure that others can't disturb our self-satisfaction and thereby fail to recognize how our satisfaction depends on this disturbance, which is why we nonetheless fantasize the possible disturbance even as we isolate ourselves from it. The contemporary turn away from public space is simultaneously a turn away from our own subjectivity and from the disturbing satisfaction that accompanies this subjectivity. Privacy promises security not just from physical threats but also from the threat of our own subjectivity, and the price of this security is the possibility of recognizing the source of our satisfaction.

Nonetheless, a key component of capitalism's appeal is the privacy—and thus the protection from the encounter with the form that our satisfaction takes—that it offers. If I remain within my own private property, I protect myself not from my neighbor's satisfaction that might intrude on my own (the blaring music, the ostentatious orgies, and so on) but from my own satisfaction. The apotheosis of privacy and private property that corresponds to the development of capitalism represents the greatest protective barrier to satisfaction that the world has ever witnessed. Universal private property functions like a universal ban on satisfaction (though this ban, like all bans, doesn't work).

In order to understand the division between public and private space, Rousseau distinguishes between two forms of subjectivity—*homme* and *citoyen*. An *homme* is a figure of the private world who pursues self-interest and neglects wider concerns, while a *citoyen* is devoted to the public world and interacts in that world. Though Rousseau has fears about the *homme* completely eclipsing the *citoyen*, it is not until the twentieth century that the threat to the public world becomes dire and seemingly irreversible. The first philosopher to pay attention to this threat was Hannah Arendt, who, in *The Human Condition*, chronicles what she calls the evanescence of action and work at the expense of labor.[4] For Arendt, labor occurs exclusively in the private realm and concerns only the reproduction of life. Because it confines itself to private reproduction, labor has no creative power.[5] Work, in contrast, creates a public world, and action represents political engagement in this world. When labor becomes our privileged or even sole mode of being, we lose these creative possibilities.

The critique of the disappearance of the *citoyen* becomes even more pronounced in the work of Giorgio Agamben and Jacques Rancière.[6] Both Agamben and Rancière notice an evanescence of politics in the contemporary world. The protection and reproduction of life—what Arendt calls labor—has invaded and subsumed the realm of politics. As Agamben points out in numerous works, a zone of indistinction between life and politics has arisen. He claims, "our private biological body has become indistinguishable from our body politic, experiences that once used to be called political suddenly were confined to our biological body, and private experiences present themselves all of a sudden outside us as body politic."[7] The transformation of politics into private concerns about life and the body is the elimination of politics proper. The *homme* comes to replace the *citoyen* completely, and with the disappearance of the *citoyen* we enter into a world dominated by privacy and bereft of public space.

This transformation is not simply a cultural transformation, a product of changing social mores. It is intrinsically connected to the development of capitalism. The premise of the capitalist economy is that the subject is fundamentally an *homme* and only secondarily a *citoyen*. Concern for one's private interest always trumps concern for the public world, and one becomes involved in public matters only to safeguard private interest, like the homeowners who protest the construction of a nuclear power plant because it would threaten their property values. The capitalist system encourages elevation of privacy as the only real concern, and it thus leads to the elimination of politics as such.

Capitalist economists, whatever their specific orientation, accurately identify the system's reliance on private interest and its opposition to the public world. As a field, economy limits its judgments on why people pursue the ends that they do and focuses on what they do. According to the foundational axiom of capitalist economics, people act as they desire. But this desire is always conceived as the desire for the advancement of private interest. From Adam Smith to the leading current capitalist economists, the pursuit of private interest has remained the governing explanation for human behavior. Smith famously claims, "It is not from the benevolence of the butcher, the brewer, or the baker that we expect our dinner, but from their regard to their own interest. We address ourselves, not to their humanity, but to their self-love, and never talk to them of our own necessities, but of their advantages."[8] Capitalism works through its reliance on private interest and its disdain for the public world, which takes care of itself when we allow private interest free reign.

The public world is at best a beneficent by-product and at worst an intransigent barrier to capitalist production. According to the theoretical champions of capitalism, this world has no independent existence because no one acts on its behalf. When people enter the public world, it is in order to advance their self-interest and affect changes in their private world, which is the only world that really counts. Capitalism disregards the public world because this world is not where our interest lies.

Capitalism only functions properly, however, when we accede to the self-interestedness of human nature. This is a claim that almost every capitalist economist repeats. For instance, in his *Principles of Economics*, marginal utility theorist Carl Menger argues, "every individual will attempt to secure his own requirements as completely as possible to the exclusion of others."[9] When capitalism runs as smoothly as it can, this pursuit of private requirements leads to the gratification of the requirements of others. Serving one's private interest benefits the public good.

Even as behavioral economists have recently begun to correct the dogmatism of rational choice theory and insist on the limits of the human pursuit of maximal self-interest or utility, the underlying assumptions of the driving forces of economic activity remain relatively the same. If choices cease to be completely rational, private self-interest is nonetheless the foundational point of departure. The behavioral revolution is less a revolution than a reform designed to keep the system—or at least our ways of understanding the system—afloat.

The rational choice theorist contends that individuals act according to the dictates of private interest. If we look at behavioral economist Richard Thaler's modification of rational choice theory, we can see how the underlying assumption of private self-interest remains the same. Thaler concludes his purportedly revolutionary *The Winner's Curse* with an argument for a new way of accounting for economic activity. He says, "rational models tend to be simple and elegant with precise predictions, while behavioral models tend to be complicated, and messy, with much vaguer predictions. But, look at it this way. Would you rather be elegant and precisely wrong, or messy and vaguely right?"[10] Thaler and other behavioral economists like Daniel Kahneman challenge our capacity for choosing rationally where our private self-interest lies, but they don't challenge the idea of private self-interest itself. This idea is implicit within the capitalist system and not just the product of some wrongheaded economists. If one invests oneself in the exigencies of the capitalist economy, one necessarily sees some form of self-interest as the motivating factor in life.

Thinking of ourselves as private and self-interested beings may seem unflattering, but at the same time, it enables us to avoid confronting the intrusion of the public world in our own satisfaction. The trauma manifested in the neighbor is the trauma of our own subjectivity that refuses to allow us to pursue our self-interest, no matter how diligently we commit ourselves to this project. The great deception of the capitalist system is that it convinces us that we are self-interested beings when we are in fact beings devoted to imperiling and even destroying our self-interest.

Capitalism and its defenders take pride in admitting that capitalism assumes the worst in people and then takes advantage of their baseness to develop widespread social prosperity. But capitalism's success doesn't stem from its brutal honesty about the human psyche. Subjects adhere to it so fervently because it protects them from confronting the traumatic nature of their mode of obtaining satisfaction. Capitalism's picture of the psyche is actually too flattering, not too pessimistic. Capitalism allows us to believe that we find satisfaction in what we successfully accumulate and not in our unending pursuit of failure.

RETREATING BEHIND THE GATE

The theorists of capitalism envision the development of social interaction, but this interaction remains just an extension of private self-interest. There is no public world—and no public space—in the capitalist world that they theorize because capitalism constantly works against the formation of this world. Capitalism's allergy to the public world inspires a thoroughgoing retreat from this world. This retreat manifests itself in massive privatization.

The contemporary impulse to privatize public areas is widespread: it manifests itself in the call to sell publicly owned land, to create privately owned and maintained roads, to build private prisons, to construct gated communities, and, in the most general terms, to privilege "austerity" in public finances. The worldwide response to the financial crisis of 2008 cogently reveals the extent of today's obsession with privacy, especially when we contrast it with Franklin Roosevelt's reaction to the Great Depression. Though there were attempts to use government money to stimulate economic growth and rescue the economy, these efforts were often inadequate and reflected a clear bias against public investment. Rather than committing substantial resources to the development of a national rail system or alternative energy plants, Barack Obama's stimulus package of 2009 had no broad public aims and included large expenses for tax cuts, a private rather than a public stimulus focused on increasing consumption.[11] This is an indication of the increased hold that capitalist thinking has on the world today.

But even Barack Obama's minimal gesture toward public investment met with severe criticism and occasioned an exaggerated concern with budget deficits. This same concern prompted the austerity movement in European countries as well, where leaders cut spending on public projects. The ostensible line of thought behind these cuts was that public debt was responsible for the economic crisis, when it was clear that the turn to privacy and away from public oversight was the culprit. The fact that private speculation, not government spending, occasioned the crisis disappeared beneath the apotheosis of privacy that followed the crisis. It was as if privacy, so self-evidently a good, couldn't possibly be to blame. As a result, the cause of the financial crisis—less investment in the public world—becomes the solution to it. Such Bizarro World thinking reveals not that people are easily manipulated but the extent to which the investment in privacy dominates our thinking today. We can't imagine that privacy might be the problem, nor can we imagine that a greater commitment to the public world might be the solution. But this degree of investment in privacy has not always been the case within the capitalist system.

Despite capitalism's inherent tendency toward privacy, the emergence of capitalism coincided with an unprecedented creation of public space and an explosion of the public sphere of political contestation. Though such space existed in classical Greece and other societies, it is only in capitalist modernity that public space and the public sphere loses the restrictiveness that characterizes it in its past manifestations. That is, the bourgeois public sphere is open, at least theoretically, to anyone who desires to enter into it. This is what Jürgen Habermas celebrates—and then laments its decline—in *The Structural Transformation of the Public Sphere*.[12] Though Habermas is not an apologist for capitalism, he does see its initial benefit for the development of a public. He claims, "Bourgeois culture was not mere ideology. The rational-critical debate of private people in the *salons*, clubs, and reading societies was not directly subject to the cycle of production and consumption, that is, to the dictates of life's necessities. Even in its merely literary form (of self-elucidation of the novel experiences of subjectivity) it possessed instead a 'political' character in the Greek sense of being emancipated from the constraints of survival requirements."[13] The emergence of public sites for political discussion did not haphazardly coincide with capitalism's rise to dominance. The two are intricately related. Capitalism leads to the development of a public world because it necessitates interaction in the form of exchange.

Though capitalism and its defenders constitute exchange as a private matter between individuals, the process of exchange tends, at least initially, to produce a public world in which exchange can occur.[14] This public world brings subjects into contact with each other and creates the political debate Habermas celebrates. But the public world of nascent capitalist society remains only a side effect of capitalist relations of production rather than an intrinsic necessity. That is to say, the structure of capitalist exchange leads to the formation of public space but doesn't necessitate that space. If exchange could occur uninterrupted without any public world, then this world would not form.

In *The Structural Transformation of the Public Sphere*, Habermas laments the disintegration of this sphere, but he doesn't try to explain this transformation in terms of changes within capitalism itself. Nonetheless, capitalism itself does change during the time of the disintegration of the public sphere. The most significant shift in the nature of capitalism occurs gradually, but most dramatically, at the end of the nineteenth century. Whereas early capitalism focuses on the act of production and the creation of dedicated laborers, twentieth-century capitalism creates consumers. Twentieth-century subjects of capitalism don't consume in order to work like their forebears, but rather work in order to consume. When consumption—an ostensibly private activity—becomes one's end, public space and public discussion cease to be a primary concern. The subject can consume in private, and as consumption becomes the only social preoccupation, public space becomes increasingly rare. Private spaces that provide arenas for consumption, like shopping malls, come to function as ersatz public spaces. The problem with these ersatz public spaces is that the rules of privacy apply there, in contrast to genuine public spaces. The private security forces of a mall can police political discussion, squelch dissent, and prohibit collective association without any repercussions whatsoever.[15] The public police force cannot act in this way in public space. Though there are countless examples of public police forces squelching dissent, they typically must keep up the appearance of respecting the right to dissent, which is what private security forces can disregard. Here appearances matter because they effectively sustain the freedom of the public world.

Many of the cultural theorists who lament the recent decline of a public space link this decline either directly or indirectly to the predominance of consumerism. Sociologist Robert Putnam, for instance, views the turn away from the public world as a consequence of a specific form of consumption—television watching. In his celebrated account of rampant privatization in *Bowling Alone*, he claims, "More television watching means less of virtually every form of civic participation and social involvement."[16] The consumption of television and video images appeals to contemporary subjects in a way that "civic participation" cannot. It allows subjects to bypass the possibility of trauma that arises from public encounters and to live within the safety of the private world. This is what Christopher Lasch labels the "culture of narcissism," a culture in which public life becomes anathema and "consumption promises to fill the aching void."[17] For theorists such as Putnam and Lasch, consumption carries with it an automatic identification with privacy.

But to lay the blame on consumption for the decline of the public world would be to proceed too quickly. Certainly capitalism depends on consumption, and consumption occurs in private transactions. With the advent of the Internet, consumption can become even more private: one need not leave one's home in order to consume as much as one wants, and one need not even rely on the public mail system to receive one's new commodities. But consumption retains a public dimension insofar as one consumes in order to make an impression on the Other. Though there are commodities that subjects buy for completely private consumption, most have a clear public effect. A designer dress, an iPhone, a minivan, even a cup of Starbucks coffee—these popular objects owe their popularity to the effects that they have on the public. We consume in order to be thought of in a certain way. I am the kind of person who drives a minivan, while you are the kind that wears a designer dress. The private purchase of the commodity speaks to the public that it ostensibly avoids.

The evanescence of the public world and of public space is not directly attributable to the turn from a production-oriented to a consumption-oriented capitalism, but is nonetheless related to the essential structure of the capitalist economy. As capitalism has developed, it has not only emphasized consumption as an economic motor over production, but it has also increasingly convinced subjects that they could attain the lost object, which has augmented hostility to the public world, the site of necessary loss. As subjects invest themselves in the ideal of unlimited satisfaction, the possibility of a public gradually disappears. The public world depends on subjects who recognize that their satisfaction depends on the encounter with the obstacle of otherness.

THE PUBLIC OBSTACLE TO PRIVACY

From its inception, psychoanalysis has taken the side of the individual subject in this subject's struggle against the demands of civilization. In this sense, it seems to be a certified opponent of the public world. Neurosis, as understood by psychoanalysis, is nothing other than the price the subject pays for its submission to the demands made by the social order. The neurotic symptom emerges out of the subject's refusal to submit completely.[18] In *Civilization and Its Discontents*, Freud goes so far as to wonder if entrance into society as such represents a good deal for the individual. He sees that the pleasure principle might be easier to fulfill without social restrictions. Freud notes, "In the developmental process of the individual, the programme of the pleasure principle, which consists in finding the satisfaction of happiness, is retained as the main aim. Integration in, or adaptation to, a human community appears as a scarcely avoidable condition which must be fulfilled before this aim of happiness can be achieved. If it could be done without that condition, it would perhaps be preferable."[19] In the end, Freud does not believe it possible to do without social restrictions altogether, even if, from some perspective, that might be "preferable."

If psychoanalysis emerges out of the suffering that integration into the social order causes, it also reveals how the subject's satisfaction depends on the public world that appears to thwart this satisfaction. This idea, as much as any other, forms the basis for psychoanalytic practice. Unlike philosophers like Descartes or Kant, Freud doesn't believe that one can arrive at the truth of one's being through private introspection. It is only when one is in public and talking to others that one reveals this truth. This is why others know us better than we know ourselves, even when we try to maintain a hidden inwardness that we reveal to no one. In order to interact with others, we must constantly pay attention not to what they say explicitly but to the desire that their words express in the act of concealing.[20] We constantly read the unconscious truth of those with whom we interact. No amount of introspection can replace public interaction for the revelation of truth.

Psychoanalysis eschews the possibility of self-analysis for precisely this reason. Although Freud claims to have performed a self-analysis, and even published the results, he doesn't develop this as a general practice or possibility. In fact, Jacques Lacan calls Freud's self-analysis the "original sin" of psychoanalysis. Self-analysis is impossible because it remains within the domain of privacy, a domain predominated by narcissistic illusion and imaginary ideals. Private analysis or self-reflection always obeys the restrictions of consciousness and never allows the disturbance of the unconscious to manifest itself. We might go so far as to seek our unconscious introspectively, but it will always remain one step ahead of our conscious self-reflection. A disturbance that we seek is never a disturbance. In public interactions, however, one often does encounter the unconscious. It erupts all the time and forces us to engage in a constant quasi psychoanalysis of each other just to navigate our daily life.

When we practice self-reflection, we pay attention to our conscious intentions rather than to the signifiers that we employ unconsciously. To psychoanalyze oneself is to fall further into one's private self-deception. Psychoanalysis requires the analyst to act as the point of connection to the public world. The lack of a face-to-face encounter in the psychoanalytic session is simultaneously an abandonment of private intimacy. The patient speaks to a public and not a private desire. This association of psychoanalysis with the public world places it at odds with the demands of capitalism.

The psychoanalytic session—and this distinguishes it, more than anything else, from other forms of therapy—occurs in a public space. Even though psychoanalysts don't typically go on television and give public accounts of their patients' private lives, the act of analysis itself is public in the sense that it publicizes what the patient would prefer to have remain private. In the act of analysis, the patient confronts a public and articulates its desire through this confrontation. The analyst stands in for the desire of the public, and the subject discovers its desire through the encounter with this desire of the Other.[21] By assisting the subject in discovering and naming its own desire, psychoanalysis hopes to lead the subject to a changed relation with its object. Subjects come to psychoanalysis without knowing the truth of their desire, and they leave, hopefully, recognizing that the satisfaction of desiring derives from the obstacle rather than from overcoming it.

This is the recognition that the logic of capitalism spares the subject. The capitalist subject views the trauma of the public encounter as a temporary barrier on the path to an immersion in the complete satisfaction of privacy. The capitalist subject enters the public world—by, say, driving on public roads—in order to arrive at a shopping mall where it can purchase a potentially satisfying object of desire and then return to enjoy that object in private. Satisfaction, for the capitalist subject, resides in the private realm because this is a realm where one can have the object without the barrier that exists in public.

Psychoanalysis provides a different relationship to the object. The capitalist subject imagines itself dissatisfied because it imagines itself constantly overcoming obstacles to arrive at the object, but in fact the obstacles are the object. If the subject can recognize its satisfaction in its obstacle, then the public world undergoes a dramatic transformation. Rather than seeking an object in this world and retreating with the object into one's private oasis, one must embrace the public world as the site of the obstacle. Without the public qua obstacle, the subject would lose its ability to satisfy itself, which is why capitalism's hostility to the public world itself is not sincere. But the subject has the ability to recognize the public obstacle to the realization of its desire as the source of its satisfaction.[22]

The changed attitude toward the obstacle permits the subject to find satisfaction where it formerly saw only dissatisfaction. The barrier to the satisfaction that capitalism posits transforms into the source of the satisfaction for the subject. Satisfaction in the obstacle replaces an unending and dissatisfying pursuit. The subject overcomes the constitutive dissatisfaction that capitalism requires by transforming the relation to the obstacle. The subject that finds satisfaction in the obstacle doesn't fit well into the role of the capitalist producer or consumer.

Our desire moves metonymically from object to object without ever successfully obtaining satisfaction in the object that it seeks. Each time that I obtain an object of desire, I quickly find this object dissatisfying and move on to another object. This is because of the key distinction between the object of desire and the object that causes desire (or what makes the object of desire desirable). The object that arouses my desire is not the object of desire itself but what prevents me from obtaining this object, the barrier to an experience of the object's complete abundance.[23] Desire depends on the obstacle, but the capitalist subject doesn't recognize this dependence and instead imagines that the obstacle is only there to be surpassed. This inability to recognize the necessity of the obstacle produces the capitalist subject's hostility to the public world, which is the obstacle as such, the obstacle that causes the subject to emerge.

While adhering to the logic of capitalism, the subject doesn't grasp the constitutive role of the limit. It is the difference between the Coke that I drink and the can that limits the amount of Coke that I have. This limit constitutes the Coke as desirable, and as a barrier, it functions as the object-cause of my desire. When I have the object of desire without the object-cause, without the limit that prevents me from fully having it, I cease to desire the object of desire, and it becomes a normal empirical object. If I could drink an unlimited amount of Coke at any time, I would simply cease to desire it.[24] It is not only the can but also concerns about health, caloric intake, and propriety that serves as obstacles to this unbridled consumption. The fact that I would become obese if I drank two liters of Coke per day institutes even the desire for a small bottle. The object-cause of desire—that is, the obstacle to the object of desire— renders the latter sublime and thus desirable. But the capitalist subject remains blind to the constitutive role of the obstacle and thus remains resistant to venturing out into the public world where obstacles abound.

Psychoanalysis reveals, in contrast, that the subject's satisfaction derives from the repetition of the failure to obtain the object, and the subject who recognizes the form of its satisfaction can see the necessity of the public world, which is the site of the subject's original loss. The satisfaction of the subject does not reside in what it accumulates but in its repeated failures to accumulate. Though the capitalist subject sees itself as avoiding repetition by moving from object to object, this subject repeats the same trajectory without knowing it. Even though the object changes, the failure remains the same. The capitalist subject, just like every subject, finds satisfaction in failure. It is just that the capitalist subject doesn't recognize the form of its own satisfaction. But this misrecognition can have dramatic effects on the structure of the social order.

We can see how the change in attitude toward the object turns the subject toward the public world at the conclusion of François Truffaut's first feature, *Les quatre cents coups* (*The 400 Blows*, 1959). The film recounts the troubled youth of Antoine Doinel (Jean-Pierre Léaud), whose constant disobedience lands him in a reform school. Truffaut places Doinel and the spectator in a position of the capitalist subject: he seeks an object that he cannot find and encounters the intractable barrier of prohibition laid down by authority figures (his father, the police, and so on). In the final sequence of the film, however, Antoine undergoes a thorough transformation: a famous tracking shot follows him as he flees the reform school and runs down a long path toward the ocean.

As Doinel arrives at the ocean, Truffaut turns the tables on the spectator with a closing shot that is almost unprecedented in its audacity. Rather than finding freedom at the shore or the realization of his desire as the spectator expects, Doinel encounters the ocean as an obstacle that forces him to turn back toward the public world he has fled throughout the film. In the final shot, Truffaut follows Doinel to the water's edge, and the film ends with a freeze-frame of Doinel as he turns around and returns to the world. This is one of the key scenes in Truffaut's filmmaking career because it clearly depicts the move from seeking the satisfying object to finding the necessity of the obstacle and its ramifications for the public world. The subject that recognizes the necessity of the obstacle, like Doinel at the end of *Les quatre cents coups*, no longer flees the public but opens itself to the public world, which is what Truffaut suggests with the turn back toward the world in the final shot.

This subject recognizes that there is nothing beyond the public world and that its satisfaction can only be found through this obstacle, not by escaping it.[25]

INVASION OF PRIVACY

The totalitarianisms of the twentieth century seem to bespeak the dangers of the public world that eclipses all privacy. Under Stalinism one could have no private life that might not at any moment become a public crime. Stalinism's universal suspicion appears to be the nefarious result of its complete elimination of privacy. Private dissent became implicitly public and treasonous—and thus punishable with the gulag or death. If capitalism has a tendency toward privatization, at least it saves us from the totalitarian rule that renders everything public. One might, along these lines, interpret the contemporary turn toward privatization as a response to a ruthless totalitarian rule that forced every bit of privacy under public scrutiny.

But as Hannah Arendt makes clear in her famous study of Nazism and Stalinism, these systems did not develop out of an embrace of universalized public space but rather out of a profound commitment to privacy. This is a point in *Origins of Totalitarianism* that few subsequent thinkers have noticed, but it fits within Arendt's critique of privacy developed in other works. For this reason, it is perhaps the key insight of her analysis. As Arendt describes how totalitarian rule emerges, she claims, "Nothing proved easier to destroy than the privacy and private morality of people who thought of nothing but safeguarding their private lives."[26] It is precisely the attempt to cling to one's private world and avoid the public that nourishes the totalitarian impulse that wipes out all privacy. A commitment to the public world itself sustains the private world as the product of the former.

In this sense, totalitarianism is not the reverse side of liberalism's insistence on sustaining the private world at all costs, but instead the ultimate end point of this insistence. The more one seeks to safeguard privacy and clear the path for capitalist relations of production, the more one also leaves space for the rise of totalitarianism. The totalitarian leader might eliminate privacy but is able to do so because a commitment to privacy predominates. One cannot imagine the rise of totalitarianism without capitalism's destruction of the public world.

Still, concern about capitalism's destruction of the public world seems misplaced in the context of contemporary events. The greatest threat today seems to be the elimination of privacy, not the destruction of the public world. There may be whistle-blowers who come forward to expose secret assaults on the public, but they are in prison or exile for bringing the evisceration of privacy to light. Our privacy appears imperiled in the face of assaults from both the state and from the corporate world. It has become increasingly difficult to exist off the capitalist grid, to find a private place in which one might challenge the dominance of the capitalist system.

We live today in a surveillance society in which there is increasingly less space where subjects can act without being observed. If capitalism ushers subjects into a private world, it is also developing a system of surveillance that appears to eliminate the possibility of privacy. Though we can be reasonably sure that no one surreptitiously opens our letters and reseals them, we can be also be reasonably certain that some system is actually monitoring our e-mail and cell phone communications as well as observing us for much of the day. Surveillance has become the norm in contemporary capitalism.

But widespread surveillance doesn't have the effect of eliminating our investment in privacy and our private worlds. Instead, surveillance—and knowledge about that surveillance—has the effect of heightening our commitment to privacy. When surveillance threatens the private world, we respond by identifying entirely as private beings, which is precisely the response the surveillance aims to trigger. The ideological function of surveillance is not the elimination of privacy but the creation of subjects who see themselves only in terms of privacy. Surveillance leads one to think of oneself as an essentially private being whose private life threatens to become visible.[27]

Whether one responds to surveillance with outrage or acquiescence, the fact of thinking about oneself as a being subjected to surveillance already indicates a turn away from the public and toward the private. In this sense, surveillance ipso facto privatizes us. This is clearest in those who see increasing surveillance as an existential threat that they must defend themselves against. They retreat into enclaves of privacy and erect more and more barriers to any public contact in order to preserve their private worlds. But by doing so, they play right into the hands of the structure they believe they are opposing. They accept that they have a private world and a private being to treasure. But one cannot defeat the privatization of the world by retreating into privacy.

Those who simply accept surveillance often do not escape its ideological hold either, though their investment in privacy is not as easy to see. Surveillance ensconces subjects in a self-relation built around privacy, and going about one's daily existence under surveillance tends to focus one's attention on one's private interests. This is evident in many consumer interactions with companies on the Internet. On the Internet, surveillance is even more thoroughgoing than it is in London, the city with the most surveillance cameras in the world.

As everyone who has ever made an online purchase knows, companies track the electronic behavior of individuals in order to know how best to market to them. They keep records on the websites individuals visit, the products they purchase, and contacts they make on social networks. Most individuals tacitly appreciate this tracking because it facilitates the act of consumption. Amazon.com knows which coupon to send to one customer, and Nike knows which shoe to advertise to another. Everyone comes out ahead. Surveillance facilitates the consumption process by eliminating barriers to the object of desire. It is easier to find what one wants on Amazon.com because the company has tracked previous purchases and browsing activity. When one accepts this easy access to the object, one has adopted the attitude toward desire that capitalist society constantly encourages in its subjects.

Other acts of surveillance, however, have no direct bearing on subjects accessing their objects of desire. Surveillance of private phone calls in the United States by the National Security Agency or the millions of surveillance cameras placed throughout Great Britain observing the minutiae of individual activity do not make it easier for me to accumulate. But these apparatuses do function as evidence for the essentially private nature of existence. They constantly remind us that we have something to hide, something that belongs to us alone.

The premise that animates the surveillance society is that the subject is an essentially private being. In public interactions the subject dissimulates and obfuscates its true desire, but in private that desire becomes evident. When I'm in public, I alter my actions according to the expectations of the Other, but when I'm in private, no such barrier exists. I'm free to be myself, which is why the system of surveillance focuses on the private sphere and increasing our investment in it.

In the face of an almost ubiquitous surveillance perpetuated by both state and corporate forces, it seems ludicrous to lament the decline of the public world. And yet, our satisfaction depends on this public world and the obstacle to desire it erects. Threats to privacy are not threats to the subject's mode of satisfaction. Privacy itself is the threat. Surveillance is only a danger insofar as it convinces us that we have an essentially private being that might be subjected to surveillance. The subject's essence is always outside of itself and readily visible to the public. For the subject that recognizes the necessity of the obstacle, there is nothing for the surveillance camera to see. The subject necessarily exposes itself in the form of its subjectivity.

In the public world, the subject is a *citoyen*, someone engaged in affairs that concern everyone. But one comes to be a *citoyen* only through recognizing that one's status as *homme* depends on the obstacles of the public world. In this sense, Rousseau's distinction breaks down when we analyze how the *homme* satisfies itself. This is also the problem with all the critiques of the emergence of the *homme* and the disappearance of the *citoyen* that populate contemporary political thought. The retreat into privacy that increasingly marks capitalist society cannot be overcome with moral calls for engagement with the commons. The most effective counter to privacy lies in showing that the retreat into privacy is actually a retreat from the subject's own satisfaction, which depends on the public world that the private subject tries to flee. As long as we remain committed to obtaining the object (whatever that object is), the private world will seem like the only site for satisfaction. But there is no satisfaction for the subject without the act of engaging the public. When we recognize the necessity of the public trauma, we accede to our status as *citoyens*.

[3]

Shielding Our Eyes
from the Gaze

THE IMAGE OF NEUTRALITY

In *The Usual Suspects* (Bryan Singer, 1995), Verbal Kint (Kevin Spacey) describes the mysterious villain Keyser Soze by comparing him to the devil and quoting, without citation, Baudelaire. He claims, "The greatest trick the Devil ever pulled was convincing the world he didn't exist."[1] By hiding his existence, the Devil can operate stealthily through seemingly self-motivated human actions. Though many on the Left equate capitalism with the Devil, capitalism operates in exactly the opposite fashion. Its basic trick consists not in hiding its existence but in proclaiming that it exists. This trick proves so effective that it blinds not just the true believers but also even some of the system's most thoughtful detractors. Of course, capitalism really exists in the sense that it functions as today's controlling economic system, but it doesn't exist as the substantial ground of our being, which is the status that it has for the capitalist subject.

Capitalism is not the default economic system that results from the failure to decide politically on some alternative. It is political through and through. Its existence depends on the collective decision that brought it into being and that continues to sustain its development, and it is in this sense that it doesn't exist. But this decision is difficult to see. Whereas one could easily link the existence of communism to a revolutionary decision that creates its rule, no such decision inaugurates capitalism. No one would mistake the communist system that arose in Russia in 1917 with the natural order of things. But capitalism appears as a neutral background that emerges out of being itself, an economic system that simply develops on its own and continues unabated unless it encounters political interference.

Capitalism owes much of its strength as an economic system to its guise of neutrality, to its illusion of belonging to the order of existence. If it isn't a system at all or even a way of life, but just *the* way of life, then the idea of contesting it is nonsensical and doomed to failure. According to this way of thinking, the communist revolutions of the twentieth century ran aground not because of their own internal contradictions but because they attempted to violate the economic laws of nature. The idea of capitalism's natural status or its correlation with human nature provides the fundamental obstacle to any attempt to contest capitalism's dominance. Before one can challenge capitalist relations of production, people must believe that capitalism doesn't exist, that it results from a break within the structure of being itself rather than simply deriving from that structure. The key to taking this step lies in an investigation of how the nonexistence of capitalism becomes evident. It does so only at moments of crisis, which is what gives crisis its theoretical fecundity.

Though subjects within the capitalist universe experience themselves as free (free to make money, free to consume what they want, and so on), the system spares them the weight of the decision. We make numerous decisions every day concerning what to do, where to go, and what to buy, but none of these decisions occurs outside the confines of the narrow limits of our given possibilities. The political decision, the decision concerning our way of life itself, disappears within the capitalist horizon. None of our everyday choices involves the risk of a radical transformation, but all offer the security of a well-known terrain instead. This security is the direct result of the belief in the substantial existence of capitalism, a belief the system itself requires and sustains.

Belief in the existence of capitalism has become especially pronounced with the absence of any economic alternative. Political theorists today often lament the absence of political engagement among subjects within the capitalist economy. The problem is not just that few actively engage in political struggle but that it is difficult to conceptualize the world in political terms. Rather than seeing themselves as incessantly confronted by political questions, subjects today tend to accept the given order as the natural state of things. This acceptance represents a retreat from politics because politics necessarily involves a rupture with what is given. By conceiving oneself as a political subject, one loosens, ipso facto, the grip of the given order. As Jacques Rancière points out, "Politics breaks with the sensory self-evidence of the 'natural' order that destines specific individuals and groups to occupy positions of rule or of being ruled, assigning them to private or public lives, pinning them down to a certain time and space, to specific 'bodies,' that is to specific ways of being, seeing and saying."[2] Taking oneself to be a political subject creates a disruption in what is given insofar as it reveals the political structure of the given. As political subjects, we see the given not as given but as the result of a political victory.

Though Rancière correctly sees the need for politicization, the marginalization of economy in his thought obscures how this politicization might occur.[3] Today politicization requires a disruption in the naturalness of the capitalist economy, but this economy works constantly to present itself as natural, which is why such a disruption is difficult to conceive or experience. It is not enough simply to call for a return to politics. As long as capitalism persists in the guise of a natural system that simply exists, such calls will go unheeded. Grasping the vulnerability of the capitalist system requires taking stock of its strength.

Capitalism's appeal as an economic system stems in part from its capacity for protecting subjects from seeing their own role in constituting the system in which they participate. Capitalism seems to run on its own. Subjects participate in it, but their decision to participate or not does not appear to affect the functioning of the system. This is why capitalists who decide to outsource their labor or to manufacture deadly products (like guns or cigarettes) defend their actions with the claim that someone else would be acting this way if they weren't. In other words, the system, not individuals themselves, is culpable for the sins committed within it. Subjectivity entails responsibility, but capitalist subjects evade any sense of responsibility because the system obscures their role in what transpires.

By keeping the awareness of this role at bay, by promulgating a sense that capitalism exists, the capitalist system produces the appearance of solid ground beneath the subject's feet. Though Marx and Engels point out the deracinating form of capitalist relations of production in *The Communist Manifesto* and elsewhere, this uprooting of traditional guarantees and realities leads to the formation of an even more deeply imbued sense of ground that capitalism offers. This sense of ground derives from the seeming emergence from being itself that inheres within the capitalist system. Capitalism's form of appearance is that of the natural order of things. Because it commands us to follow our own self-interest rather than question where this interest lies, capitalism can present itself as the economic system most proximate to the givens of our biology.

Capitalism's reliance on the idea of self-interest is the foundation for its claim to a connection with human nature. But it is this connection that Freud thoroughly demolishes. Though we often think of Freud as the cynical thinker who discovers self-interest at the heart of every altruistic action, the basis of his thought—the discovery of psychoanalysis itself—derives from subjects acting contrary to their self-interest with maddening consistency. Acting according to self-interest is not the default subjective position but actually represents, for Freud, a psychic impossibility (even under capitalism, a system that rewards such action). What characterizes the subject's state of being is not self-interest but a process that involves the repeated subversion of self-interest. If I am to attain satisfaction, I must sacrifice my self-interest, and this is what subjects constantly do, even those who believe themselves to be fervently pursuing it.

Though capitalism demands that subjects act out of their self-interest, it sustains itself through their self-sabotage. If subjects were able to pursue self-interest, they would immediately unite to overthrow the capitalist system and create a more efficient and equitable economic system.[4] Capitalism is not in anyone's interest, not even that of the most successful capitalists. Bill Gates must endure the burden of capitalist dissatisfaction with what he has every bit as much as the worker in a sweatshop. Capitalism does not permit anyone to avoid the dissatisfaction that inheres in a universe based on the demand for ever increasing accumulation. But as long as subjects remain within the capitalist universe, they can derive satisfaction from their self-sabotage, while disavowing this form of satisfaction and believing themselves to be purely self-interested—and thus purely natural—beings.

Freud tries to cure neurotics, but he has no illusions about rendering them happy by allowing them to pursue their self-interest. Even Freud cannot turn a neurotic into an alien. His melancholy statement at the end of *Studies on Hysteria* testifies directly to this conclusion. He defines therapeutic success not as allowing the realization of self-interest but as "transforming your hysterical misery into common unhappiness."[5] *Common unhappiness* is Freud's term for the subject's inability simply to pursue its self-interest. A system structured around the pursuit of self-interest is in no way suited to the inherent structure of subjectivity, but instead results from a political decision that subjects continue to make unconsciously through their participation in the capitalist system. But capitalism relies on disguising this decision through the appearance of naturalness.

LIFE DURING WARTIME

It is no coincidence that the great ideologues of unrestrained capitalism base their support for capitalism as an economic system on the fact that it coincides with the nature of being itself. For such figures, capitalism is not so much an economic system as the way of the world. This is clearly the position of Ayn Rand, whose novel *Atlas Shrugged* represents perhaps the leading treatise of capitalist ideology.[6] The unrepentant boldness of its claims—its celebration of self-interest as the only virtue—suffices to recommend it above the relative timidity of F. A. Hayek or Milton Friedman, who accept some mitigation of rampant self-interest. In the novel, Rand divides characters into the producers who actually create value and the moochers who just appropriate the value created by the producers. Whereas Marx views the working class as the producers and the capitalist class as the appropriators of the value created by the working class, Rand conceives capitalists as the only true producers.

In an explanation to a fellow producer, the character Francisco d'Anconia posits a natural world in which the production of money exists outside any societal structure that makes this production possible. He proclaims, "Money is *made*—before it can be looted or mooched—made by the effort of every honest man, each to the extent of his ability. An honest man is one who knows that he can't consume more than he has produced."[7] As Rand sees it, the capitalist engages in a pure act of production that takes place outside any system that would regulate it. It is a natural act. Production relies solely on the effort of the productive few, people like Francisco d'Anconia, Henry Reardon, Dagny Taggart, and John Galt in *Atlas Shrugged*.

Rand envisions all the producers going on strike in order to protest the political system that interferes with their natural productivity. Her polemic becomes ideological insofar as it fails to account for the political structure of the capitalist economy in which these producers dominate. They succeed not simply by virtue of their own productivity or ingenuity but also through the systematic regulations and structures that create the conditions of possibility in which this productivity can thrive. Regulations of capitalist society are not simply barriers to capitalist productivity but also its very condition of possibility. Capitalist production, in other words, cannot exist except against the background of the capitalist political decision that produces an unnatural (despite its appearance) economic system. Without stable capitalist social relations, neither Henry Reardon's new metal nor Dagny Taggart's trains would be conceivable. Rand misses this important dimension of the producers' success because she assumes that capitalist relations of production are the natural or neutral background against which all human activity takes place. For Rand, capitalist relations of production are ubiquitous, which is why capitalism has a substantial existence.

Rand's philosophy of identity (which she claims wrongly to take from Aristotle) depends on this same misperception produced by capitalism's form of appearance.[8] She believes that identity simply is, that a = a. But the statement of identity—the claim that a = a—transfigures the fact of identity. The statement of identity implies a political decision to assert a claim about the world and a psychic investment in the claim about identity. This claim distorts the world that it constitutes. The claim of identity becomes an inextricable part of the identity, and this is what Rand's philosophy cannot accommodate. Her blindness to the distortion of subjectivity finds its crowning avowal in the name that she gives to her philosophy—*objectivism*. Objectivism is not just Rand's personal way of thinking; it is also the philosophy that capitalism's obfuscation of subjective distortion demands. The purported objectivity of the journalist under capitalism is the not-so-distant cousin of Rand the objectivist thinker.[9]

One can trace this error back to the founding theorists of capitalism. In the *Wealth of Nations*, though he doesn't use the term *capitalism*, Adam Smith defines the capitalist economy as an economy based on the pursuit of self-interest, but self-interest remains a pure presupposition of Smith's philosophy. He never attempts to argue for his conception of humans as self-interested beings because he associates self-interest with nature itself. It is in this sense that capitalism is the natural economic system. Once Smith adopts this starting point, the justification for capitalism necessarily follows. The pursuit of individual self-interest, given the market logic of supply and demand, leads to societal good. Though Smith avoids Rand's absolute libertarianism, he does share her insistence on an identification of the pursuit of self-interest with the inherent structure of humanity.[10]

This is not, unfortunately, an error confined to champions of capitalism such as Rand and Smith. One can even find it among communist philosophers in their attacks against capitalism. Throughout his writing, Marx is careful to stress just how unnatural capitalism is, even though he doesn't always say this in a critical way. But for someone like Alain Badiou, capitalism and reliance on self-interest equate with nature itself. Like other students of Louis Althusser (such as Jacques Rancière), Badiou's communist philosophy represents a plea for a political intervention that would displace the priority that economy has in capitalist society. Economy has no place in Badiou's political vision of revolution. But the emphasis Badiou places on political as opposed to economic intervention causes him to grant capitalism a natural status, to presuppose its existence.

In Badiou's thought, capitalism exists: it has the status of being the background of pure animality against which we might act. As he points out in his treatise on former French president Nicolas Sarkozy, "Whoever does not clarify the coming-to-be of humanity with the communist hypothesis—whatever words they use, because the words have little importance—reduces humanity, as far as its collective becoming is concerned, to animality. As we know, the contemporary, that is to say capitalist, name for this animality is: competition. The war dictated by self-interest, and nothing more."[11] Though Badiou champions communism as the alternative to capitalism, what is significant about these lines is his characterization of capitalism. Here as elsewhere, Badiou equates the capitalist system with human animality and thereby takes the capitalist system at face value when it presents itself as a system emerging out of nature. According to Badiou, there was no event that occasioned capitalism, no capitalist event, and there can be no economic event or rupture within the realm of economy. In explicit contrast to politics, economy is definitely not a truth procedure. Any economic intervention in society plays into the hands of capitalism, according to Badiou, because economy itself is de facto capitalist. Capitalism is economy as such.

By equating capitalism with economy as such, Badiou creates a broader target for critique and a clearer path for politics. Revolutionary politics becomes the political decision itself, not just the decision for communism. But the theoretical cost of this wager is too high. Badiou grants capitalism its fundamental ideological contention—its association with nature. He admits, in other words, that capitalism exists. In so doing, he implicitly concedes that Ayn Rand's premises are correct, even if her conclusions are not. He agrees to fight the battle for communism on a capitalist terrain.

In contrast to Marx, Badiou sees economy as an alternative to politics rather than conceiving the economy in political terms. This gesture from one of capitalism's most thoughtful opponents suggests just how widespread capitalism's image of neutrality has become. Marx's conceptualization of capitalism through its historical emergence represents perhaps his most significant achievement insofar as it provides a counterweight to the image of neutrality. This way of thinking about capitalism gives the lie to its alignment with natural being, but one need not be Marx or a Marxist to recognize this.

SEEING THAT ONE SEES

The difficulty of seeing the unnatural status of capitalism is akin to the problem that besets subjects confronted with the visual field. The relationship between the subject and the visual field provides a homology for the subject's relationship to the capitalist system, a homology that enables us to see capitalism's unnatural status and its power to hide this unnaturalness. Though capitalism is a system that shapes the activities of subjects within it and not a field that captures their look, it does nonetheless share a key element with the field of vision. In both cases the terrain appears natural and given to us as subjects irrespective of our engagement in it. That is to say, capitalism and the visual field seem to exist on their own in a neutral state with regard to the subjects who engage them. They present themselves as simply partaking in the order of things. Just as no political decision inaugurates the capitalist system, none constitutes the visual field.

This appearance of naturalness is more pronounced in the visual field than with any of the other sensory fields. While touch, taste, hearing, and smell often result from an evident and active decision—someone moves forward to embrace us or bakes us a cake to eat, for instance— sight most often makes use of what lies before our eyes apparently without any act that forges what we see. In the other sensory fields, it is easier to discern the subjective distortion or decision that constitutes the field. Perhaps this is clearest in the case of taste, where the subject's own desire so evidently determines the status of the field. If I hate spinach, this will shape how I experience the green leafy substance in my mouth. Though I may believe that spinach simply tastes awful, I can grasp how it tastes awful for me and how my taste plays a role in its status as awful. I can even, through an act of radical imagination, consider the existence of someone who might take pleasure in eating it.

With vision the situation is much more difficult. What I see and how I see it appears to exist in front of my eyes, and the role that my desire plays in constituting this scene is not at all evident. The visual field, in other words, does not appear distorted by desire. I assume that others, standing where I stand, will see what I see in the way that I see it. Vision, ironically, does not seem to be a question of my act of seeing. The illusion of naturalness renders the subjective distortion of the visual field—its reliance on our act of seeing to constitute it—almost impossible to detect. But it is not quite impossible. We see this distortion of desire primarily in works of art, like films or paintings, where the constitutive role of our subjectivity can become more prominent.

In his *Seminar XI* Jacques Lacan names the distortion that desire produces in the visual field *le regard* or the gaze. The introduction of this term immediately opens Lacan to a horrible misunderstanding that derailed Anglo-American film theory for decades.[12] The gaze, as Lacan theorizes it, is not the simple act of looking and the mastery involved in that act (as the English-speaking interpreters of Lacan had it), but rather the point at which the distortion caused by the subject's desire becomes visible as a disruption in the visual field.[13] In short, the gaze is nothing but the way that the subject's desire deforms what it sees. It is the impossibility of a neutral or natural field of vision. At the point of the gaze, the subject is an absent presence in the visual field that is responsible for the field's distorted character, its lack of neutrality. The gaze is political in the sense that it exposes the unnatural status of the apparently natural visible world.

When we see the gaze, we see that the visual field is not simply there to be seen but constituted around our vision of it, distorted by our desire. This distortion then forces us to reexamine everything that we see. As Joan Copjec notes in her account of the gaze, "At the moment the gaze is discerned, the image, the entire visual field, takes on a terrifying alterity."[14] We see that our desire has been taken into account by what appears to be a neutral visual field. The neutrality of this field vanishes, and the political decision that inaugurates it becomes apparent. The encounter with the gaze transforms the subject by creating an awareness in the subject of its role in producing what it sees.

The typical Hollywood film obscures the gaze by presenting the visual field as simply there for the spectator to see. In the same way, capitalism presents the economic field as existing apart from the activity of the subjects whose activity constitutes it. The typical Hollywood film doesn't just propagate capitalist ideology; it utilizes the form of capitalist economy and acts on the spectator the way that capitalism acts on the subject. In both cases one cannot readily recognize one's involvement in the system. The obfuscation of the gaze enables subjects to believe that the economic and visual fields operate without the subject's activity.

The gaze exposes the tendentious nature of the apparently neutral visual field: what seems to be simply there to be seen becomes evident as a structure created around the subject's desire. What appears in front of the subject thus loses its independent and external status for the subject. The distance that inheres in the act of looking collapses through the emergence of the gaze. In this sense, the trauma of encountering the gaze is nothing but the trauma of encountering the constitutive power of one's own desire in shaping what one sees even before one sees it. The gaze as an object that causes our desire is most powerful in the visual field due to the apparent independence that this field has for us. Its manifestation always occasions a traumatic shock.[15]

We can see an instance of an encounter with the gaze in Nicolas Winding Refn's *Drive* (2011). The film recounts the travails of an unnamed driver (Ryan Gosling) who helps his neighbor, Standard (Oscar Isaac), to commit a robbery in order to pay a debt that he incurred while in prison. Even though he sees the folly of the plan, the driver agrees to go along because he has fallen for Standard's wife Irene (Carey Mulligan). During the robbery, Standard is killed by the same criminals who forced him into the crime, and after the driver escapes with the money, they come after him. The film's key scene occurs in an elevator at the driver's apartment building, where a hit man rides with the driver and Irene.

Understanding that both his own life and Irene's are at stake, the driver attacks the hit man with extreme violence and brutally kills him by beating him to a bloody pulp. Though Irene had begun to fall in love with the driver, especially after the death of her husband, here she looks on with complete shock. Though she recognizes that the driver is saving her, the violence he displays reveals the impossibility of any life together with him. He shows that he is capable of a level of brutality with which she could not simply coexist. The scene concludes in a striking fashion: Irene exits the elevator, and the shot focuses on the door as it closes in front of her disoriented look. This is the encounter with the gaze.

The shot of Irene's shocked face does not itself represent the gaze. The horror of her look exposes the gaze or distortion within the elevator. Her exclusion from the scene as the elevator door shuts reveals the unnatural or distorted status of what we have just witnessed. The driver's brutality—necessary as it might have been—was not simply a natural response to a threat but a horrible display of excess. Irene's look shows it to be unnatural, inadmissible within the bounds of social interaction—a gaze. Her look signals to the spectator that the driver's extreme violence did not fit within the spectator's field of vision, and this look makes it impossible to take voyeuristic pleasure in the violence. In this sense, the film, despite its graphic violence, represents one of the most thoroughgoing critiques of such violence in contemporary cinema. It exposes this violence as the result of a political decision or a desire, and it associates both the film's protagonist and the spectator with this decision. From this moment on, there is no possibility of any romantic bond between the driver and Irene. The driver exists in a position that the film exposes as excessive.

When the elevator door closes in *Drive*, the camera remains within the elevator and thus leaves the spectator with the driver rather than with Irene. The spectator is positioned within the distortion or the gaze itself. The possibility of a typical life within society lies on the other side of the elevator door. In this sense, the film alludes to a similar exclusion in one of the most famous scenes in American cinema, an exclusion that also involves an encounter with the gaze. At the end of John Ford's *The Searchers* (1956), the door shuts on Ethan Edwards (John Wayne), the violent war veteran who has finally returned his niece to her family after years of Indian captivity. Though both films facilitate an encounter with the gaze that reveals the distortion of the visual field, the position that each film takes relative to this encounter is completely opposed.

While *Drive* leaves the spectator with the driver to inhabit the distortion, *The Searchers* remains inside the house as it excludes Ethan Edwards and the distorting gaze from the visual field. The film's point here is that social normalcy depends on the exclusion of the gaze, which exposes the unnatural status of this normalcy. But *Drive* pushes this logic even further by locating the spectator within the distortion itself. With this gesture, it becomes apparent that the distortion is inescapable. One can shut the door on it, but we remain on this side of the barrier.[16] Most films, to be sure, do not expose the gaze in this way. Instead, they work to hide the spectator's investment in the image.

The link between the cinematic gaze and capitalism becomes most evident in Frank Capra's *It's a Wonderful Life* (1946), a film most often seen as a straightforward capitalist fantasy. This fantasy shows the importance of the individual and the ability of a network of family and friends to overcome the machinations of a big capitalist. In the fantasy proffered by the film, the capitalist system takes care of the working class and allows them to succeed. Though the big capitalist, Henry Potter (Lionel Barrymore), is the film's villain, Capra nonetheless shows how the small capitalist can thrive and provide the backbone for the formation of a supportive community. When the community comes to the rescue of George Bailey (James Stewart) at the end of the film and supplies the money that he owes to Potter, it seems as if capitalism is compatible with the values that its insistence on self-interest would appear to thwart. Though this ideological fantasy is certainly operative, the film's relationship to the capitalist system is much more complex and involves its depiction of a neutral field of vision. This image of neutrality is much more ideological than the capitalist fantasy that the film proffers.

The decisive section of *It's a Wonderful Life* is the fantasy sequence in which the angel Clarence (Henry Travers) shows George Bailey what life would be like without him. We see the quaint small town of Bedford Falls transformed into the squalid Pottersville, a city where corruption and self-interest are ubiquitous. Others have noted that this fantasy sequence simply provides Capra the opportunity to present the capitalist reality of his time, but what we see is not simply the social reality. Instead, by subtracting George Bailey from the filmic universe, the film shows us the distortion of the capitalist gaze. George's presence obscures the gaze, and his absence unleashes it. The excesses and horrors of the capitalist system become visible because George's crisis leads to an encounter with the gaze. Clarence exposes him to the gaze not just in order to convince George to remain alive but also to reassure him about his investment in the capitalist system. It is this investment that renders Pottersville invisible, and when George accepts his former role at the end of the film, the image of Pottersville once again recedes from view. Bedford Falls tames the gaze and thereby allows us to believe that the capitalist system simply exists.

In the cinema the gaze emerges at moments of narrative crisis, at moments when the spectator's sense of mastery and distance evaporates. When the gaze emerges, the visual field loses its illusion of neutrality, and the distortion produced by the spectator's desire that stains the image becomes visible. This distortion most often remains hidden, but it manifests itself whenever we encounter the gaze, during any crisis when the cinema reveals how our investment as spectators skews what we see. In the same way, the moment of crisis exposes the capitalist gaze— its status as one economic system among others that we must either accept or reject. The moment of crisis within capitalism makes the unnaturalness of capitalism evident. These moments represent political opportunities or opportunities for politics. They stage what we might call an encounter with the gaze.

OCCUPY THE CRISIS

Capitalism functions through the same illusion of neutrality or naturalness as the visual field. The possibility for an encounter with the gaze or the subjective distortion that produces capitalism exists also within the field of capitalist economics. Here the encounter is just as difficult to produce as it is within the field of vision. Most of the time, capitalist relations of production create enough prosperity that few question the neutrality of these relations. But the gaze is ever present within capitalism and always ready to appear. When it does, the political decision undergirding the capitalist economic system becomes visible.

The tendentious status of capitalism—the gaze within capitalism—becomes most visible during crises. This is why it is not surprising that the clearest challenges to capitalism have occurred during times of economic tumult. We can see three undeniable instances in the United States in the twentieth and twenty-first centuries. The Great Depression occasioned the emergence of a social safety net in the United States, a definitive political intervention into the economic realm designed to modify the structure of capitalist relations of production. Even if Franklin Roosevelt attempted to save capitalism from the threat of communism with the New Deal, this intervention nevertheless shifted the terrain of the discussion and exposed the unnatural nature of capitalism. The capitalist system left capital itself idle and unable to stimulate economic activity. There was no capitalist solution to this failure. The United States needed the New Deal because capitalism could not simply work on its own without destroying itself.

The American economy in the early 1970s was not in the same moribund condition that it was in during the 1930s, but Richard Nixon's decision to sever the link between the U.S. dollar and gold—the elimination of the gold standard—represents another instance where capitalism's nonexistence becomes apparent. On August 15, 1971, Nixon tried to stem the tide of inflation and massive foreign redemption of dollars for gold by freeing the dollar from its link to the American supply of gold. As a result, the Federal Reserve could print dollars in response to impending or actual economic crises and thereby work to abate them. The turn away from gold ushered in a much more flexible and much more evidently political monetary policy. Though monetary policy had always been political, Nixon's action exposed its tendentiousness—and the tendentiousness of capitalism as a whole.

Even more than Roosevelt, Nixon was attempting to save or harmonize capitalism rather than destroy it. But his response to the economic crisis he confronted makes even clearer capitalism's break from the natural world. The link to gold enables us to believe that capitalism functions on a solid foundation, that it is rooted in an element of the natural world. We can find gold on the periodic table and identify its atomic number, in that way assuring ourselves of its natural status.[17] The dollar has no atomic number. One needn't be an alchemist to create dollars, just the owner of the proper printing press. The dollar doesn't provide any reassuring link to the natural world but makes evident the act of faith on which all monetary systems rest. This is why Nixon's act eliminates the illusory connection to nature. During the crisis of 1971, the American economy would bear the mark of politics.

The financial crisis of 2008 produced a phenomenon almost exactly the converse. Rather than exposing the politicized structure of the economy, it ushered the capitalist economy onto the political scene. The question of the injustice inherent in capitalism emerged as the salient political question. This indicated a disruption in the usual order of American politics, which has historically worked to marginalize fundamental capitalist questions in favor of cultural ones or small economic ones. Even the widespread use of the signifier *capitalism* revealed an expansion of the political field to include the terrain of capitalist economy.

The birth of the Occupy movement out of the 2008 financial crisis was the vehicle for this expansion: the crisis in which financial managers became even wealthier through the immiseration of others and the government intervention to save the banking system laid bare the interpenetration of politics and the capitalist economy. Operating according to its own logic, the system self-destructed, and it required an extraordinary political act to avoid complete collapse. Once this became evident, the Occupy movement could make the case that the antagonism between the 1 percent and the 99 percent had a political, rather than a natural, status.[18]

Due to the specific nature of the capitalist crisis, it reveals capitalist relations of production as unnatural. Though it is possible to denaturalize capitalism at other times, the moment of the crisis marks one of the few times that capitalism's distance from nature manifests itself. The crisis acts on the capitalist system as the film does on the visual field: it facilitates an encounter with the distortion that constitutes the system but remains repressed within it.

Of course, crises do not begin with capitalism. Throughout its history, humanity has endured crisis after crisis. Crises even predate humanity: the object from space that crashed into Earth and killed the dinosaurs provoked a crisis not just for the beings that became extinct but for all life. In this case, and in those involving precapitalist humanity, the crisis is always a bout of scarcity when natural conditions obstruct the production of goods necessary for survival. Capitalism does not eliminate the crisis, but radically transforms it from the crisis of scarcity into the crisis of overproduction. In one sense, who cares? A crisis is grave whether it results from scarcity or overproduction. But their political status is completely different. This transformation of the crisis reveals the wholly unnatural status or nonexistence of the capitalist system.

The natural world engages in a constant struggle with scarcity. Plants and animals must either fight with each other or cooperate—neither strategy is more natural than the other, despite what appears self-evident—in order to survive in a world that provides a limited number of resources for them. A crisis comes about for animals, for instance, when they can no longer find enough food in their particular locality. Precapitalist humans suffer the same types of crises as animals and thus appear to be simply human animals, to be natural beings. But capitalism revolutionizes the crisis that humanity confronts and thereby exposes humanity's fundamental break from the natural world.

The capitalist economy enters into crisis not through scarcity but through overproduction, the production of an excess of commodities with a paucity of consumers for these commodities. Recessions and depressions are the result of too many goods, not too few. What is telling is not only the form of the capitalist crisis but the measures taken to ameliorate it. All attempts to create a stable system reveal its unnatural and unharmonious status. For instance, the Keynesian solution of excessive state spending shows that capitalism doesn't properly function as a natural order. The immiseration that capitalism causes is not the result of its inability to produce enough commodities for consumers to buy but the by-product of the excess it produces. Even on the most commonsensical level, the fact that an excess of production leads to a crisis can only seem bizarre.

The housing crisis of 2008 makes this logic perfectly clear. The crisis was not the result of a lack of houses for people who needed them but of an excess of houses with no one to pay for them. Vacant houses began to proliferate, which led to a drop in the value of existing houses and a near total collapse in the production of new houses.[19] The term used to describe the precursor to the crisis—the *housing bubble*—testifies to the problem of overproduction. Whereas early humanity struggled to find enough shelter, subjects of capitalism suffer from having too much of it.

The 2008 crisis didn't just leave us with a surplus of housing, however. Surpluses were evident throughout the economic landscape. As David Harvey notes, the postcrisis world was "short on cash and awash with surplus houses, surplus offices and shopping malls, surplus productive capacity and even more surplus labour than before."[20] No one could mistake an excess of commodities and an excess of the capacity for producing more as a natural problem. All of a sudden, with the crisis of overproduction, capitalism ceases to exist and becomes the product of a political decision. Overproduction renders the capitalist system as such visible.

But the crisis of overproduction creates an awareness that doesn't exist at any other time. Marx recognizes this in the *Grundrisse*, where he notes, "capital has no awareness whatever of the nature of its process of realization, and has an interest in having an awareness of it only in times of *crisis*."[21] The crisis forces capitalism to take stock of how it realizes value and to control this process in a conscious way. But the problem with this awareness, from Marx's perspective, is that it will always be fleeting: when the crisis passes, the awareness will pass as well. The crisis of capitalism will never facilitate a lasting consciousness of capitalist relations of production because such a consciousness would destroy these very relations. But for those not invested in the preservation of capitalist relations of production, the crisis represents an unparalleled opportunity. The crisis reveals the capitalist gaze, the unnatural status of capitalism, the decision that sustains its relations of production. Just as the subject can experience the gaze in its field of vision, it can also experience the gaze, even though this gaze is not visual, within the structure of capitalism.

Although the structure of capitalism is not homologous with the structure of the visual field, thinking about capitalism in terms of the gaze follows from the apparent neutrality that both structures share. When we look at a visual field, it appears not as a field constructed around our desire but rather as field already there to be seen. No background lights fall from the sky as in Peter Weir's *The Truman Show* (1998) in order to reveal to us that our look has informed what is visible to us. Visual reality successfully presents itself as a background against which and in which we desire rather than as a field thoroughly colored by our desire. In the same way, when we confront capitalism, it appears as a neutral economic system that simply exists in the absence of any political intervention. Capitalism passes itself off as the economic system given by being itself, just as the visual field does. It passes itself off as existing.

The traumatic encounter with the gaze, the moment of confronting one's own desire as a distortion of the world in which one exists, renders this world unnatural and foreign. The world ceases to be a habitual space in which one can dwell and becomes a groundless field based solely on the desire of the subjects that exist within it. The gaze exposes the world itself as nothing but a presupposition of the desiring subject, a structure lacking any independent existence or substantive weight. The world is not the background in which we desire but emerges only through the force of desire. What appears as substantial and preexisting subjectivity depends for its substantiality on the subject's role in its constitution. This is not to say that there is no objective material reality, that everything exists only in an ideal realm, but rather that this objective reality is inextricable from a subjective distortion, a gaze, that divides it from itself and on which it depends. The dependence of objectivity on this subjective distortion makes the world *unheimlich*, which is why we seek refuge from the gaze.

When the crisis occurs, capital ceases to flow smoothly, and the money necessary to buy commodities and restart this flow of capital remains dormant. The crisis causes capital to lose its productivity, and even Rand's producers cannot rediscover it. We see that capitalism does not work like a neutral background but rather distorts social relations. The failure of capital itself to resolve the crisis—its reliance on state intervention— exposes its unnaturalness and the decision that permits its survival. The crisis confronts us with the possibility that capitalism might fail, with evidence that it exists only through our efforts to bring it into being. The danger of the crisis for capitalism is not that it will bring about an economic catastrophe from which the system cannot recover but that it will expose the system's nonexistence and thus create an opportunity for the encounter with the gaze. And this encounter would make possible another form of economic decision, an economic event.

FASCISM OR EMANCIPATION

Moments of crisis within capitalism facilitate an encounter with the gaze, but they are not necessarily always revolutionary. Oftentimes, the response to this encounter is a fascist reaction. The same economic crisis that occasioned the New Deal in the United States gave birth to Nazism in Germany. The moment of the gaze's emergence makes the political dimension of the economy evident, but it does not point in any necessary political direction. The gaze presents us with a political opening that can either lead toward a leftist or a rightist mobilization.

The key to the political valence of the encounter with the gaze lies in the interpretation of the gaze itself. If we interpret the gaze as the distortion of an otherwise balanced and neutral system, then we will respond with fascistic efforts to restore the capitalist system's imaginary neutrality through the violent exclusion of the source of the distortion. In other words, the fascist believes that the gaze—the distortion of the capitalist system—is not inherent in the system but an excess that corrupts the system from the outside. Fascism is the attempt to purify capitalism, but it necessarily fails because capitalism's impurity inheres within the capitalist system itself. There is no such thing as a purified capitalism, which is why the fascist project of eliminating the impurities is always an unending one. The more Jews the Nazis sent to the death camps, the greater the Jewish threat loomed.

Emacipatory politics, in contrast, interprets the gaze not as an external distortion of the neutral capitalist system but as the indication of the system's inherent imbalance and partiality. That is, the distortion of the crisis is nothing but capitalism's own inherent imbalance. The point of emancipatory politics is not the elimination of the gaze but identification with it. The struggle between the forces of fascism and the forces of emancipation is one between two fundamentally opposed responses to the crises of capitalism. Fascism views the crisis as an anomaly that one might repair, while emancipatory politics sees the crisis as the moment at which capitalism reveals the truth of the distortion lurking in its own structure. The appeal of fascism is almost always stronger because it offers the assurance that a neutral background exists and enables us to avoid confronting the trauma of a political decision.[22] But fascism preserves and extends the very crisis that it promises to ameliorate.

In *The Usual Suspects*, a moment of crisis occurs that occasions just the effect that a crisis in capitalism does, and it points the spectator toward emancipation rather than fascism. After hearing the testimony of Verbal Kint, customs investigator Dave Kujan (Chazz Palminteri), along with the spectator, comes to the conclusion that he will not discover the identity of the criminal responsible for the death of twenty-seven people in a boat explosion at the harbor. But as Kint walks free, Kujan looks around his office and recognizes various terms that Kint used during his testimony on various items (a coffee cup, a poster on the wall, and so on). As the film cuts from item to item, the fictionality of Kint's account of the incident becomes evident to both Kujan and the spectator. Through the juxtaposition of these images, director Bryan Singer creates an encounter with the gaze.

At this point we must revisit the entire experience of the film and reinterpret what we have seen. Rather than being a neutral account of the events that preceded the explosion, the film has depicted a fiction structured around the desire of Verbal Kint—who is, in fact, Keyser Soze. Whatever assurance we felt about the events we were seeing evaporates with this encounter with the gaze produced by the crisis within the narrative. Our investment as spectators in the desire of Keyser Soze himself becomes apparent during this encounter. The crises of capitalism create a similar opportunity for radical reinterpretation that the encounter with the gaze offers. Rather than viewing capitalism as the background for our actions, we might view it as the product of them. In this way we lose the guarantee of a neutral playing field and gain responsibility for the very turf on which we exist.

The Persistence of Sacrifice
After Its Obsolescence

SACRIFICE BECOMING SECULAR

Capitalism doesn't require the sacrifice of virgins. In contrast to most other modes of social organization, it has no specified rituals of sacrifice that it cannot do without. In this sense, there is a clear philosophical continuity between capitalism and the Enlightenment, which aims at overcoming the superstitious belief in the necessity for sacrifice. An ethic of utility shapes the structure of both capitalism and the Enlightenment, and it leads each to reject rituals of sacrifice as a massive waste of time and misuse of precious energy. In fact, capitalist theorists argue that the logic of capitalism includes a penalty for any residual sacrifice to which subjects adhere. Time spent attending the sacrifice of the latest virgin might be better used designing a way to fit more people inside an airplane in order to increase its efficiency. This ostensible preference for the useful over the sacred distinguishes capitalist modernity.

Nonetheless, there are points at which sacrifices become visible within capitalism. The most self-evident form of sacrifice in capitalist society lies in the "creative destruction" theorized first by Joseph Schumpeter. In his landmark work, *Capitalism, Socialism, and Democracy*, Schumpeter argues, "This process of Creative Destruction is the essential fact about capitalism. It is what capitalism consists in and what every capitalist concern has got to live in."[1] Capitalism constantly sacrifices old mechanisms of production and old products for new ones, and this sacrificial procedure is the lifeblood of the capitalist system. But the problem with Schumpeter's image of sacrifice is precisely his avoidance of the term *sacrifice*. Rather than emphasizing sacrifice, Schumpeter stresses destruction and creation. It is a wholly secular process, a process befitting capitalist modernity. One might argue that it is not really a case of sacrifice at all.[2]

For many social theorists, however, there is no getting around sacrifice and the sacred.[3] Freud sees the collective sacrifice of individual enjoyment as the foundation of the social order itself, a foundation that subsequent sacrificial rituals commemorate and reaffirm. For René Girard, sacrifice puts an end to the exchange of retributive violence and thereby makes coexistence possible. Marcel Mauss, for his part, identifies sacrifice as the basis for the sense of obligation that holds groups together and creates cohesiveness. What these theorists (and all modern theorists of sacrifice) have in common is their effort to come to terms with the persistence of sacrifice in society after the onset of capitalism and the Enlightenment, both of which disdain it.

If we look closely at this disdain, however, its self-evident status becomes less certain. It is true that one need not slaughter a ram to fit in capitalist society—we would probably feel uncomfortable if someone attempted this method of social belonging—but sacrifice nonetheless plays an essential role for capitalism (as it does for the Enlightenment, which, as Hegel argues in *The Phenomenology of Spirit*, depends on the thoroughgoing sacrifice of the sensual world).[4] Sacrifice appears in the workers' sacrifice of their time for the production of the commodity, which profits the capitalist in the stead of the workers. It also appears in the act of consumption, where consumers sacrifice their wealth for commodities that they don't need. Sacrifice manifests itself in a hidden form in the production and consumption of the commodity.

Rather than overcoming sacrifice, capitalism secularizes it. This is the essence of capitalism's relation to sacrifice. Sacrifice survives within capitalism, though its form of appearance undergoes a complete overhaul. Sacrifice migrates from the transcendent site of the ritual into everyday life. This migration of sacrifice from the sacred realm to the everyday has the effect of rendering sacrifice common and simultaneously making it seem a thing of the past. Whereas sacrifice used to be confined to specific highly visible rituals, it now manifests itself in an almost invisible way in everyday activities. This migration is part of the genius of capitalism.[5]

The migration of sacrifice from the realm of specified rituals to the everyday world of producing and consuming commodities has the effect of obscuring the act of sacrifice. Overt sacrifice troubles the equilibrium of the modern subject, but it becomes completely acceptable in the hidden form that capitalism proffers. In capitalism, subjects can enjoy sacrifice while believing that they aren't. We can enjoy sacrifice in and through its very invisibility when it becomes secular.

The secularization of sacrifice not only eliminates its visibility but also destroys its cohesive power. Public rituals of sacrifice have the effect of constituting or cementing the social bond by involving all subjects in the loss that occurs through sacrifice. Secularized sacrifice, on the other hand, is private sacrifice, and it enforces the privacy of the subject rather than opening the subject to the public. This is, as I argued earlier, the fundamental trajectory of capitalism itself: a path from public to private. As a result, capitalist subjects almost necessarily fail to see their own psychic investment in the public world. One lives in isolation, but this isolation is undergirded by an extensive social network that makes it possible. This public bond can only become visible when we recognize the inevitability and constitutive status of sacrifice. Seeing this is implicitly moving beyond the strictures of the capitalist economy.

But capitalism has a crucial role to play in the understanding of sacrifice. Despite the absence of sacrificial rituals within capitalist society, the connection between the demands of the capitalist system and sacrifice help to explain the centrality of sacrifice in every social order. It is only after sacrifice seems obsolete that it becomes comprehensible. Far from being actually marginalized within capitalism, sacrifice is essential to the creation of profit and to the desire to consume. Without the act of sacrifice, no capitalist would turn a profit, and no one would find the purchase of a commodity satisfying.

As capitalism makes plain, societies sacrifice because loss is the source of value.[6] At first glance, this statement seems crazy. Of course, there are objects that have a value not mediated by loss, like the food and shelter necessary for us to survive. But seeing some objects as inherently valuable for their contribution to our survival assumes that the fundamental goal of our life is to perpetuate itself. This is the vitalist assumption that subtends the thought of every theorist who sets out to defend the social benefits of capitalism.[7] But the assumption that there is a value in life itself or that life just aims at perpetuating itself is only an ideological assumption without any philosophical legitimacy. If one examines the physical universe—and especially if one accepts the Second Law of Thermodynamics—the notion that life or even energy aims at perpetuating itself becomes much less tenable. Its only possible legitimacy lies in the claims of biology, and if human animals don't act like natural beings, this assumption loses its status as self-evident.

Furthermore, the belief that life itself has value is not at all present across different historical epochs and different societies. Hannah Arendt and Giorgio Agamben take great pains to illustrate that the Greeks of antiquity held animal life as valueless. According to Arendt, the Greeks believed that "what men share with all other forms of animal life was not considered to be human."[8] Anyone could survive, but value required engagement in the speculations of civic life. The contemporary belief that survival and prosperity are themselves unimpeachable values bespeaks not the real value of life itself but the victory of the capitalist system and the mode of thought that must support it.

As subjects of the signifier, we are no longer just living beings, and this is what ancient Greek society properly understood.[9] The signifier cuts into the living body and implants a little piece of death in us. Our immediate instinctual needs for the presence of objects (like food and shelter) become desires mediated by the structure of loss. In contrast to the animal, the subject's satisfaction will always depend on the absence of the object it enjoys. Even when an object is wholly present (like the BMW one drives), one's satisfaction depends on what is absent (like the invisible others watching one drive the nice car).

We can see this at work in the satisfaction of basic needs: the speaking subject does not have sex just with another flesh and blood object but also with the fantasy of an object that isn't there. Every actual partner substitutes for the lost object in the sex act. The subject of the signifier gets off on what isn't there, not on what is (even when actually having sex rather than surfing the Internet for pornography). This is equally the case with eating. While eating a perfect slice of pizza, I ponder the piece of cake that I'll have for dessert. And when I'm eating a bite of the cake, I anticipate the next one, which promises to be even tastier. Even if I immerse myself in the moment and devote myself entirely to the cake itself, the fleetingness of the experience—the way that absence haunts it—is essential to the satisfaction that it provides. This structure is the product of the signifier's effect on the subject.[10] For this subject, every actual and present object pales in comparison with the lost object, and sacrifice provides a way of creating this object and existing proximate to it. Societies privilege sacrifice out of a proper sense of sacrifice's fecundity, a sense of its capacity for producing a satisfaction that would otherwise be impossible.

EVIL, BE THOU MY GOOD

Prior to capitalist modernity, one could look at the prevalence of sacrifice and chalk it up to the unenlightened state of society. People sacrificed because they simply weren't all that smart. An absence of scientific knowledge about the nature of the universe, for instance, might have led people to believe that sacrificial rituals influenced the weather or brought God's grace. After the Enlightenment, ignorance could no longer be the culprit. If sacrifice persisted, it must have appealed to the structure of subjectivity itself. This is borne out increasingly in today's world as knowledge increases rather than decreases the tendency to sacrifice. Though some critics of capitalism cling to the idea of ideological manipulation as the source of the investment in capitalist sacrifice, this thesis seems difficult to accept given the prevalence of this investment.[11]

Capitalism thrives not because we are self-interested beings looking to get ahead in any way that we can but because we are looking for new ways to sacrifice ourselves. This propensity for sacrifice stems from a recognition that no satisfaction is possible without loss. Sacrifice does not exist just at the margins of capitalist society. It is omnipresent within capitalism and provides the key to its enduring popularity as an economic system. Sacrifice occurs when the worker creates the commodity and when the consumer buys it. The worker sacrifices time to produce the commodity, and the consumer sacrifices money to purchase it. Though the worker receives pay for this time and the consumer receives a commodity for this money, the pay is never equal to the value the worker creates, and the commodity is never equal to money the consumer gives for it. The satisfaction the capitalist receives from employing workers and the satisfaction the consumer receives from buying a commodity depends on the imbalance rather than the fairness of the exchange. But these imbalances are hidden within the capitalist structure. Capitalism employs sacrifice in the backroom.

Penetrating the invisibility of sacrifice within capitalism necessitates a look at the origin of profit. The commonsensical understanding of profit locates it in the oscillations of supply and demand. The capitalist profits by buying low and selling high, and if we focus on the stock market, this image of profit seems irrefutable. But this is an image that the first theorists of capitalism were careful to explode. The labor theory of value, as discovered by Adam Smith and developed by David Ricardo, locates value in the quantity of labor required to produce a commodity. Commodities that require a greater quantity of labor have more value than those that require less. The laws of supply and demand cover small variations in price, but labor time remains the source of value itself and will quickly outstrip the changes produced by these variations. The amount of labor invested in a product tells us how much we are willing to sacrifice for it. The more time someone will sacrifice to create a commodity, the more value it has. If no one will or has to work to produce something, capitalism ascribes no value at all to it.

This is true even of a commodity like gold, which seems to acquire its value simply from its scarcity. Ricardo insists that gold has its great value because of the labor time that it takes to mine, a time multiplied by its natural scarcity. Useful objects that require no labor to have—like air and water—have no value. In order to make water valuable, a capitalist must create the idea of its scarcity and then use labor time to produce it. This has, of course, occurred with bottled water, and the animated film *The Lorax* (Chris Renaud and Kyle Balda, 2012) envisions the same process happening with air. An inventive capitalist, Mr. O'Hare (Rob Riggle), aided by massive air pollution, convinces consumers that air is scarce and then hires workers to bottle it for sale. When watching, one laughs not at the ridiculousness but at the likelihood of the conceit. Any object can become a commodity as long as we can imagine a way to attach the sacrifice of labor time to its production.

The noxiousness of profit for Marx resides in its obfuscation of the workers' sacrifice that creates the value of the commodity. The capitalist profits from a sacrifice and then hides this sacrifice. As Marx sees it, workers exchange their labor time for a wage, and this exchange does not involve exploitation. But exploitation enters into the relationship through the workers' production of surplus value, the result of the excessive productivity of labor. If the exchange were just an even exchange—labor time for the production of the commodity—the capitalist would be left with no way to profit from it because no value would have been created. Value requires the act of sacrifice, and this is what occurs when labor produces surplus value. During the production of surplus value, workers sacrifice themselves for the profit of the capitalist. Marx's revolutionary idea is that workers should enjoy the value that their sacrifice creates.

The essence of the capitalist system involves workers producing an excess that they give to the capitalist without any reimbursement. This is an act of sacrifice on the part of workers. Both capitalist economists and Marxists agree on this point. The different between them is that the former believe that the capitalist deserves to profit on the workers' sacrifice because she or he has risked capital to start a company and in this way made the sacrifice possible in the first place, while the latter see the capitalist as an exploiter of another's sacrifice (that rightly belongs to the one making it). In either case, sacrifice, even if that's not what we call it, remains essential to the creation of value.

If one abandons the theory of surplus value and the labor theory of value, the sacrifice involved with labor does not disappear. In fact, even theories that don't attempt to account for the creation of value, like the General Equilibrium Theory, nonetheless posit a form of calculated sacrifice made by the worker. The worker sacrifices time for money, and no amount of money can ever create time. As Lionel Robbins puts it in his discussion of economic choices, "The time at our disposal is limited. There are only twenty-four hours in the day. We have to choose between the different uses to which they may be put."[12] The time that the worker spends working is thus sacrificed time.

We can also see this devotion to the worker's sacrifice in the behavior of contemporary industry. Capitalism is not content with granting workers a comfortable wage and making a sizable profit. Instead, it constantly seeks out new workers willing to work for less, thereby pitting workers in industrialized countries against those in economically marginalized ones. The capitalist economy drives workers to increasing sacrifices for the sake of profit, but profit is just an alibi for sacrifice. Sacrifice, as the source of value, has a far more fundamental role within capitalist society than profit, just as it does within every society.

This constant pressure to further the workers' immiseration is not an accidental feature resulting from the actions of a few evil capitalists. It is endemic to the system itself. The struggle for greater and greater profit is the form of appearance of the struggle for more and more sacrifice. Brutal labor conditions in India are the sort of sacrifice that capitalism relies on to produce satisfying commodities. These working conditions are not anomalies of the capitalist system but rather its sacrificial blood and guts.

The enjoyment of the sacrifice embodied in the commodity depends on the obscurity of this sacrifice. If we know, for instance, that child laborers in a sweatshop worked eighteen hours a day to produce the shoes that we want to buy, they will seem less attractive. This is why, just as slaughterhouses are not located next to steakhouses, factories are not placed in the vicinity of shopping malls. This is also why the "Made in China" tag on garments is not prominently featured. We must be able not to know that the production of the commodity required sacrifice. The labor embodied in the commodity must remain hidden, though we must also maintain an unconscious awareness of it.

The consumer's enjoyment of the worker's sacrifice—the enjoyment of the value given to the commodity by the worker's sacrifice of time—occurs through an act of fetishistic disavowal. For psychoanalysis, the fetish enables the subject to disavow the necessity of loss. It is a failure of knowing that implies another level of knowledge. In other words, fetishists don't know that they know and work to ensure that they will never know this. The disavowal permits knowledge and ignorance to coexist. This coexistence is vital for the modern subject.

CONDITIONS OF THE WORKING CLASS IN THE CONGO

The sacrifice that capitalism demands from the working class is a constant that has not changed through the centuries. We take it as an article of faith that the sacrifices of the working class have lessened, but this faith requires an active ignorance of what is happening around the world today. Though working conditions in some industries and regions are appreciably better than they were at the beginning of the industrial revolution, there are also areas where conditions have clearly deteriorated. One would rather be a young woman toiling in garment manufacturing in the 1840s Manchester than a child mining coltan in the Congo in the 2000s.

Exploitative working conditions are not a contingent aspect of the capitalist system but a result of the form of sacrifice that it demands. If one capitalist refuses to sacrifice the lives of workers ruthlessly enough, another capitalist with less scruples will surely drive the former out of business.[13] If we look at the situation of workers in Manchester, England, in the 1840s and compare this situation to that of workers in China or the Congo today, not only is it difficult to conclude that capitalism has progressed, but the reverse seems to be the case: the condition of the working class has for some worsened over the last 150 years.

Capital demands the maximum possible exploitation of labor—the highest possible quantity of work for the least possible pay—because increasing productivity while lessening cost is the only path toward augmenting accumulation. More accumulation leads to a richer future, which is the sole aim of the capitalist system. A richer future marks the fulfillment of the promise that animates capitalist production and consumption. The immiseration of workers is a means to this end. And yet, this immiseration—the sacrifice of workers' lives—also provides the satisfaction that keeps the psychic investment in the capitalist system going. If capitalism could produce more efficiently without the workers' sacrifice, it would not do so. Though consumers might protest against sweatshops and other horrific working conditions, their enjoyment of the commodities they purchase demands some sacrifice on the part of the workers who produce them. But consumers must be able not to know about it.

In the middle of the nineteenth century, this sacrifice was more visible, at least to some. Friedrich Engels sheds light on the travails of laborers under capitalism in his classic, *The Condition of the Working Class in England.* Engels begins this exposé by describing the absolute squalor in which the working class in Manchester lives and then he turns to an account of the factory conditions. The manufacture of fabrics and clothing exemplify these conditions at their worst.

The fabric industry found children best suited to the required labor and thus made use of them in order to maximize efficiency (and minimize pay). Engels chronicles a series of tasks and their nefarious effects on the children working on them. Those who thread needles, he argues, suffer the most. Engels states,

> Most unwholesome of all is the work of the runners, who are usually children of 7, and even of 5 and 4, years old. Commissioner Grainger actually found one child of 2 years old employed at this work. Following a thread which is to be withdrawn by a needle from an intricate texture, is very bad for the eyes, especially when, as is usually the case, the work is continued fourteen to sixteen hours. In the least unfavourable case, aggravated nearsightedness follows; in the worst case, which is frequent enough, incurable blindness from amaurosis. But, apart from that, the children, in consequence of sitting perpetually bent up, become feeble, narrow-chested, and scrofulous from bad digestion.[14]

The children used in the manufacture of lace were economical and enabled capitalists to produce elegant clothes for women to wear. But the sacrifice of these children's sight or their well-being is not just incidental to the value of what they produce.

The children's sacrifice ensures that the lace is not simply commonplace and imbues it with a worth that it otherwise wouldn't have, even if the women who wear it simultaneously decry the fate of these children. Lace created through the destruction of children's lives has a value that leaves or flowers picked off the ground to adorn my clothing do not. If anyone can obtain a product without sacrifice, it has no value for the subject.

Of course, an examination of working conditions in England in the nineteenth century cannot be decisive for the whole of the capitalist epoch. After all, even a rabid apologist for capitalism today would admit that Engels (at least on this point) was correct and that working conditions were horrible. But this same proponent of capitalism would quickly add that the situation has changed, that the capitalist system always ameliorates the conditions of the working class, as well as the standard of living for the whole society. Thus, if one wants to counter this point and argue that the sacrifice of workers is essential to the capitalist system, it must persist in all systemic manifestations.

The England of today does not resemble the England that Engels describes. Working conditions there evince an exponential improvement since the middle of the nineteenth century. But horrible conditions have not disappeared. They have migrated and remain integral to capitalist production. Capital actively seeks out regions where it can exploit labor and develop working conditions on par with those in a nineteenth-century British lace factory.

In the contemporary capitalist landscape, it is easy to find systemic instances of what amounts to human sacrifice. The worst of these sacrifices do not occur in Manchester, England, but they are nonetheless pivotal to the operations of capital in England and other prosperous regions of capitalist society. If one examines the manufacture of electronics in today's economy, the situation sounds akin to what Engels encountered. Even socially aware companies, if they want to remain competitive, must not just turn a blind eye to brutal exploitation of workers but must actively encourage it through their corporate policies.

Retailers such as Walmart play a decisive role in the horrible working conditions in countries such as China, India, and Vietnam. Walmart's insistence on the lowest prices necessarily leads to worker mistreatment among its suppliers in nations with lax labor laws or enforcement. Suppliers operate with a slim profit margin and must keep labor costs (including spending on labor safety) to an absolute minimum. Workers end up in dismal conditions earning typically much less than 1 percent of the price of the inexpensive products sold at Walmart. But almost everyone who enters Walmart understands the cost of the store's low prices (which is why many refuse to shop there). What is less obvious to consumers— yet even more significant—is similar or even more shocking horrors wrought by electronic companies that present themselves as socially responsible.

Apple is not Walmart. Steve Jobs is not Sam Walton. Though Jobs founded Apple in order to sell personal computers, his vision, like that of his fellow founders, went beyond simply making a profit. Apple envisioned changing the world and making lives better through its products. But even an enlightened company like Apple must sacrifice the lives of workers in order to produce iPods, iPads, and iPhones.[15] This sacrifice occurs in two distinct phases during the production process—the mining of raw materials and the assembly of the various devices.

According to the Enough Project (a group fighting crimes against humanity), Apple was historically one of the worst culprits among electronic manufacturers who relied on minerals mined in the Congo.[16] The four minerals that are most essential for electronic products include columbite-tantalite, or coltan (for tantalum), cassiterite (for tin), wolframite (for tungsten), and gold. Tantalum, tin, tungsten, and gold each play important roles in the functioning of electronic devices like the iPad and iPhone. Because the mines were under the control of various militia groups, they could enforce the most deplorable working conditions imaginable: forty-eight consecutive hours in unlit and gas-filled tunnels, child slave labor, rape of workers, death for the failure to achieve mining quotas, and so on.[17]

Civil war made this situation possible, but firms like Apple exploited and perpetuated the strife to obtain cheap elements for their commodities. This is why David Renton, David Seddon, and Leo Zeilig can claim that the war "was a human catastrophe linked to globalisation, profit and Western manipulation. The war was not simply an African affair, a regional war fought on Congolese territory. Behind the countries and the rebel groups involved in fighting it were Western companies and interests which played a crucial role in setting these forces into motion."[18] Despite the geographical distance that separates the retail outlets selling iPhones and the mines in the Congo, these two sites enjoy an intimate connection. The sacrifice of workers in the Congo is the condition of possibility for the consumer's enjoyment of the iPhone, though this consumer must remain able to disavow any knowledge of this sacrifice.

Apple's reliance on unimaginable mining conditions and civil war for the minerals that make up its products has ameliorated in recent years, thanks to groups like the Enough Project and the conflict mineral provision in the Dodd-Frank Act of 2010.[19] But the company's reliance on the extreme exploitation of workers continues at the assembly plants. The manufacture of iPads has led to great death and destruction in China, including worker suicides, plant explosions, and daily interaction with poisonous chemicals. One of Apple's suppliers in China, Foxconn, ran into such a problem with worker suicides that it constructed netting around the factory to curb the practice and forced workers to sign pledges saying that they would not do themselves in while working at Foxconn.

The relation between Apple and the sacrifice of workers in China is indirect but clear. According to the *New York Times*, "Apple typically asks suppliers to specify how much each part costs, how many workers are needed and the size of their salaries. Executives want to know every financial detail. Afterward, Apple calculates how much it will pay for a part. Most suppliers are allows on the slimmest of profits. So suppliers often try to cut corners, replace expensive chemicals with less costly alternatives, or push their employees to work faster and longer."[20] In order to develop exciting new products that consumers can afford, Apple must act this way. If it doesn't, another company will gladly take advantage of the possibility.[21]

No matter how much awareness rises among human rights groups and consumers, there will always be the equivalent of mines in the Congo and factories in China under the capitalist system. If labor becomes organized and powerful in China, the factories will—and already have— move to Vietnam or some other region where labor groups cannot check the demands of a major corporation. Capital seeks out vulnerable workers because their vulnerability holds the key to the creation of value. The most vulnerable workers create the most value for the capitalist.

The sacrifice of workers' lives for the sake of an unnecessary commodity like the iPad does not detract from our ability to enjoy iPads. In fact, we cannot enjoy without some sacrifice—either of ourselves or of others— because sacrifice is the source of all value. We value objects through the loss that they embody. The psychic or financial cost of an object is inextricable from the worth that we assign to it. When we can obtain an object without any sacrifice, we will also freely part with it because we know we can simply obtain it again. This logic of sacrifice operates independently of the capitalist system, but capitalism permits us to enjoy sacrifice while fetishistically disavowing it. We can ensure that we are unaware that Congolese children labored in a pitch-black mine or that Chinese workers died in explosions for the sake of our iPads.

INVENTING FORMS OF WASTE

The onset of modernity makes the direct enjoyment of sacrifice impossible.[22] The modern subject has to believe in its own commitment to utility and rationality, even in the face of its unconscious dependence on sacrifice. There is thus no going back to the sacrificial rituals of the past. But modernity continues to require sacrifice in order to satisfy its subjects, and the result of this confluence is the turn to fetishistic disavowal, which permits an unconscious satisfaction for modern consciousness. Only through the fetish can the modern consumer enjoy the miseries that produce the objects to be consumed.

The enjoyment of the commodity in contemporary capitalist society requires a delicate balancing act between ignorance and knowledge. On the one hand, the consumer must know that some sacrifice went into the making of the commodity, but on the other hand, the consumer must be able to claim ignorance about this sacrifice to avoid feelings of guilt. What renders us guilty is always our ignorance, not our knowledge. Our efforts to remain ignorant about coltan mines in the Congo reflect our complicity with the militias that run them. The consumer's ignorance is not just the result of a lack of desire to know but of a genuine passion for ignorance.

The satisfaction in consumption doesn't derive only from the sacrifice of the worker's time to create the commodity. Working alongside this sacrifice is the consumer's own sacrifice of money for an object that serves no useful function. There is no question that consumers enjoy purchasing commodities. Shopping is for many the top-rated leisure activity, and the lines outside stores during sales before the Christmas holidays around the world testify to the eagerness with which many consume.[23] This satisfaction has an inverse relationship to the utility of what one buys. Buying gasoline to fuel one's car is seldom arousing (despite the metaphorical similarity to sexual activity, down to the term *pumping gas*), but buying a new video game or seeing the newest Hollywood blockbuster often is. When we buy useful items that contribute to our self-interest, like broccoli or underwear, we experience the purchase as an act of exchange.[24] We obtain a product in exchange for the labor time accumulated in our money. But when we buy useless or even self-destructive objects, like Oreos or wine, the purchase becomes an act of self-sacrifice in which we can take satisfaction. Almost everyone enjoys buying a fine wine more than stalks of broccoli. This is not an accident. When giving our money for the former, we can experience sacrifice instead of exchange, and this sacrifice is the basis of our capacity to enjoy.[25]

The spirit of sacrifice is also present among the most prosperous capitalists themselves. These figures spend almost all of their time in the service of accumulation, an accumulation that bears no relationship to utility. Even after they have accumulated enough capital for the grandchildren of their grandchildren, most capitalists continue to strive to accumulate even more. They don't enjoy the free time they have earned because their enjoyment resides in the sacrifice of this time for the sake of ever more accumulation. The future prosperity of the capitalist's descendants simply allows the sacrifice to take place with a good conscience. The capitalist's desire to accumulate allows for the sacrifice of great amounts of time and energy for capital that will not provide much additional satisfaction for the capitalist.

From the marketing director of a small company to the owner of Microsoft, the capitalist spends more time on questions of accumulation than is necessary for the most comfortable life imaginable. This differentiates the ruling class in the capitalist system from the ruling class in all hitherto existing societies. Formerly, the ruling class used its position of mastery to avoid all forms of sacrifice. This class imposed terrible sacrifice on others in order to avoid experiencing sacrifice itself in the form of labor. Servants dedicated their lives to the ease of masters, and, though servitude certainly endures within a capitalist economy, mastery also becomes associated with sacrifice.

The sacrifice that the capitalist makes is all the more confusing for its senselessness. The capitalist sacrifices for more after already having enough and gives up time for minor profits. In his *The Quintessence of Capitalism*, Werner Sombart puzzles over the devotion that the capitalist shows toward economic activity. He asks, "What is to be said of the phenomenon that perfectly healthy, good-natured people, often enough with mental gifts above the average, should care for such a thing as economic activity? Not, mind you, because they regard it as a duty or as a necessary evil, but because they love it, because they have devoted themselves to it with heart and soul, with mind and body!"[26] Capitalists devote themselves to economic activity because they enjoy it, and this enjoyment, as Sombart hints at without explicitly stating it, depends on the sacrifice that occurs when one preoccupies oneself with economic activity. The banality of economic activity is not an argument against it but the ultimate argument for it. One can sacrifice one's life for nothing and in this way find a satisfaction that would otherwise be impossible.

Sombart's statement underlines the insignificance that defines the capitalist's sacrifice. Whereas workers sacrifice for the sake of their survival, capitalists sacrifice their free time for the sake of a few pennies added to an already large fortune. Just as in the sphere of consumption, sacrifice in production has the greatest appeal when it has the least utility, and this is where capitalism's unique psychic attraction lies. Capitalism provides innumerable opportunities for subjects to sacrifice their time and resources for what is socially and personally useless. Spending one's days scanning the reports from the stock market offers much more satisfaction than building a shelter for the homeless. The utility of the latter activity detracts from the satisfaction that it offers, while the former has the thrill of smoking a cigarette without its carcinogenic quality.

The most important insight into the part that sacrifice plays in capitalism comes from John Maynard Keynes. In his effort to think through solutions to the crises of capitalism, Keynes discovers that wasteful or sacrificial spending actually creates more wealth than productive spending. The problem with productive spending, Keynes argues, is that it can always reach a point of abundance where it will cause a crisis. If a company invests in food production and makes plenty of food available, the demand will lessen and lessen, and the prospects for future growth will disappear altogether. This will have the effect of dampening investment in the company, even if the time of abundance lies well in the future. Abundance is an investment killer, as Keynes correctly sees. If a company produces enough tables, they will cut into the demand for their product and thus scare off potential investors. Today's success portends tomorrow's failure when one is dealing with a useful commodity, like roads and tables.[27]

Capital investment depends on the prospect of future increases in consumption, and this is impossible with useful commodities. According to Keynes, "New capital-investment can only take place in excess of current capital-disinvestment if *future* expenditure on consumption is expected to increase. Each time we secure to-day's equilibrium by increased investment we are aggravating the difficulty of securing equilibrium to-morrow."[28] It is not the fact of future abundance (and thus overproduction) that leads to crisis but the expectation of this result. There is only one way to avoid this deadlock, and Keynes makes it into the central plank of his response to the Great Depression.

Keynes arrives at the idea that wasteful spending avoids the deadlock of future abundance. Unlike useful spending, wasteful spending—acts of pure sacrifice of money—have no future prospect of abundance. Spending on war will never result in abundance because the demand is infinite. One can keep fighting wars until there is no one left to fight—and, even then, one can continue to produce useless weapons by imagining the emergence of future enemies. In the same way, investment in gold mining wastes resources without any prospect of cutting into demand. The appeal of wasteful spending lies in its inability to satiate a demand and thus in its infinite status. It puts people to work without the prospect of their work eliminating its own utility through overproduction.[29]

When they perform useful labor, workers are digging their own graves, pushing toward a state of abundance when they will no longer be necessary. Ironically, the act of actually digging graves frees workers from this dilemma. Keynes explains the prosperity of ancient Egypt by noting the immense resources that they directed toward the completely unproductive act of building large tombs for the dead. This kind of inexhaustible domain provides an avenue for constant economic growth. As Keynes puts it, "Two pyramids . . . are twice as good as one; but not so two railways from London to York."[30] Even useful public spending programs run into the problem of future abundance, which is why nothing solves an economic crisis like a war.[31]

Keynes puts the final nail in the coffin of the capitalist myth of utility, but capitalist economists—even Keynesians—continue to cling to this myth till this day. Without the idea that capitalism adequately provides for human needs, one could not remain a believer in the capitalist system. Keynes's own attachment to the system grew out of the fantasy that one could permanently stave off crisis by accepting small growth. He thought, to put it in the terms of psychoanalysis, that keeping to the reality principle and avoiding the pleasure principle would keep the system's self-destructiveness at bay. But this is an illusion. No amount of compromise can eliminate the drive for sacrifice. Once Keynes shows the vacuity of capitalist claims to utility, there is no going back, despite his personal effort to do so.

Nonetheless, capitalist ideology depends on the idea of utility. Utility is the sacred cow of the theory of capitalism. The fact that capitalism avoids unnecessary sacrifice is the basis of most theories of capitalist economics. For instance, as general equilibrium theorist Léon Walras notes, "Only useful things limited in quantity can be produced by industry."[32] If a commodity were useless, industry would have no incentive to produce it because no consumer would take an interest in purchasing it. This schema of complete utility leaves no room for sacrifice—and certainly no room for the ritualized unnecessary sacrifice that populates precapitalist societies.[33]

The justification for the violence of the free market derives from its ability to supply society with the goods that it needs to reproduce itself and to grow. Critics of capitalism point out the failures of capitalism on this count: it doesn't provide enough shelter, enough food, or enough pleasure for everyone to survive and prosper. Capitalism's ruthless insistence on profitability ensures that many needs will be left unfulfilled. But the problem with this emphasis on capitalism's utility goes much further. It devotes enormous resources to products that are socially unnecessary and even incredibly destructive.

If we think about some of the major industries of today, the falsity of capitalism's commitment to social utility becomes evident. Enormous resources are devoted to weapons, sports teams, cigarettes, alcohol, and luxury cars—just to name a few areas of production with no evident social benefit. In fact, if we think about the industries to which capitalism devotes most of its resources, social utility does not come out well at all, and it seems as if capitalism serves the reproduction of society very reluctantly.

This becomes completely clear if we look at the companies dedicated to the most socially essential product—the food industry. Makers of food, which is the basis of social reproduction, today spend an inordinate amount of time transforming food into a socially destructive product. Rather than simply growing healthy food and distributing it to stores where people could purchase it, food companies create an almost infinite number of products designed to lure the consumer into purchasing something destructive. They prefer to sell Cheetos to bananas because there is more sacrifice—and thus more profit—in the former. If corporations serve social utility, its importance is always secondary to the creation of a destructive new desire, like the desire for junk food.

Desires do not preexist the product that arrives on the market to sate them. The product and the desiring consumer form in a dialectic relation with each other: the commodity speaks to the possibility of a desire in the consumer, and if it speaks successfully, the desire will form. This is a process that Marx uncovers in the *Grundrisse*. He notes, "Production not only supplies a material for the need, but it also supplies a need for the material. . . . The need which consumption feels for the object is created by the perception of it. The object of art—like every other product—creates a public which is sensitive to art and enjoys beauty. Production thus not only creates an object for the subject, but also a subject for the object."[34] Here Marx attributes all creative power to the producer, and if this were the case, there would be no possibility of a failed commodity.[35] But he does grasp the essential role that the production of commodities plays in creating its own market, which is what political economists like Smith and Ricardo don't comprehend. Capitalists are not trying to create socially useful products but rather products that foment socially useless desires.

The apologists for capitalism get around this argument against capitalism's self-justification by redefining the term *utility* in a tautological way. Capitalism doesn't have to provide what we define as socially useful; what is socially useful is socially useful because capitalism provides it. As David Ricardo, the inventor of this idea, puts it, "If a commodity were in no way useful—in other words, if it could in no way contribute to our gratification—it would be destitute of exchangeable value, however scarce it might be, or whatever quantity of labour might be necessary to procure it."[36] Our acts of consumption themselves respond to the exigencies of utility, and any commodity that doesn't speak to our "gratification" will go unsold. That is to say, there is no such thing as a superfluous need or what Marx identifies as the creation of needs. If an industry can create a market for a commodity, the incipient need for this commodity must have already existed in consumers.

The brilliance of Ricardo's formulation has stood the test of time, and we should have a proper appreciation for it. Prominent defenders of

capitalism in the twentieth century, like F. A. Hayek and Milton Friedman, continued to reason like this in order to justify the ways of capitalism to humanity. Ricardo's logic cannot be countered because it is perfectly circular: capitalism gratifies human desires, but it is only through
the free market that we can know those desires. Ricardo never articulates the nature of human desires prior to their fulfillment, which renders his solution so elegant and utterly irrefutable. From this perspective, any attempt to argue for an alternative would ipso facto represent a
loss of touch with desire as such. Though Ricardo's argument is irrefutable, it does rest on the vitalist assumption that desire is natural, that it
emerges out of life itself. According to this assumption, we simply cannot be made to desire what we don't already desire.

This vitalism founds capitalist ideology, but it founders when it runs
into the problem of sacrifice. According to vitalist thesis, sacrifice must
be the result of some type of deception—either people being deceived or
deceiving themselves. The vitalist analysis thus consists of denouncing
those responsible for this deception, those who coerce others into accepting the negation of life. In *A Thousand Plateaus*, Gilles Deleuze and
Félix Guattari place the blame on the figure of the priest.[37] Anyone who
insists on the necessity of sacrifice and lack, like the psychoanalyst or the
Hegelian philosopher, occupies, according to Deleuze and Guattari, the
position of the priest and contributes to the denial of desire.

But what neither Deleuze and Guattari nor the defenders of capitalism can explain is how the denial of desire emerges as a possibility. If
there is only life, and sacrifice comes as a monstrous deviation from life,
the vitalist cannot explain what enables this deviation to occur. In other
words, life must already negate itself—being must be self-negating—in
order for subjects to have the capacity for sacrificing themselves. There
must be a space within life for sacrifice in order for priests to come along
and convince people to sacrifice themselves. The victims are either some-
what invested in their own victimization or completely stupid, and even
this stupidity would have to receive a philosophical reckoning.

Despite its conceptual beauty, Ricardo's vision of a closed loop between
capitalism and desire must be rejected for its failure to account for the
origin of desire. The test of capitalism as an economic system is not that
it meets all the needs that appear within it, since this is one it can't fail.
The test is rather whether or not capitalism can permit the avowal of

the satisfaction that it produces. This is a test that capitalism does in fact fail. Capitalism relies on the violent sacrifice of workers, consumers, and even capitalists themselves, and it uses this sacrifice to produce satisfied subjects. But this sacrifice can play no part in capitalism's ideological self-understanding. In response to this failure to make sacrifice explicit, reactionary alternatives to capitalism have proliferated. These alternatives seek a system in which they can rediscover the sacrifice that capitalism appears to deny to us. The first thinker to focus the critique of capitalism on its failure with regard to sacrifice was Georges Bataille, an anticapitalist apostle of sacrifice.

HIDDEN ENJOYMENT AND ITS VICISSITUDES

Bataille was also the first thinker to identify sacrifice with enjoyment. His critique of capitalism focuses on its turn away from sacrifice and thus from the possibility for a true satisfaction. In his riposte to the assumptions of political economists like Smith and Ricardo, Bataille locates satisfaction not in accumulation of goods but in their sacrifice. Since sacrifice functions as our basic mode of satisfying ourselves, capitalism represents an ontological retreat and an abandonment of our mode of enjoyment. Bataille notes, "The practice of sacrifice has today fallen into disuse and yet it has been, due to its universality, a human action more significant than any other. Independently of each other, different peoples invented different forms of sacrifice, with the goal of answering a need as inevitable as hunger. It is therefore not astonishing that the necessity of satisfying such a need, under the conditions of present-day life, leads an isolated man into disconnected and even stupid behavior."[38] Capitalism has failed us, Bataille claims, through its marginalization of sacrifice. In his own life, Bataille attempted to struggle against this evacuation of sacrifice, even once going so far as to spread the rumor that he had been involved in a human sacrifice.[39]

The problem with Bataille, however, is that his theory of sacrifice is grounded in an ontology of excess energy. We enjoy sacrifice because we are burdened with too much energy: there is enjoyment in the diminution of this burden. But Bataille never explains how this excess arises and how we obtain it. In this way, he misses the creative power of sacrifice, its capacity to form something out of nothing. We don't begin with too much but with undifferentiated being, and sacrifice enables us to differentiate, to create a value where none otherwise exists. It is the creative power of sacrifice that generates its appeal.

In terms of his analysis of capitalism, Bataille's emphasis on the impoverishment of sacrifice leads him astray. He mistakes the secularization of sacrifice for its evanescence, and this error leads him to underestimate capitalism's appeal. If sacrifice was "a need as inevitable as hunger" as he says, capitalism could not endure while turning away from it. The invisibility of sacrifice is not its disuse but its multiplication. But Bataille nonetheless captures the experience of the capitalist subject reacting to the hiddenness of sacrifice in the capitalist world. His thought functions not so much as a critical analysis of capitalist society but as a phenomenology of capitalist life, a life that hides its dependence on sacrifice.

The hiddenness of sacrifice often produces outbursts of sacrifice that attempt to compensate for its apparent absence. The secularization of sacrifice creates the image of a world in which all objects are equal and thus one in which no object has any value. Where everything has a price, nothing is worth anything. Outbursts of sacrifice occur most prominently with contemporary terrorists. The true terrorist is the one who is not fighting for a particular ethnic or nationalist cause but rather struggling against capitalist modernity. This figure finds the absence of visible sacrifice in modernity suffocating. Modern subjects appear to exist without any sacrificial demands: they can display their bodies openly, watch obscene films, and even engage publicly in overtly sexualized behavior. They seem to enjoy in lieu of sacrificing, and the terrorist aims at reintroducing sacrifice into this abyss.

The terrorist always sacrifices others and often sacrifices herself or himself to create value in the monotony of the modern world. Though terrorism involves destruction, it is always also creation. The terrorist tries to gives existence a value that it seems to have lost. But this judgment on the part of the terrorist reflects a failure to recognize how the capitalist system actually functions.

It is true that the tedium of capitalist existence appears valueless. But this is just the result of the transmutation of sacrifice performed by capitalism, not its absence. Capitalism's secularization of sacrifice actually multiplies its frequency in the social order. Though no one in capitalist society cuts out the beating heart of a sacrificial victim, nuclear warheads, elaborate churches, and slaughterhouses testify to the persistence of sacrifice. And unlike the Aztecs and the Mayans, modern subjects have lost the alibi of ignorance, which makes the presence of sacrifice within capitalism so instructive.

Because sacrifice becomes less explicit and more integrated into everyday life under capitalism, subjects often fail to see its presence and seek out more direct forms of sacrifice out of a sense of dissatisfaction with modernity. This is the dissatisfaction that produces terrorist attacks, fundamentalist revivals, and bungee jumpers. The reactionaries that take up these activities are the direct result of capitalism's ideological commitment to utility. They sacrifice themselves in senseless activities to proclaim their disgust with utility and their adherence to something of value. But the hatred of capitalism's universe of utility reflects a failure to diagnose that universe and its mobilization of sacrifice.

To hate capitalist modernity for the abandonment of sacrifice and the desecration of value is to accept capitalist ideology at face value. Though capitalist ideology professes that capitalism is the most efficient economic system because it is the most responsive to human needs and eliminates the unnecessary sacrifices of time and energy that haunt other economic systems, sacrifice remains the sine qua non of capitalism, just as it was for earlier economies. But responses like terrorism, fundamentalism, and bungee jumping themselves play a part in furthering this ideology as well. They work to convince us that capitalism does really eliminate sacrifice and simply gratify needs by implicitly criticizing it for doing so. Their failure to see capitalist sacrifice helps to render it more invisible. But the answer to these reactionary positions should be an analysis of capitalism's structural similarity to them.

One must only look and see in order to become aware of the ubiquity of sacrifice in the capitalist economy. The moments of satisfaction that capitalism offers are themselves replete with sacrifice, but the system shields us from confronting it. As a result, we accept the capitalist myth that sacrifice belongs to a prior epoch, and either we accommodate ourselves to this world or violently revolt against it. But this violent revolt rests on a fundamental misunderstanding of how capitalism sustains itself. One need not turn to terrorism in order to rediscover the spirit of sacrifice. This spirit has never left. Every act that we perform in the capitalist system involves us in forms of sacrifice, even if the system renders them invisible. Instead of flying a plane into a building, all one need do to experience the most violent sacrifice is to buy a new iPhone.

[5]

A God We Can Believe In

NOT GOD BUT AN OTHER

Capitalist modernity creates the possibility of conceiving human freedom. Unlike other socioeconomic systems, capitalism doesn't demand
widespread obedience of a transcendent entity in order to function.
Though hierarchical relations remain, they are not rooted in a divine
justification that would render free actions impossible. This marks a dramatic break from past systems. At the same time, modern science also
entails a rejection of divine intervention as a factor in its calculations
about the universe. Scientists can believe in God (though most do not),
but they cannot explain human or natural actions with recourse to God
and continue to have a serious standing among other scientists. This absence of God in capitalist modernity creates the space in which subjects
can, for the first time in human history, believe in freedom without contradiction. Freedom is only thinkable without the presence of a divine
force active in the world.

If God's absence from the world becomes evident after the birth of
capitalist modernity, capitalism simultaneously erects a new form of
divinity, one even more tyrannical than the old form. The new god is the
market, and unlike the omnipotent and omniscient God of the monothe-
istic traditions, the market doesn't make its tyranny clear. It never proclaims itself to be a jealous god in the way that Yahweh does. It doesn't
appear to restrain freedom, as God does, but rather to foster it. The free
market replaces God and acts as the Other, as a social authority, in capi-

talist modernity. Like God, it tells subjects what to desire and directs their actions, but it does so in a surreptitious fashion. The methods of God and those of the market are thus at odds, even though their function as the guarantee of social existence is the same. The traditional God and the market are bastions against the trauma of freedom. Capitalist modernity opens up the possibility of freedom only to close it off, but this opening is nonetheless the decisive event of the modern epoch.

God doesn't disappear in modernity—one is still permitted to believe—but this epoch does away with God as a physical presence within the world. As long as God exists as a physical being governing the movements of the world, there is no possibility for human freedom because all human activity occurs in reference to an actually existing—rather than a spiritual—Other. The geocentric conception of the world enables humanity not just to see itself as the center of creation but to find assurance in the certain existence of a substantial Other (that is, in a substantial figure of authority). With this background, we can make sense of a historical mystery.

From a contemporary perspective, it is difficult to understand why the Copernican heliocentric system had such a radical effect on Catholic authorities. For the faithful, why would it matter if the Earth or the Sun were the center of the solar system? If one consulted believers today, probably not a single one would claim that the collapse of geocentrism troubles their sleep. Copernicus himself never had to worry about the wrath of the Church since he had the good fortune to die on the day that *De revolutionibus orbium coelestium* appeared in 1543. Others were not so lucky. A belief in heliocentrism played a major role in the Inquisition's execution of Giordano Bruno in 1600 and led to Galileo Galilei denying his own publicly stated support for the Copernican thesis in order to avoid a similar fate. Bruno's courage and Galileo's capitulation were both the result of the intense pressure that the Church felt to maintain the geocentric system. The assault on geocentrism had the effect of an assault on the nature of God.

Though there are no biblical passages stating unequivocally that the Earth is the center of the universe, the heliocentric hypothesis nonetheless bothered Church authorities greatly. It did so because it uprooted God from the specific location that this being could have within the Ptolemaic or Aristotelian system. God could continue to exist and be ubiquitous or even simply spiritual, but God could never again have a definitive place. With the theoretical development of the heliocentric system, God ceases to be a substance.[1] This is the perhaps modernity's greatest disruption of tradition. The displacement of God can lead (and has led) to all sorts of fideism, but it also tears away the transcendent ground of social authority. It is just a small step from the displacement or spiritualization of God to the freedom that makes possible the execution of the monarch.[2]

As a being with a definite place in the structure of the world, God could function as the ultimate cause or prime mover of every action within the world. The spiritualization of God does not immediately eliminate the possibility of God's causal relation to the world, but it renders this relation problematic. Just as Descartes requires the pineal gland to link causes in the mind with physical effects in the body, a sort of cosmic pineal gland would be necessary to connect the spiritual nature of God with the actions taking place in the physical universe. As with Descartes's postulation, no amount of research is likely to turn up the existence of such a cosmic gland. Thus, a barrier between God qua cause and the physical universe qua effect emerges for the first time with heliocentric modernity. It becomes possible, even necessary, to separate religious belief from scientific research due to the intractability of the barrier. But this barrier is also the source of the freedom that modernity bequeaths to the subject. A spiritualized God, a God without a physical place, ceases to hold all the cards in advance for those playing in the physical universe.

Freedom is never simply the freedom to do what one wants.[3] As thinkers from Plato onward have insisted, what one wants is always socially mediated and thus necessary before it is free. We don't generate our own wants but inherit them from our milieu and its constraints. We are never more determined than when we are doing what we want, which is why freedom must not simply be equivalent to the ability to act in any way we please.

Freedom involves an absence of reliance on the Other as a substantial figure of authority. For the free subject, the Other does not have a substantial existence. There is no guarantee undergirding and taking responsibility for the decisions the subject makes. This means that the most significant barrier to freedom is not a member of the police forcing me to eat celery instead of a Twinkie, but a television advertisement telling me that George Clooney (or any representative of social authority) likes Twinkies. Freedom is freedom from the figure of the Other qua social authority providing an ontological support for my acts.

Though Descartes glimpses this conception of freedom when he adopts subjectivity rather than divinity as his philosophical starting point, his fully developed philosophy relies on an Other (in the form of God) as the guarantee of truth. The turn toward God in the Third Meditation represents Descartes's tacit admission that the subject cannot stand on its own.[4] Descartes, the first philosopher of capitalist modernity, retreats from freedom because he recognizes the horror that it manifests. Freedom implies the absence of any substantial Other, the lack of guarantees to guide the subject's choices. The free subject exists alone with its decisions, and whatever morality it adopts stems from it alone, not from God or from any authorized figure. Many after Descartes have effected similar retreats from freedom and into the arms of various forms of the Other—Nation for the fascist, History for the communist, Jesus for the Christian fundamentalist, and so on.

The one thinker who refused to retreat into the arms of the Other on the question of freedom was Immanuel Kant. Kant's moral philosophy represents a landmark in the history of philosophy because the moral subject must derive its guidelines from itself rather than from any external source. Even though the moral law is universal, the subject must define that universality itself, which is the crucial problem. Alenka Zupančič recognizes this in her analysis of the great leap forward that Kant accomplishes with his conception of morality. She argues, "That which can in no way be reduced without abolishing ethics as such is not the multicoloured variability of every situation, but the gesture by which every subject, by means of his action, posits the universal, performs a certain operation of universalization."[5] Even reason, which alerts the subject to the existence of the moral law, does not constitute the law or direct its implementation. Instead, the subject must decide for itself.

Kant identifies the bare existence of the moral law as the source and index of the subject's freedom. No unfree entity, as Kant sees it, could have the capacity to give itself laws and disrupt its instinctual being. Though Kant ultimately believes that the moral law enables us to assume the existence of God, God provides no moral guidance in Kant's philosophy. Morality leads to God rather than God leading to morality. This means that we are completely free, without any Other to guide our actions.

If God exists for Kant, God does not provide the key to moral action and thereby obviate our radical freedom. This is why Kant insists that the moral law—the subject's own free decision—must serve as the final arbiter of good and evil. God does not have a say. In the *Critique of Practical Reason*, Kant claims, *"the concept of good and evil must not be determined before the moral law (for which, as it would seem, this concept would have to be made the basis) but only (as was done here) after it and by means of it."*[6] The subject is free because it has no external authority on which it might rely. Kant's greatness as a philosopher lies primarily in his grasp of the implications for the subject's freedom implicit in modernity.[7]

Though Georg Lukács tries to reduce Kant to being the philosopher of the antinomies of bourgeois thought, he is able to do so only by confining himself to the theoretical Kant of the *Critique of Pure Reason*. In the second *Critique*, Kant's distance from capitalism becomes apparent through his insistence on a form of freedom that capitalism cannot stomach. The *Critique of Practical Reason* shows that freedom is not simply subject to the undecidability that the attempt to theorize it in the first *Critique* encounters. Instead, we know that we are free and that this freedom rests on no external guarantees (like God or the good). We know this through the experience of constraint that the moral law effectuates. But the moral law is not another substance that might replace God or even a new God. The moral law is not the Other but its absence. It is the site of authentic freedom because it is nothing but the subject's own self-division. Thus, its existence is the index of the radical freedom of modernity's break from God.[8]

If modernity inaugurates the possibility of freedom and Kant develops it philosophically, capitalism provides the perfect avenue for retreat from the trauma inherent within freedom. This is ironic given that every apologist for capitalism begins by foregrounding the role that freedom plays within the capitalist system. Even if capitalism produces injustice, even if capitalism leads to immorality, it nonetheless enables subjects to act freely. From Adam Smith to Ayn Rand to Donald Trump, freedom is the capitalist watchword always on the lips of its defenders. But capitalism's conception of freedom has little to recommend it. It has more in common with the freedom of the communists who believe that they are acting on behalf of the objective forces of history than with the genuine freedom that Kant extols. Capitalist freedom is utterly false, which is why we cling to it so vehemently.

THE POVERTY OF FREEDOM

Capitalism's impoverished conception of freedom manifests itself in the thought of almost every capitalist economist. These economists do not betray authentic capitalist freedom through their conception of it but make apparent the deleterious effect that capitalism has on actual freedom, that is, on freedom from the Other and its guarantees guiding our existence. Capitalism furnishes the freedom to accumulate but determines how that accumulation will take place. Despite the complete identification of capitalism with freedom, subjects in this system are not even free to choose their careers, their possessions, or what they will build. As almost every capitalist economist shows, the free market doesn't allow for freedom.

Nowhere is this contradiction more apparent than in the work of Ludwig von Mises. Unlike most other exponents of the free market (like, for instance, Milton Friedman), von Mises doesn't grant the existence of any form of freedom other than that produced by the market. He says, "There is no kind of freedom and liberty other than the kind which the market economy brings about."[9] Political freedom is entirely secondary and even inconsequential for von Mises. Economic freedom—the freedom to buy and sell one's own commodities without restriction—is what renders social life endurable. When one can buy and sell freely, one can have the kind of satisfaction that would be impossible under any other economic system. This freedom is an end in itself for von Mises, a good that should exist throughout every social order and that we should promulgate at all costs.

The panegyric to the free market that animates the thought of von Mises is representative of that found in every defender of the capitalist economy. But the ideal of freedom to buy and sell what one wants to buy and sell is not just capitalist ideology. One really has this freedom in the capitalist system, and it separates capitalism from other economic forms in which the state or some other organization restricts what one can buy or sell. Though every market has some restrictions—the local department store cannot sell nuclear bombs or snuff films—the market in a capitalist economy has only minimal restrictions justified in the name of public safety. Though certain companies may work to limit the production of certain commodities (as oil companies did with the electric car), these instances represent violations of the inherent ideal of capitalism, and they do not eliminate the real effects of this ideal. Nonetheless, the free market, even in its ideal unrestricted form, is not a bastion of freedom, as von Mises himself surprisingly reveals.

Von Mises presents himself as an apostle of freedom, as someone so committed to freedom that he will countenance extreme inequality to sustain it.[10] But then, when he extols the virtues of the market, he praises its ability to rescue us from our freedom. This is one of those shocking moments when a thinker inadvertently exposes the unconscious desire at stake in her or his conscious project. According to von Mises, "The market process is the adjustment of the individual actions of the various members of the market society to the requirements of mutual cooperation. The market prices tell the producers what to produce, how to produce, and in what quantity."[11] Rather than confronting the burden of freedom when we decide on our life's work, von Mises believes that the market decides for us. This is the crucial move in the thought of von Mises and many other champions of capitalism. They give the market the status of the Other for subjects within the capitalist economy. These defenders are even more perspicacious than Marx himself in displaying capitalism's retreat from freedom at the precise point—the market— where it posits an absolute freedom.

The market replaces God insofar as it tells us what we should desire. But it is an improved version of God because it permits us to retain the idea of ourselves as free beings. Whereas Christian theologians must constantly wrestle with the problem of human freedom in the face of an omnipotent God, the apologist for capitalism never confronts a similar problem because the free market incessantly assures us, even with its moniker, of our freedom. That is, the capitalist Other, unlike God, doesn't force us to question how we could reconcile freedom and the Other's omnipotence, and yet the market relieves us from our freedom much more effectively than God. God leaves room for doubt, whereas the market rarely does.[12]

When we think about the difference between God and the market, it seems easy to judge which is the more oppressive form of the Other. The partisans of the Christian God in the Middle Ages burned at the stake the heretics who refused to accept God's abridgement of their freedom. Capitalism, in contrast, leaves heretics alone. Those who reject the market can forge an existence outside its exigencies without any legal ramifications. Capitalism does not condemn nonbelievers to hell. But this explicit tolerance hides an ideological severity much more extreme than that of the Inquisition. The association of the market with freedom is so widespread in the capitalist universe that it is almost impossible to think outside these terms. Even those who opt out of the system most often seek the form of freedom that the capitalist system itself promulgates—the freedom to control their economic destiny. Heresy might not have been commonplace in the medieval world, but it becomes rarer once the market replaces God because the market is an improved form of God, a deity that insulates us from freedom, insisting all the while that we are free.[13]

In *The Road to Serfdom*, F. A. Hayek repeats the same contradiction that entraps von Mises, though he discusses it in terms of the worker rather than the businessperson. Hayek argues that society should not provide any security of employment but instead allow workers to lose their jobs when these jobs cease to be socially necessary. Rather than seeing this position as coldhearted, Hayek views it as enlightened. One of the virtues of capitalism is that it eliminates socially unnecessary labor by rendering that labor unprofitable. Utility rules the capitalist universe and quickly eliminates positions that no longer contribute to the collective good.

When I examine the field of possibilities for my life's work, the choice seems impossible. I could devote myself to medical research, stock trading, exploration of the cosmos, garbage collection, the study of history, or an almost infinite amount of other options. But when I look at the absence of career opportunities for history professors and the bevy for stock traders, the choice becomes clear. Even those who lack the privilege of choosing a career and must simply decide where to apply for a job receive guidance from the market, which tells them to apply at Walmart rather than at the local bookstore. The free market rescues me from the horrible freedom of having no grounds for deciding what I desire to take up as an occupation.

The way that parents and teachers talk to us about this decision reveals the profound link between the guidance offered by the market and that which comes from God. They explain that we will know we've found our calling when we find it. We will find ourselves struck like Paul on the road to Damascus. But the voice indicating our career path is not the voice of God. It is the voice, as Hayek makes clear, of the free market.

What Hayek likes about this economic verdict is the extreme clarity that it provides for the worker faced with a free decision about employment. He notes, "Even with the best will in the world it would be impossible for anyone intelligently to choose between various alternatives if the advantages they offered to him stood in no relation to their usefulness to society. To know whether as the result of a change a man ought to leave a trade and an environment which he has come to like, and exchange it for another, it is necessary that the changed relative value of these occupations in society should find expression in the remunerations they offer."[14] We don't have to flounder around searching for what to do within the capitalist system. The magic of the market will direct us to the proper, socially necessary line of work. Despite Hayek's insistence that only capitalism ensures our absolute liberty, here he describes its brake on that liberty as a virtue.

It is difficult to express enough shock at the presence of this passage, given Hayek's zealous commitment to freedom. Toward the beginning of *The Constitution of Liberty*, an extended homily to freedom, he provides his definition of the concept. He contends that freedom is nothing but the absence of coercion, the ability to act without being compelled in one way or another.[15] This is a sentiment that Hayek echoes throughout *The Road to Serfdom* as well: freedom is the foundational value for Hayek, and yet he celebrates capitalism for freeing us from its burden by directing our desire. Capitalism places an Other in the place of the modernity's displaced God. By resurrecting this God, Hayek betrays the freedom he celebrates. This resurrection is not simply his theological misinterpretation of capitalism. He correctly sees that capitalism does provide subjects with a new form of social authority, a new Other to guide their actions, even if that authority is invisible.

In an ontological sense, my freedom has its basis in the nonexistence of the Other, in the fact that there is no Other to tell me how to desire. I must interpret the desire of the Other that does not exist in order to constitute my own subjectivity as desiring. We are condemned to freedom not, as Jean-Paul Sartre would have it, because we could also decide to act differently but because there is no authoritative and substantial Other to tell us how to desire. Any such figure that we call on is the product of an act of belief, and this is what occurs with capitalism, as Hayek rightfully describes. In the form of the market, capitalism provides us with the image a substantial Other that we can believe in.

Given the thoroughgoing hostility to any abridgement of freedom to choose expressed during the entirety of *Human Action* and *The Road to Serfdom*, the passages cited above are startling. Von Mises and Hayek extol the virtue of capitalism for providing respite from our freedom to choose what we want to devote our lives to. Under capitalism we don't have to decide wholly on our own; instead, the system, through its formulation of demand and its allocation of salaries, lets us know what business we should start and what work would be socially useful, and what is socially useful is what, according to von Mises and Hayek, we should choose.

Capitalism, in other words, tells us how to belong to our social order, how to fit in with the demands of society. There is no possibility here of the freedom to do something that does not fulfill the social demand. We can only act according to this demand, and capitalism excels by making this demand completely clear. Though we can believe that we freely chose our job—and Hayek argues that we always do—capitalism takes the weight of this burden off our shoulders by showing where we should direct our energies. The system of salaries and the announcement of positions available offer a schema for understanding the Other's desire. This schema is the fantasy structure through which capitalism permits us to escape the nonexistence of the Other and thus the horror of recognizing that there is no one and nothing to tell us how to desire.

But capitalism's installation of this new Other or new form of God comes on the heels of the destruction of the earlier form. In short, capitalism killed God.[16] It is only after the onset of capitalist modernity that it became possible for Spinoza to imagine a horizontal rather than a vertical conception of substance in which God would be wholly immanent to creation. Spinoza's God no longer "acts with an end in view" because he no longer has a status outside or above the world.[17] This dethroning of God is the direct result of the introduction of capitalist relations of production. Capitalism dismantles hierarchies, levels social relations, and eliminates privileges. Even God cannot survive this process.

Of course, people in modernity still believe in God—and not just in Spinoza's immanent version. But God no longer functions as the master signifier for the social order in the capitalist universe. God no longer tells subjects what they should desire. But it is difficult to endure this absence of God qua social authority, which is why we find refuge in other forms of social activity once the God hypothesis is no longer tenable as the ground for the social order. Belief in God is so appealing because God provides respite from the confrontation with the nonexistence of the Other. If God provides this type of guidance, it requires a leap of faith to gain access to it. God's directives on desire are not publicly disseminated within the capitalist social order. Belief remains widespread, but the capitalist universe is incompatible with the traditional figure of God.

The true horror of God's spiritualization or the Other's nonexistence is not that the subject can't interpret what God or the Other wants. It is that the Other itself ceases to know and begins to bombard the subject with questions about desire. One turns to suicide bombing or begins watching reality television shows—they are similar responses to the same problem—in order to discover what the Other wants, but one continues to confront the Other's nonexistence even in the midst of these activities. The contemporary Other doesn't offer the commandments of the traditional God.

Though capitalist modernity eliminates the transcendent God of tradition religion, it introduces an immanent God. This is not Spinoza's God, which is correlative to the created world, but rather a God who tells us what to desire. This figure is the market itself. Instead of leaving us on our own with just our freedom and no idea of what we should desire, the market frees us of the burden of freedom, but we are able to keep the word. In the capitalist universe "freedom" saves us from freedom.

For all capitalism's success in directing the desire of subjects when it comes to production and work, the most conspicuous destruction of freedom in the capitalist system occurs in the act of consumption. The capitalist universe today centers around consumption rather than production or work, and it is here that the new form of God becomes fully evident. Advertising exists not simply—or even primarily—to sell products but to save subjects from their freedom. Advertisements provide an image of the Other that enables us to believe that we are not simply on our own when it comes to how we should consume.

The advertisement doesn't tell us directly what to desire—no successful advertisement would say, "Drink a beer right now," for instance—but instead works to create a belief in the existence of a particular Other. The beer commercial shows the Other rewarding us for the act of drinking beer. We see the male drinker surrounded by a group of young women attired only in bathing suits, an image that shows the social support one receives for choosing this beer. One fits in the social order and attains the maximum recognition. In this way, one knows how to desire and thereby avoids the trauma of one's freedom.

The advertisement enables the capitalist subject to believe that in every consumer choice it makes it is being seen. That is to say, the Other rewards the consumer for its choices through the recognition that stems from the proper purchase. When I am drinking a certain kind of beer, I don't necessarily imagine myself surrounded by adoring women, but I do imagine the Other seeing my choice and approving it. The advertisement tells me that my choice has the Other's stamp of approval, and the best advertisements enable the subject to disavow this reliance on the Other's approval at the same time that they offer it most thoroughly.

The beer commercial is often the most straightforward in its evocation of the Other. The Other exists in the form of a group of potential love objects, friends watching a football game together, or Clydesdale horses nostalgically reminding the viewer of a former era when choices were clearer. In each case the advertisement offers a point of identification from which the subject can see itself being seen. This point is the Other who exists and who authorizes the subject's choices. The proper viewer of these advertisements gains from them a sense of belonging that has the effect of saving the subject from its freedom.

More successful—and more dangerous—advertisements proffer the image of belonging through freedom or detachment from the Other. In such advertisements the Other forms through the image of its nonexistence and thus becomes even more firmly entrenched. One of the great instances of this phenomenon was the Monster.com commercial from the 1990s. Here a group of young children ironically express their desire to fit in the capitalist system. One says, "I want to be forced into early retirement," while another proclaims, "I want to work my way up to middle management." This series of damning indictments of the hopelessness of the capitalist system serves to support an investment in Monster.com as respite from this hopelessness and as a form of the Other that will create a region within the capitalist economy where one can fit without sacrificing one's freedom. In this way, Monster.com, like Google or Apple, presents itself as a vehicle for the subject's liberation from the conformity that the market demands while sustaining an image of the Other that is the basis for the market's success. The appeal of the Monster.com advertisement is inextricable from its nefariousness. It is an even more potent obfuscation of freedom than the Budweiser Clydesdales. We can believe ourselves to be rejecting the market while nonetheless finding recognition in this new form of God.

The link between the advertisement and God stands out in one of the key scenes from F. Scott Fitzgerald's *The Great Gatsby*. The novel recounts the story of Jay Gatsby's pursuit of his lost love Daisy Buchanan, whom he is trying to lure away from her husband Tom. After a confrontation between Tom, Daisy, and Gatsby, they flee New York City back to their homes on Long Island. Daisy drives with Gatsby, and Tom goes in another car. While traversing the Valley of Ashes that separates the city from its wealthy suburbs, Daisy hits and kills Myrtle Wilson, who is having an affair with her husband Tom. Though Daisy doesn't intend to hit Myrtle, she drives carelessly and then doesn't even stop after the accident. Though Daisy's behavior reveals the insularity of the ruling class, the importance of the scene lies primarily in what happens in the aftermath of Myrtle's death and in the reaction of her husband George.

George responds to Myrtle's death with recourse to an advertisement. Fitzgerald's description of the Valley of Ashes highlights a prominent billboard that hangs over the industrial wasteland. This billboard presents what the narrator, Nick Caraway, describes as "the eyes of Dr. T. J. Eckleberg." The fading billboard advertises an optometrist by showing a massive pair of eyes with glasses that look out over the Valley of Ashes. Throughout the novel, the eyes of Dr. T. J. Eckleberg function as the Other, the modern form of God that guarantees and directs our actions. When Myrtle dies, George identifies the role of the billboard and of all advertisements in capitalist modernity.

When discussing what he plans to do with his neighbor Michaelus, George looks up at the eyes of Dr. T. J. Eckleberg for assurance. He tells Michaelus, "God sees everything," and then his neighbor replies, "That's just an advertisement."[18] With this exchange, Fitzgerald perfectly captures the relationship between advertising and God, as well as the change in the status of God in modernity. Though advertising now plays the role of God—the eyes of Dr. T. J. Eckleberg tell us how to desire and how to evade our freedom—this new form of God is absent rather than present. Thus, we can proclaim, with Michaelus, that the Other does not exist, even though this requires abandoning the security that the all-seeing Other provides.

When we conceive of God in the modern world, we should abandon the idea of a transcendent being and instead take Fitzgerald's image as our point of departure. The eyes of Dr. T. J. Eckleberg soothe George because they permit him to imagine that our actions occur with an ontological support. These eyes authorize his misplaced vengeance when he kills Gatsby for Daisy's crime. In the same way, advertisements provide a salve for all consumers by offering an image of what we should want.

Even if we don't buy the products that the advertisements try to sell us, we take solace in the idea of the Other that they sustain. George's conclusion about the billboard was wrong—God doesn't see everything—but his error is nonetheless completely understandable. Dr. T. J. Eckleberg is the new god. Just like the old God, this one exists in order that we don't have to be free, but unlike the old version, this one exists in an epoch where its existence has been thoroughly questioned.[19]

Understanding capitalism's new version of God enables us to grasp the solution to the oft-debated question concerning the relationship between Adam Smith's two great works, *The Theory of Moral Sentiments* and *The Wealth of Nations*. This debate has aroused such furor that it has even acquired its own name: *Das Adam Smith Problem*. The basic problem is that Smith's two major works don't appear to jibe philosophically. He argues in his moral philosophy for a sentimental attachment to others and in his economic work for an emphasis on private interest in lieu of public concerns. This problem gains renewed interest in light of understanding the free market as the new form of the Other. The solution to Das Adam Smith Problem lies in the free market replacing God and saving capitalist subjects from freedom.

The solution requires that we think about Das Adam Smith Problem in different terms than those often used to approach it. The commonsensical answer to this problem was for a long time a historicist one: Smith's position simply evolved over time from the writing of his moral philosophy in 1759 and his economic treatise in 1776. Today this answer no longer has many adherents, and the task has become one of identifying the sources of continuity rather than emphasizing the differences.

Though the problem of the difference between the moral Smith and the capitalist Smith has largely disappeared, the question of the shared concerns of his two books remains up in the air. As David Wilson and William Dixon note, "an Adam Smith problem of sorts endures: there is still no widely agreed version of what it is that links these two texts, aside from their common author; no widely agreed version of how, if at all, Smith's postulation of self-interest as the organising principle of economic activity fits in with his wider moral-ethical concerns."[20] Das Adam Smith Problem comes about because Smith's two books appear almost completely at odds with each other. The first argues for the existence of human morality on the basis of a sentimental attachment to others, while the second contends that self-interest drives the human being.

In the opening of *The Theory of Moral Sentiments*, Smith argues for a fundamental limitation on human selfishness that seems utterly incompatible with his later economic proclamations. He says, "How selfish soever man may be supposed, there are evidently some principles in his nature, which interest him in the fortune of others, and render their happiness necessary to him, though he derives nothing from it except the pleasure of seeing it. Of this kind is pity or compassion, the emotion which we feel for the misery of others, when we either see it, or are made to conceive it in a very lively manner."[21] Emotion connects us to others even when we fail to see the connection. Compassion might not be conscious, but it nonetheless functions and governs our interactions with others. Smith's entire moral philosophy has its basis in the emotional or sentimental identification that people experience with each other, and this type of identification plays no role in his conception of the activity of the economic world. It is thus no wonder that the attempt to reconcile Smith's two famous texts became enough of a theoretical problem to earn its own name.

It takes only a brief glance at the juxtaposition of Smith's moral philosophy with his treatise on economy to recognize that his concerns in the two texts are disparate. In *The Wealth of Nations*, Smith famously argues that self-interest provides the basis for human interaction. We benefit from others because they act according to their self-interest, and when we appeal to them for commodities that we require, we do so on the basis of fulfilling this self-interest. In Smith's later work, self-interest is the guiding thread and emotional connection seems entirely absent. The emphasis on an unbreakable sense of compassion that dominates the earlier book has no place in this economic outlook. There is a connection between subjects, but this connection derives from the unconscious manifestations of self-love, not from unconscious compassion for the distress or misery of others.

Most solutions to Das Adam Smith Problem focus on the ethical status of Smith's conception of capitalism. Samuel Fleischacker is one exponent of this position. His defense doesn't claim that capitalism necessarily leads to the kind of virtue that Smith espouses in *The Theory of Moral Sentiments* but rather that it lays the groundwork for this virtue. That is to say, capitalism isn't inherently moral; it facilitates morality. It provides the structural basis for the development of morality.

Capitalism does so though its production of prosperity. According to Fleischacker, "Commerce tends to bring freedom in its train, and to improve the lodging, clothing, and sustenance of the worst off. These basic goods are all that one needs to lead a decent life—and therefore enough to make commercial society worth striving for and preserving."[22] Fleischacker flirts with the idea that capitalism provides training in the virtues and ultimately leads to the end of violence, but he abandons this thesis as too strong and reconciles himself to a weaker vision of the connection between the two texts. He sees that a profound gap does exist with only certain points of overlap, despite his own efforts at reconciliation.

It is the case that the two texts are disparate works and that Smith's concerns in his treatise on economy run far afield from his concerns in the discussion of morality. On the whole, it seems that we cannot reconcile them except through the statement that the same author wrote each. But there is nonetheless a nodal point that unites the two works—Smith's vision of God. This is the fundamental overlap between *The Theory of Moral Sentiments* and *The Wealth of Nations,* and it is all the more revelatory given God's relative absence from Smith's thought.

Nowhere in either work does Smith make explicit mention of a traditional deity. Nonetheless, the modern notion of God—the capitalist reformulation of God—makes an appearance in both books as the Other who would direct our desire and lead it out of the abyss. Though Smith writes both works (in 1759 and 1776) before Kant's *Critique of Practical Reason* (in 1788), they represent a retreat from modern Kantian freedom before the fact. It is as if Smith read Kant and then constructed a moral and an economic theory that would enable us to escape the traumatic ramifications of Kantian freedom.[23] In fact, the defining trait of Smith's thought, like that of so many defenders of capitalism, is the flight from freedom. Smith conceives of subjects as free, but this freedom has a support in an Other, as both *The Theory of Moral Sentiments* and *The Wealth of Nations* make evident.

The great convergence of Smith's two books occurs when he mentions—it occurs only once in each text—the invisible hand. This is Smith's metaphor for the modern God, the social authority who gives a direction for the subject's desire. In *The Theory of Moral Sentiments*, Smith presents the invisible hand in a less ideological form than he does in the later work. In a shocking section of the book, Smith admits that wealth, contrary to what we and the wealthy themselves believe, doesn't bring happiness. For a champion of capitalism, this is a potentially damning admission, and it would be difficult to imagine it in the mouths of today's capitalist believers. We pursue wealth, as Smith sees it, from a completely misguided premise, but this pursuit brings with it great benefit for society. The pursuit of wealth functions like Hegel's cunning of reason: the universal benefits from the sacrifices made by particulars.[24] The pursuit of wealth enables the social order to develop and advances the interest of society, even though it doesn't bring the promised happiness to the one who pursues it.

When Smith turns to a discussion of the distribution of resources that derive from the pursuit of wealth, he has recourse to the metaphor of the invisible hand. Commenting on the wealthy, he notes, "They are led by an invisible hand to make nearly the same distribution of the necessaries of life, which would have been made, had the earth been divided into equal portions among all its inhabitants, and thus without intending it, without knowing it, advance the interest of the society, and afford means to the multiplication of the species."[25] The invisible hand functions like God, directing the rich to invest and spend their money in the proper avenues. Without the invisible hand, we would be morally adrift, and nothing would guarantee that our actions correlated with each other for the good. The concept of the invisible hand, in other words, enables Smith to sustain an idea of a social safety net that holds subjects together and coordinates their desires. It also frees them from their own freedom in the face of the Other's absence.

The far more famous mention of the metaphor of the invisible hand occurs in *The Wealth of Nations,* where Smith argues for the socially beneficial effect of the pursuit of self-interest. Here the invisible hand coordinates otherwise competing sites of self-interest into a coherent whole. Smith says, "by directing that industry in such a manner as its produce may be of the greatest value, he intends only his own gain; and he is in this, as in many other cases, led by an invisible hand to promote an end which was no part of his intention. Nor is it always the worse for the society that it was no part of it. By pursuing his own interest, he frequently promotes that of the society more effectually than when he really intends to promote it."[26] Though later champions of capitalism pick up on Smith's insistence on the pursuit of one's own gain, what stands out even more in this passage is the direction that the invisible hand provides to all self-interested activity. There is no risk of the system destroying itself, as Smith sees it, because an invisible hand watches over it, just as it watches over the moral "distribution of the necessities of life." This is the modern version of God: a force that provides assurances that all our activities will work out for the good despite our intentions. This is the point at which *The Theory of Moral Sentiments* and *The Wealth of Nations* perfectly align.[27]

The solution to Das Adam Smith Problem is also the solution to capitalism's hold on us as subjects. Capitalist modernity does away with God as a present force in social relations, but it installs him as a determining absence. The Other as an absent field that directs the desire of subjects arises with capitalism just as modernity destroys the figure of God as the guide for our desire. That is to say, God ceases to be a visible hand and becomes an invisible hand. The invisible hand traverses Smith's disparate books as the unifying force between them. It also represents Smith's most important contribution to the understanding of capitalism's success.

The conception of God as an invisible hand is not just an idiosyncrasy of Smith's two books. The fact that the term appears a single time in each work permits it to stand out, but the concept undergirds the entirety of both works and the capitalist economy as such. The invisible hand is not just capitalist ideology, a conception generated to smooth out the antagonisms of the capitalist system. It is rather an inextricable part of that system, its necessary product.

The lovers of capitalism—and who doesn't belong to this group, even if unconsciously?—love it precisely for its invisible hand. Through this figure, it resurrects in a much more palatable form the God that it killed. The invisible hand doesn't demand that we abandon enjoyable activities like bearing false witness and coveting our neighbor's wife. Far from prohibiting them, it integrates these activities into the alignment of competing desires within the capitalist universe. This universe is one in which we all have a place and from which none need be cast out as long as we abandon our freedom and accept the verdict of the new god. The invisible hand not only solves Das Adam Smith Problem but also the problem of a horrible freedom.

THE OTHER DOES EXIST

The fundamental project of psychoanalysis is its combat against the belief in the invisible hand. In psychoanalytic terms, the precise name for a believer in the invisible hand is *neurotic*. The neurotic seeks refuge from her or his own freedom in the idea of an Other who provides a hidden guidance for what the neurotic should desire. As long as God exists as a physical presence within the world directing desire, neurosis cannot develop.[28] The guide for the subject's desire is clearly stated in the dictates of God. But when modernity eliminates God or consigns God to a spiritual realm, the subject turns toward a new Other that exists only in its absence. This Other—Smith's invisible hand of the market—tells the subject how to desire, and the subject who accepts this Other becomes neurotic. The struggle against neurosis is thus the struggle against the underlying belief that sustains the capitalist economy. If we are all neurotic to some extent or another, this means that we all have some degree of investment in the capitalist system.

One of the chief complaints of psychoanalytic Marxists in the twentieth century concerned capitalism's tendency to render its subjects neurotic. For most of these thinkers, the problem lies in the repression that capitalism demands. Even a non-Marxist like Karen Horney identifies the capitalist economic system as the source of what she calls "the neurotic personality of our time." In Horney's book of this title, she states, "From its economic center competition radiates into all other activities and permeates love, social relations and play. Therefore competition is a problem for everyone in our culture, and it is not at all surprising to find it an unfailing center of neurotic conflicts."[29] Capitalist competition does not lead to free subjects but to neurotic ones. It requires repression in order to fit subjects into the limited positions that the market economy requires.

The association of capitalism with neurosis represents an accurate diagnosis with a mistaken cause. Michel Foucault is undoubtedly correct to call into question the attack on capitalism as a purely repressive system, but Foucault's critique misses another possible link between capitalism and neurosis. Capitalism doesn't feed the neurotic subject through its repressiveness but through its capacity for fostering the illusion that the Other exists. The basis of neurosis is not just the repression of sexual desire and its replacement with a symptom but the belief in the substantial existence of the Other, the belief that a self-identical social authority can issue clear demands that solve the problems of subjectivity and freedom. Neurosis is dependence on an external authority that enables the subject to avoid taking responsibility for its own acts. This redefinition of neurosis is crucial both for understanding the neurotic structure of capitalism and for avoiding Foucault's critique of this diagnosis.

The problem with neurosis is that the social authority the neurotic obeys doesn't exist. Though social authorities do make constant demands on subjects, they do not know their own desire and thus cannot direct the desire of subjects who look to them. That is to say, the authority cannot say what it really wants.[30] Like the subject, social authority has an unconscious that prevents its unambiguous articulation of demands. Like the subject, social authority suffers from the divide between what it says and the point from which it articulates this demand. The demand is always articulated with signifiers, and signifiers always create a divided subject out of the pretension of authority.

The divide in social authority becomes evident if we examine how authority figures respond to those who comply with their demands to the letter. For instance, the student who always comes to class prepared, always turns in assignments early, and always has her hand up to provide the correct answer to the question annoys the teacher rather than winning the teacher's love. The student who knows when to disobey and when to challenge the teacher's authority stands a much better chance of becoming the beloved student. The perfectly obedient student equates the teacher's demand with the teacher's desire, while the student who sometimes challenges authority reads the teacher's desire as distinct from the demand. The student who challenges authority recognizes that social authority does not exist, even if the flesh-and-blood teacher does. The obedient student, in contrast, neurotically clings to the idea of a substantial authority embodied in the teacher, an authority that knows and can say what it wants.

In his *Seminar XII*, entitled *Problèmes cruciaux pour la psychanalyse*, Jacques Lacan identifies neurosis with desire of the Other's demand, which is another way of saying that the neurotic subject believes in the substantial existence of the Other. Lacan says, "In the neurosis . . . it is in relation to the demand of the Other that the subject's desire is constituted."[31] The neurotic thinks that strict obedience of the Other's demand—not exceeding the speed limit by even a little bit, for instance—works to capture the Other's desire. But this alignment of the Other's demand with the Other's desire never occurs. The driver who never speeds earns not the respect of social authority but its suspicion, just like the student who fails to see that the teacher doesn't desire the perfect obedience she or he demands. The Other doesn't really want what it demands because it has an unconscious just like the subject itself.

The mistake of the neurotic is the belief that the Other exists, that the Other has no unconscious, which leads the neurotic to cling to the Other's demand rather than confront the abyss of its own subjectivity. This attempt to cling to the Other's demand always leads the subject astray—and represents the weak link in the capitalist chain—because the Other never wants the subject to do what it demands. The result is a neurotic failure on the part of the subject to find its satisfaction satisfying. Capitalism necessarily produces neurosis. It is not, as the contemporary world constantly reminds us, a repressive system, but it is, all the same, a neurotic one insofar as it allows us to find refuge in the market qua social authority.

Capitalism requires a belief in the existence of the Other. This is what Adam Smith makes clear in his discussion of the invisible hand, and it is the reason for the lasting popularity of this image among capitalism's defenders. The idea of an invisible hand or an Other guiding our desire enables us to believe in our freedom—there is no clearly delineated God or authority telling us what to do—and to find respite from this freedom at the same time. It is thus the perfect system for the destruction of the freedom that modernity offers to its subjects.

The fundamental catastrophe of modernity is the disappearance of God as a substantial Other. Subjects like Donald Trump attempt to compensate for this catastrophe by buying their way into popularity, which is simply a situation where the Other offers clear and distinct demands. But popularity, like capitalism, always leads to disappointment. One is never popular enough, just as one never has quite enough capital. The invisible hand ultimately betrays us. As subjects of modernity, we must exist without a visible or an invisible hand. We must dissociate modernity from capitalism—a dissociation that is the only path to authentic freedom.

[6]

A More Tolerable Infinity

THE SPURIOUSNESS OF THE BAD INFINITY

Many Marxists, including Marx himself, see Hegel as the apogee of bourgeois thought. Georg Lukács, however, assigns this status to Kant and seeks to redeem Hegel on behalf of socialism. Lukács credits him with being the first to address himself seriously to the ramifications of the capitalist economy. In his description of Hegel's materialist achievement, he states, "it is undoubtedly no accident that the man who completed the edifice of idealist dialectics was the *only* philosopher of the age to have made a *serious* attempt to get to grips with the economic structure of capitalist society."[1] Though Lukács acknowledges that Hegel requires the corrective that Marx subsequently supplies, he sees in Hegel a great diagnostician of the logic of capitalism.[2] But what Lukács fails to notice is that Hegel doesn't just provide a trenchant analysis of capitalist society. He already points beyond this society.

What makes Hegel the most important anticapitalist philosopher, inclusive of Marx, is his conception of infinity. Up to Kant and Fichte, philosophers could only formulate what Hegel calls the bad infinite (*die schlechte Unendlichkeit*).[3] That is, they portray the infinite externally, as the inability to reach an endpoint. To this day, this is how we commonly think of infinity. The break that Hegel introduces—a break more philosophically significant than any other he authors—is that of the true infinite. The idea of true infinite enables Hegel to simultaneously avoid two pitfalls—the finitude of the closed world of traditional society and the infinite progress implicit in modernity.

The bad infinite, for Hegel, has no limit. Like the series of whole numbers, it simply keeps going and going without reaching an endpoint. The finite, in contrast, has an external limit that it can never surpass. Animal life, which always ends in death, is finite. The true infinite adopts the limit from the finite, but this limit does not come externally. Rather than escaping limitation, the true infinite limits itself, like the subject that confines itself to a single project out of a multitude of possibilities.[4]

In this sense, the true infinite is opposed to both the bad infinite that has no limit and the finite that has an external limit. For the true infinite, the limit emerges out of the infinite's articulation of its infinitude. In the *Science of Logic*, Hegel offers a contrast between the bad and good versions of the infinite. He says, "The image of progression in infinity is the straight *line*; the infinite is only at the two limits of this line, and always only where the latter (which is existence) is not but *transcends itself*, and in its non-existence, that is, in the indeterminate. As true infinite, bent back upon itself, its image becomes the *circle*, the line that has reached itself, closed and wholly present, without *beginning* and *end*."[5] This idea of self-limitation or exclusion of its own limit allows Hegel to envision an alternative to capitalist modernity without regressing to the finite logic of traditional society. Though it occurs on the terrain of logic, it represents his great political breakthrough. His new version of infinity offers an alternative to capitalism that remains nonetheless within the spirit of modernity.

To understand how Hegel's true infinite, which shares the structure of the subject as psychoanalysis conceives it, represents an alternative to the capitalist system, we must explore capitalism's complex relationship to infinity. The infinite has a clear role in capitalist society. Capitalist economy predicates itself on the possibility of infinite growth, and any idea of an ultimate barrier—even the eventual heat death of the universe—disturbs the development the functioning of the capitalist economy, which depends on constant and unending expansion.[6] There is an infinite capacity for economic expansion, and if capitalism encounters limitations on the earth, this will necessitate the financing of interstellar space travel.

Though the first efforts at space exploration were public ventures, funding for these missions was always tenuous. The seventh human trip to the Moon by Apollo 18 fell victim to financial exigencies and ended the era of public voyages to the Moon. It is almost undoubtedly the case that private space voyages will soon come to replace public ones, with the result that space will become a genuine site for the expansion of capitalism. The logic of capitalism and its inherent relation to the bad infinite lend it to the conquest of space.

But capitalism's identification with infinite expansion runs into an irreducible stumbling block with the entropy law. The development of the Second Law of Thermodynamics by Rudolf Clausius in the early 1850s created a theoretical dilemma for the defenders of capitalism. The entropy law predicts the eventual heat death of the universe, and even if capitalism is able to capitalize on its own waste (and thereby feed itself), it can never overcome the ultimate endpoint that the entropy law establishes. Waste is a genuine barrier to capitalist expansion, but we can imagine ways around this barrier—such as perfect recycling projects— that enable us to remain within the infinitely expanding capitalist system. The entropy law is a different story. It portends not just human extinction (which one might imagine capitalist production surviving) but the end of all movement in a total diffusion of energy.

The opposition between capitalist production and the entropy law becomes apparent in Nicholas Georgescu-Roegen's *The Entropy Law and the Economic Process*. Georgescu-Roegen attempts to integrate the conclusions of entropy into economic theory, but he also recognizes that the act of capitalist production itself occurs in opposition to entropy and thus would in the last instance founder on it. He claims, "The dissipation of energy, as [the entropy law] proclaims, goes on automatically everywhere. This is precisely why the entropy reversal as seen in every line of production bears the indelible mark of purposive activity."[7] Capitalist production resists the tendency of energy to dissipate by using energy in a creative act. Capitalism struggles against the fundamental law of the natural world, despite an ideology that proclaims its natural status as an economic system.

Foregrounding the entropy law is antithetical to the basic functioning of capitalism. The system reproduces itself through an investment in a future that it cannot squarely face. The entropy law signals the limits of newness, and capitalism subsists on nothing but newness. Capitalist society would collapse in a static state. It constantly aims beyond itself and seeks new laborers, new commodities, and new markets. The development of corporations and even trade on the stock market depends on the implicit possibility of infinite expansion. In this sense, capitalism is both nonmessianic and nonapocalyptic. It can't envision an interruption of chronological time in the manner of messianism or the end of time in the manner of apocalypticism. This is why thinkers like Walter Benjamin see in messianism a distinctly anticapitalist politics. But the political valence of apocalypticism is not so clear, despite the nonapocalyptic status of capitalism itself.

Capitalism's need for the infinite explains the proliferation of catastrophic narratives within the capitalist universe. On the one hand, the narrative of catastrophe presents the worst future imaginable to show that capitalism can survive even this extreme catastrophe, that disaster will not impede its infinite future movement. Roland Emmerich's *2012* (2009) envisions not just the survival but the flourishing of capitalist society after the near total destruction of the world. Destruction here almost seems to have a purgative effect for the system. On the other hand, the catastrophic narrative can represent an attempt to counter the capitalist infinity, to show that this infinity will run into a limit.

This is evident in the disaster films *Earthquake* (Mark Robson, 1974) and *The Towering Inferno* (John Guillermin, 1974), both of which show the ability of a disaster to put an end to some aspect of capitalist society. *Earthquake* concludes with an admission of defeat—the proclamation "This used to be a helluva town." Though the larger capitalist society goes on, its limitations become evident. The same dynamic occurs in *The Towering Inferno*, which concludes with a firefighter's plea to an architect to limit the size of buildings he designs in order to make them safer. Both events— the earthquake and the fire—reveal constraints on the dynamic power of capitalist economy. The disaster represents the ultimate limit of capitalism, which the system can never overcome. At best, it can delay the encounter with this limit, but the limit will not disappear, as the disaster reveals. There is no direct political valence of catastrophe: the politics depends on the attitude that fiction takes up to the possible end of capitalist expansion.

But no matter what attitude we adopt toward the end, capitalism as a system cannot continue to function in the face of an authentic and unsurpassable barrier. The barrier must remain receding in the distance rather than actually existing. Because it borrows its energy for today from the future, it requires an image of constant expansion in that future. To imagine an intractable barrier is to challenge the capitalist system, even if it ultimately integrates that challenge.

The limit that capitalism cannot integrate is that of the true infinite. This limit is internal, a self-limitation of the socioeconomic system itself. A self-limiting system, precisely what Hegel theorizes with his concept of the true infinite, is the only tenable alternative to capitalism. It doesn't pose an arbitrary limit that the capitalist system can quickly subsume but clings to the limit as constitutive of the system itself. To subsume the limit thus becomes unthinkable.

JOUIR SANS ENTRAVES

Capitalism's allergy to the limit indicates its inextricable commitment to the bad infinite, which simply goes on and on without stopping. This allergy is apparent in both macroeconomic and microeconomic forms. The financial system as a whole develops through constant expansion. The system's functioning depends on an ever larger circle of growth. If this growth stalls or stops, the incentives for the economy's self-perpetuation and survival disappear at the same time. Reproduction within capitalism depends on increasing production. The incentives for production and consumption are tied inextricably to growth, and the abandonment of growth would destroy the system.

The capitalist system demands the idea of constant expansion as much as it relies on the fact of it. In *The Road to Serfdom*, F. A. Hayek gives voice to this fundamental tenet of capitalism with his expression of dismay for any intractable limits. He says, "Nothing makes conditions more unbearable than the knowledge that no effort of ours can change them; and even if we should never have the strength of mind to make the necessary sacrifice, the knowledge that we could escape if only we strove hard enough make many otherwise intolerable positions bearable."[8] Hayek accepts that we can imagine a limit, but he finds the idea nonetheless intolerable. The repulsion stems directly from the structure of capitalism itself, which accepts limits only in order to surpass them.

The capitalist bent on the accumulation of capital cannot pursue this endeavor while accepting the idea of an intractable limit. The accumulation of capital works insofar as one can envision its infinite expansion. The moment the capitalist foresees a future obstacle that would put an end to accumulation, she or he will turn to another form of accumulation (such as making a different product or investing in a new company). It is not simply the fact of a limit that derails the individual capitalist's accumulation but the mere idea of this limit. One invests in future growth, not in present productivity, which is why firms downsize or outsource when they are still making huge profits. The firm's survival depends on what it will do, not on what it is doing. This same dynamic exists on a systemic level as well.

Any investment in capitalism as a system demands an investment in the idea of constant expansion. Capitalism maintains its equilibrium not by sustaining a stable level of production but through increasing production, without any notion of an end to this increase. When the capitalist system confronts an obstacle (in the form, say, of a crisis), the answer is always increasing production. The future will necessarily be more productive than the present, just as the present is more productive than the past. Reversals can only be temporary.

One finds an expression of the insistence on constant expansion in almost every champion of capitalism. For instance, in his history of finance, Niall Ferguson contends, "There have been great reverses, contractions and dyings, to be sure. But not even the worst has set us permanently back. Though the line of financial history has a saw-tooth quality, its trajectory is unquestionably upwards."[9] Ferguson's choice of the term *upwards* conjures an image of space exploration in order to continue the expansion after the Earth itself became exhausted. Thinking about capitalism requires the abandonment of the possibility of an endpoint or of a static point where relations of production have completely stabilized.

Capitalism has developed through an unprecedented growth of population, income, and production. It both feeds this growth and feeds off it. In *The World Economy: A Millennial Perspective*, Angus Maddison provides a quantitative chronicle of this growth. He claims that there was almost no growth in the first millennium of the modern era and very little in the second before the development of capitalism. But then a radical change takes place. After 1820—after capitalism installs itself as the world's economic system—growth changes exponentially. According to Maddison, "Since 1820, world development has been much more dynamic. Per capita income rose more than eightfold, population more than fivefold."[10] This incredible rate of growth relative to prior epochs of human history is not just a contingent fact but rather the sine qua non of capitalism.

The need for population growth to accommodate the expansion of capital leads even some defenders of capitalism to worry about the capacity of the system to include the excess population that it fosters.[11] Capitalism demands an increasing population as both a labor force and a consumption force, but it also requires that there be too many laborers and too many consumers. Like capital itself, population expands to the point of instability rather than stability. In every aspect of capitalist society, expansion plays a central role because expansiveness inheres in the idea of capitalist production.[12] For most of its champions, this is its great virtue; for many of its detractors, this is its great defect. But no one disagrees that one cannot even think the capitalist system without the idea that infinite expansion is possible. To render capitalism finite would be to destroy it.[13] On the level of microeconomics, we can see the same requirement.

The idea of unending progress governs corporate behavior, investor decisions, and consumer choices. It functions in all aspects of economic planning within the capitalist system, from family budgets to the policy decisions of international economic organizations. At no point can anyone accept the possibility of stagnation or shrinkage. The worker must earn more next year than this year; the company must predict more growth next year; and the nation's gross domestic product must increase next year. These demands stem from the structure of the capitalist system, not from greedy individuals or corporations. Greed for more is integral to the process of growth and thus has a central place in this system.[14]

Though greed as a structural necessity brings with it many psychic difficulties, the prominence of the bad infinity relieves capitalist subjects of the burden of the true infinite. This psychic relief is an essential part of capitalism's appeal. The bad infinite focuses the subject on the future and the possibility of a form of satisfaction that will never be realized. As capitalism was in its nascent moments, Blaise Pascal considered why turning our attention to the future would provide respite. He notes, "the present is usually painful. We hide it from our sight because it distresses us; and, if it is agreeable, we regret seeing it slip away. We try to support it with the future and think of arranging things we cannot control, for a time we have no certainty of reaching."[15] Pascal reveals here why we look to future accumulation rather than contenting ourselves with what we have. He diagnoses the logic of capitalism. But Pascal's description of the present nonetheless highlights the form of satisfaction associated with the true infinite. It includes an awareness of loss, whereas the bad infinite associated with the future posits a definite separation between the dissatisfaction of loss and the experience of satisfaction.

Theoretical speculation about the goal of capitalist subjects inevitably invokes the bad infinite, even as the conception of this goal undergoes significant changes. For classical economists, subjects pursued wealth, whereas for neoclassical economists they pursued the satisfaction of their needs. In both cases the point is that the object is infinite. I always require more wealth, and I always have more needs to satisfy (or I can satisfy them more fully). Even though neoclassical economists base their calculations on needs, they assume that these needs are not finite. Though a particular desire is necessarily finite—I can only eat so many packages of M&Ms—desires themselves are not.

In this sense, the multitude of different desires solves the problem of the finitude of particular wants. Our particular wants can reach a saturation point, but another want will always emerge in its stead. In his *Principles of Economics*, Alfred Marshall makes clear this basic principle of capitalist economics. He says, "There is an endless variety of wants, but there is still a limit to each separate want."[16] Marshall is able to grant some finitude within the economic structure, but the bad infinite of perpetual increase trumps it. Particular wants are finite; wants as such are infinite. Later, Marshall describes the infinite of endless progress in more detail, noting, "On every side further openings are sure to offer themselves, all of which will tend to change the character of our social and industrial life, and to enable us to turn to account vast stores of capital in providing new gratifications and new ways of economizing effort by expending it in anticipation of distant wants."[17] The capitalist subject will never attain full satisfaction because it cannot satisfy or even anticipate its "distant wants." The infinite of desire justifies the infinite of production and consumption.

The infinite can even manifest itself within particular desires. If we examine, for instance, the very particular desire for potato chips, the infinite reappears in response to this limited desire. Capitalist production continues to add new products—and aims to do so infinitely—in order to expand this desire. Thus, the consumer can choose from regular chips, wavy chips, sour cream and onion chips, wavy sour cream and onion chips, and so on. Just when one imagines it's safe to return to the supermarket without finding a new form of potato chip, Lays invents the wavy, fat-free chip flavored with sea salt. Capitalism has the capacity to transform an apparently limited desire into an infinite one.

The infinite does not only reside in different desires but also in the subject's overall project. The project is infinite because its ideal is clouded in obscurity. This obfuscation starts at the beginning of the attempt to understand capitalism and continues without any abatement today. In *The Wealth of Nations*, Adam Smith posits the existence of a "natural effort of every individual to better his own condition."[18] He assumes no limit to this process of betterment, and the ambiguity of the terms *better* and *condition* makes it impossible to say when the project might have reached its end. This ambiguity becomes exacerbated as the theorizing about capitalism and the satisfaction it produces expands on and breaks from Smith's initial account. Even when later theorists of capitalism reject Smith's understanding of why people do what they do, they accept his assumption of an infinite movement forward.[19]

THE DIFFICULTIES OF HAPPINESS

For both the rational choice theorist and the behavioral economist, Smith fails to adequately grasp the driving forces of human activity with his idea of betterment. The rational choice theorist believes that we specifically want more rather than less of what we value as goods. This investment in more extends further than Smith's betterment, into every domain of human desire. But it shares with Smith an infinite conception of the subject's desire. The subject never reaches a saturation point, where more finally becomes enough. Rational choice theory is tied to the bad infinite, perhaps even more so than Smith.

Behavioral economics develops in response to the image of humans as beings who rationally pursue their aims. In launching this critique, however, behavioral economics remains on the same terrain as both rational choice theory and Adam Smith. It accepts that our desire is infinite even though it points out the ways that we irrationally sabotage the pursuit of our ends.[20] Our irrationality in decision making actually provides more possibility for improvement in the project of realizing our desires, but this project itself has no limit as they conceive it. Even if we sabotage our goals through bouts of irrationality, this sabotage is only a disruption on the path to an infinite end, not the source of our satisfaction itself, which is what it would be if we thought in terms of the true infinite.[21] Hegel's true infinite, because it views us as fundamentally self-limiting beings, recognizes that satisfaction necessitates self-sabotage, which is to say, an internal limit.

Happiness economics takes as its starting point the behavioral position, and its focus on happiness represents the ultimate contemporary development of the bad infinite. Happiness economics isn't wrong necessarily but simply provides the most recent expression of the central role that the bad infinite—the ideal of infinite progress—plays within capitalism. In this sense, it is just a new version of the same story. Nonetheless, proponents of happiness economics insist they are overturning the assumptions that have guided the history of economic research. We can see this belief manifest in Bruno Frey's *Happiness: A Revolution in Economics.* The title itself bespeaks Frey's belief about the radicality of happiness economics. According to Frey, "For a long time, economics has taken income as a suitable though incomplete proxy for human welfare. Happiness research shows that reported subjective well-being is a far better measure of individual welfare."[22] Though it may be the case that reports of happiness outstrip wealth as an indicator of well-being, it is nonetheless also true that the level of happiness always has room for improvement.[23]

Just like income level, happiness level partakes of the bad infinite or the infinite that never encounters a limit. No matter how much happiness I have, I'm always looking for more, for additional and future ways of augmenting my happiness. Though the theorists of happiness take note of the failure of additional wealth to improve happiness after a certain point, they fail to see the precariousness and ambiguity of happiness itself as a standard. Whether capitalism relies on a desire for wealth or a desire for happiness, in either case it has a necessary attachment to an infinite and incessant progression.

The inexorable striving toward more finds a memorable articulation in the television series *Mad Men*, which focuses on a New York advertising agency in the 1960s and shows repeatedly how advertising both feeds on and furthers the belief in the bad infinity. Don Draper (Jon Hamm), the star of the agency Sterling Cooper (and then Sterling Cooper Draper Pryce), succeeds in advertising because he sees how to construct an image of future happiness, even if he locates that future in a nostalgic ideal of the past, as he does when he invents the term *carousel* for the Kodak slide projector. All of Don's advertising campaigns create an image of happiness that the commodity being sold promises to bring to the consumer, and they include the idea of the infinite expansion of this happiness. This is his particular genius—his great understanding of how to appeal to the bad infinite and the idea of an unceasing increase in happiness.

The show constructs a parallel between Don's advertising campaigns that illustrate happiness just in the future (and yet infinitely far away) and his personal life. Despite his professional success, Don constantly moves from illicit affair to illicit affair without finding any satisfaction in this series of liaisons. Even his marriage to another woman after his divorce fails to end his quest for more happiness. As *Mad Men* chronicles it, capitalism creates an ideal of success that makes it impossible to see the satisfaction that inheres in our failures.[24]

This depiction reaches its most straightforward statement toward the end of the show's fifth season, when Don decides that he no longer wants to work at a middling advertiser with mid-level clients. Instead, he wants to persuade a major corporation to advertise with the agency. He has another partner arrange a pitch meeting with Dow Chemical, a corporation that has already assured Don that it will not advertise with his mediocre agency. The step requires Don to formulate a new type of pitch that will wow the most cynical capitalists.

When Don comes to the meeting, the viewer has no hint of what his pitch will be, but we typically witness Don generate an idea that speaks directly to the incipient desire of the consumer. Don surprises the spectator as often as he does the client, and these displays of ingenuity form a key part of the show's appeal. But in this scene Don surprises both his interlocutors and us in a completely unprecedented way, not with a startling marketing strategy but with a proclamation about the nature of the psyche. In response to their claim that they already have 50 percent of the market, he tells the executives at Dow, "You don't want most of it. You want all of it. And I won't stop till you get all of it." After making this particular appeal to the capitalist desire for more, Don turns to a philosophical claim that expresses perfectly the underlying capitalist imperative. He asks, "What is happiness? It's a moment before you need more happiness." Instead of pitching a particular commodity, Don lays bare the infinite logic of capitalism. As much as self-help manuals in the capitalist system preach the gospel of happiness, Don recognizes that happiness cannot be a lasting state. Within capitalism one must ever pursue more happiness, or else unhappiness will break out.

The identification of capitalism with the bad infinite produces a visceral form of resistance that asserts the claims of finitude. This type of argument is most prominent among environmentalists who see the natural world as a finite barrier to capitalist expansion. As a result, the strategy of many ecological movements is to challenge capitalism with the finitude of the natural world. This begins in earnest in 1962 with Rachel Carson's *Silent Spring*, a book that preaches the acceptance of limits on human activity. Carson contends that we must work not to transcend our natural world through capitalist innovation but to grasp that "nature is not so easily molded."[25] The natural world, according to Carson and many other ecological activists following in her wake, will resist our attempts to domesticate it, whether through the poisoning of necessary resources or the warming of the planet. The problem with this tack is that, because it presents an external limit, it provokes a capitalist response rather than obviating it. Capitalism views any external limit presented by the natural world as a barrier to be overcome, not as an absolute boundary.

One popular alternative in the ecological movement, Ted Nordhaus and Michael Shellenberger's *Break Through*, tries to counter the narrative of the acceptance of human finitude proffered by earlier environmentalists like Carson and James Lovelock (in *The Revenge of Gaia*). Against this narrative, which they label "tragic," they call for an optimistic ecology.[26] At the end of their treatise, they ask those concerned about the current ecological crisis to have the courage to dream about large-scale transformative projects that would enable humanity to shatter the limits that have hitherto functioned as absolute boundaries for both thought and action.

Nordhaus and Shellenberger's political program successfully escapes the lure of finitude that ensnares earlier environmentalists like Carson. They will not just erect another limit that capital will attempt to transcend. But their success is ultimately also what undermines this program. Rather than react against the logic of capitalism like the environmentalists they attack, they freely adopt this logic through their insistence on the wealth of possibilities for the future. In this sense, they produce an ecology even more in tune with the demands of capitalism.

An ecological alternative to capitalism must elude the Scylla of finitude and the Charybdis of the bad infinite, the Scylla of Rachel Carson and the Charybdis of Ted Nordhaus and Michael Shellenberger. Doing so requires reconceiving nature not as an external limit to capitalism nor as a site of infinite possibility but as the internal limit of human society. The social order requires the natural world in order to function, but the unpredictability of this world constantly throws off social progress. Whether it's an earthquake in Lisbon, the eruption of Mt. Krakatoa, or widespread death of honeybees, nature has the capacity at any time to throw social productivity out of joint. But this limit—this unpredictability and violence of the natural world—can become an internal limit of the social order, the basis for a true infinite.[27] By starting with this unpredictability as the limit, social production would orient itself around addressing this limit without any possibility of ever transcending it.

FAKING THE LIMIT

Other attempts to erect barriers to the expansion of capitalism inevitably run into the same problem that besets environmentalism. The barriers do not deter but rather inspire the process of commodification. Michal Sandel's *What Money Can't Buy: The Moral Limits of Markets* and Debra Satz's *Why Some Things Should Not Be for Sale* both lament this increasing commodification and propose that we set limits on it. Sandel claims that we are now witnessing "the growing reach of money and markets into spheres of life once governed by nonmarket norms."[28] Sandel is particularly upset about the intrusion of advertising into the sports arena, but he also documents the introduction of private inequalities into formerly public domains, like highway lanes in which one can pay extra for the privilege of using. Sandel wants to introduce some finitude into capitalism's infinite expansion, and he argues for this position on the basis of moral grounds. As he sees it, the claims of the market should not decide every question. Some things are priceless.

But there is really nothing to separate Sandel's position from that of MasterCard. In its very successful advertising campaign touting the ability of MasterCard to pay for almost everything, the company admits that there are some objects that have no price. Perhaps the most famous of these commercials depicts an elephant assembling a care package for his ailing keeper. The elephant takes a MasterCard to various stores, and as he purchases the supplies, a voiceover announces their cost. The voiceover says, "Hot soup: $4. Cold medicine: $11. Tissues: $1. Blanket: $24. Making it all better: priceless." Just like Sandel, MasterCard is perfectly willing to grant that some elements of life cannot be figured in terms of the market. The company doesn't just use the fantasy of a terrain outside the market to sell their product. Capitalism actually requires this barrier in order to constitute itself as infinitely expanding. What is priceless today, one can be sure, will have a price tomorrow, when something else will miraculously become priceless.

The link between Michael Sandel and MasterCard becomes even clearer when one moves beyond *What Money Can't Buy* and examines Sandel's involvement in massive open online courses (MOOCs). These courses represent an unprecedented expansion of capitalism into the university system and have the potential to unleash widespread privatization of higher education while transforming the majority of professors into the equivalent of glorified teaching assistants for a few luminaries like Sandel himself. For this reason, numerous other philosophers have directed sharp criticisms at Sandel. We should not see this as an inconsistency on Sandel's part, but as a logical outgrowth of his attempt to set external limits on capitalism. It is just that in this case Sandel is the proponent both of the limit and the expansion beyond the limit. He stands for finitude in his book and the bad infinite in his teaching practice, and he illustrates nicely how compatible the two are.

As Anna Kornbluh points out, the attempt to limit capitalism testifies to an investment in capitalism's bad infinite, even as it imagines itself responding to this structure. She says, "when capitalism is widely understood to be caused by our material desires, the corollary for moderating or controlling capitalism is to limit our desires."[29] But the call for limiting our desires—or limiting the encroaching of private enterprise on the public world—fails to see that desire always functions on the basis of a limit. This is Kornbluh's ultimate point, and it points toward Hegel's true infinite as the only viable response to capitalism's bad infinite.

In this sense, moral philosophers like Sandel who insist on sustaining some terrain outside capitalist production are indispensible for the functioning of the capitalist system. This is not to say that Sandel is a capitalist stooge or a double agent planted by capitalist powers in the world of moral philosophy—though, given his involvement with MOOCs, one can't be sure—but that the challenge to capitalism cannot occur through the attempt to limit the system. If capitalism requires a limit to transcend (which it does), every introduction of a new limit will be inherently self-defeating for the would-be limiter of the market's reach. One must instead rethink the form that the limit takes.

By articulating the difference between the bad and the true infinite, Hegel anticipates the psychoanalytic understanding of how the subject satisfies itself. Though the subject consciously imagines itself making infinite progress toward its goal of total satisfaction, it never arrives at this goal because the totally satisfying object exists insofar as it is lost. When the subject successfully obtains the object that it seeks, this object ceases to embody the lost object. But capitalism promulgates images of the bad infinite and hides the inescapability of the true infinite. The concept of the true infinite was Hegel's way, given the conceptual tools available to him at the time, of formulating the self-limiting structure of subjectivity.

By structuring our existence around the bad infinite and its ideal of constant movement forward, capitalism focuses all our despair on death and aging. Though human beings have always despaired in the face of death, capitalist society brings this despair to a head. The end of one's individual existence implies a failure of growth, the keystone of the system. The imminence of our death and our inability to continue growing becomes the fundamental limit that we must confront. And it comes to us as an external limit. Unless we drive wildly on the wrong side of the highway or take eighty-five pills of Valium or eat Twinkies with abandon, most of us will not cause our own deaths. Though we work to find ways to prevent death or offset aging, we know that ultimately we will fail in these efforts. This is the cause of incredible despair for the subjects of capitalism.

This despair leads us to spend vast amounts of money on products that promise to help keep the body fit, hide signs of aging, or hold death off as long as possible.[30] To be aging or dying is to betray the bad infinite, to cease to develop, which adds to the existential horror. Not only does one cease to exist, but one also feels guilty for succumbing to this cessation. One should have done more to stay young looking (like tanning) and to avoid death (like staying out of the sun). The imperative of infinite progress manifests most clearly in the anxiety produced by aging and death under capitalism.

Even though he is certainly an anticapitalist philosopher, one could not imagine Martin Heidegger constructing a philosophy around the problem of death prior to the capitalist epoch. According to the early Heidegger, death individualizes us and creates the possibility for authenticity because it is the one event that no one can do for us. While we talk, eat, and work following the model of others, no one can die in this way. Death brings an end to our possibilities and forces the recognition of our constitutive finitude. Its very unavoidability gives death its existential importance for Heidegger.[31] Certainly, capitalist life helps people to elude this confrontation with death, and this is a large part of why Heidegger thinks of capitalist modernity as a grave danger. But this danger elevates the significance of death and its centrality. Though people died in traditional society, death was not yet an ontological scandal.

Death is certainly a problem of existence. But when one lives according to the demand of the bad infinite, the centrality of this problem becomes magnified and obfuscates other, more traumatic, problems, such as that of eternity. The problem of eternity, however one considers it, is more vexing than that of death. On the surface, this verdict seems absurd. We might understand it coming from God or some other eternal being, but coming from a human being it appears to reflect an inadequate understanding of the finitude of earthly existence. If subjects were simply finite beings, this objection would be a winning one. But we are burdened by the weight of our infinitude as well as our finitude. We are beings not only of infinite striving toward the future but also of the true infinite—an encircling of our own limit.

Despite his opposition to Hegel, Søren Kierkegaard provides an almost perfect formulation of the true infinite through his conception of the sickness unto death. The idea of a sickness unto death seems to imply, as with Heidegger, a concern with anxiety in the face of one's imminent demise. But Kierkegaard has something entirely different in mind. For him, the sickness unto death is the result of the subject's confrontation with eternity.

Unlike other animals, the subject, as Kierkegaard sees it, cannot simply die. As he puts it, "to be sick *unto* death is to be unable to die, yet not as if there were hope of life; no, the hopelessness is that there is not even the ultimate hope, death. When death is the greatest danger, we hope for life; but when we learn to know the even greater danger, we hope for death. When the danger is so great that death becomes the hope, then despair is the hopelessness of not even being able to die."[32] Despair is the result of an inability to find respite in death, of a confrontation with eternity. One need not have Kierkegaard's belief in eternal life to recognize the nature of his insight here. He sees that the focus on death actually causes us to miss the real existential bind that ensnares us as subjects. We must find a reason to act, a passion to drive us, and no reason is given to us by the universe.

The eternal is the realm in which one must find a reason for acting in the world. Many of our actions have a motivation in finite exigencies—like the desire for food. But we need a reason to continue living and not simply to abandon ourselves to death. This is where we encounter the eternal. In eternity everything is possible, and nothing makes a lasting difference because no temporal constraints exist. There is an unlimited time to explore all alternatives. This eternity is constantly present for us when we confront the decision of our existence. We face the burden of having to act and to posit the cause of our own act. In this act, we take part in the true infinite with no assistance from external sources. But capitalism relieves us of this burden of the true infinite by translating the existential problem into a question of survival.[33]

Even though the structure of capitalism is that of the bad infinite, its constantly realized destiny is that of the true infinity. That is to say, it creates its own limit rather than encountering this limit in an external form. It relies on the very structure that it disdains and cannot avow. This does not necessitate the eventual end of capitalism as an economic system, as Marx thinks, but it does imply that this economic system will never escape the crises that periodically cripple and threaten to end it. Every moment of hope for a stable and prosperous economic future will run aground on capitalism's internal limit, a limit that derives, ironically, from the system's infinite need to expand itself.

When Marx discusses the contradictions of capitalism, he is really describing the system as one of true infinitude. This becomes evident in the middle of the third volume of *Capital*, where he makes a famous proclamation about the limits of capitalism. He says, "The *true barrier* to capitalist production is *capital itself*."[34] The project of infinitely expanding the forces of production encounters the barrier of capital's need to become profitable. A bit later, Marx contrasts capitalist means with the capitalist end, noting that "the means—the unrestricted development of the social forces of production—comes into persistent conflict with the restricted end, the valorization of the existing capital."[35] The limit is not external to capitalism but the product of its own striving to transcend every limit. In the capitalist universe the logic of the bad infinite leads the system directly to the true infinite, and this infinite spells its failure. Marx is able to see this but then goes awry when he tries to imagine communism in response to this contradiction.

The problem with Marx's conception of communist society derives from his investment in the capitalist bad infinite. In other words, Marx would have been a better revolutionary if he had remained a Hegelian. The revolution, as Marx sees it, would unleash the forces of production without any restriction at all from the mode of production, from capital's need for self-valorization. This image of a future of unrestricted production jettisons the limit altogether. Instead of continually surpassing their limit (which is what occurs under capitalism), the forces of production would experience no limit at all. They would continue to grow unabated in concert with the growth of desire.

Marx's image of a society without a limit errs not just due to its fantasmatic nature, as many critics claim. The problem with this vision of the future is that it is not fantasmatic enough. In an actual fantasy the subject does not just envision the complete evanescence of the limit and untrammeled access to the object. Instead, the fantasy introduces an external limit where none exists, thereby enabling the subject to enjoy the object through this barrier. Fantasy focuses on the loss of the object and then shows its reacquisition, but the loss has primacy, which is why only the last few minutes of Hollywood fantasies are devoted to the object's reacquisition. By completely eliminating the barrier when it comes to imagining the economy of the future, Marx betrays his own critique of capitalism and the communist fantasy of escaping it.

Here Marx's analysis undergoes a shocking change: he compellingly identifies how capitalism stumbles on the true infinite while pursuing the bad infinite of endless progress, but then he theorizes communism as the perfect realization of the bad infinite when he proclaims that communism will remove all restraints on the forces of production. It is commonplace to laud Marx as a critic of capitalism and criticize him as a prophet of communism, but in this passage from the third volume of *Capital* the reason for this discrepancy becomes clear. The true infinite simply drops out of the analysis. This departure from Hegel right at the point of Hegel's key insight creates a chasm between Marx's analysis of capitalism and his image of the communist future. The one benefits from the conception of the true infinite while the other is handicapped by its absence.

The failure to sustain the idea of the true infinite leads Marx to misrepresent the nature of the dialectical shift that would occur with the transition from capitalism to communism. For Marx, communism will solve the contradiction between the forces of production and the means of production in capitalism—and thus allow for unfettered productivity. Hegel never conceives of dialectical transitions in this way. The transition or *Aufhebung* does not involve an elimination of the limit that haunts the prior structure, as it does for Marx. Instead, it involves a recognition that the limit is internal to the structure rather than external. *Aufhebung* requires, in other words, a recognition that the limit is not a contingent barrier but a necessary obstacle constituted through the structure's own logical requirements.

To take an example from *The Phenomenology of Spirit*, Hegel insists that stoicism as a philosophy runs aground on its own internal obstacle. Stoicism preaches a retreat from the external world into the serenity of the self, but at the same time, it requires the hostile external world from which the stoic can execute a retreat. The unconscious focus of the stoic is on the external world that the stoic claims to disdain. The dialectical move out of stoicism, for Hegel, involves making the unconscious focus on the external world qua obstacle into the basis of a new philosophy—skepticism. The skeptic doesn't retreat from the external world but calls its reality into question. In this way, the obstacle undergoes a dramatic transformation and becomes the center of the new philosophy.

If we follow Hegel's line of thought about change, then we must rethink the relationship to the obstacle or limit that capitalism establishes. It cannot simply be a question of dispensing with this limit altogether. To try to do so is to fall into the capitalist trap, as Marx himself does, despite—or perhaps because of—his fervent anticapitalism. Capitalism demands the notion of the natural world as an external limit that it will constantly work to overcome, but it cannot integrate any limit as internal to its own functioning.[36] This is what Hegel's dialectic would demand. His version of communism or socialism would thus be significantly different from Marx's.

Marx, as everyone who reads him knows, offers very little description of the nature of communist society. The most famous of these moments occurs in *The German Ideology*, when he and Engels pause during their opening diatribe against Ludwig Feuerbach to offer their vision of the postrevolutionary future. In their brief account of communist society, they portray a world in which limits do not exist. They claim that one will be able "to do one thing today and another tomorrow, to hunt in the morning, fish in the afternoon, rear cattle in the evening, criticise after dinner, just as I have a mind, without ever becoming hunter, fisherman, shepherd or critic."[37] Marx and Engels provide a description of how socialist society would strip away fixed social identity

The problem with this image of the future is its resemblance to the capitalist present. Today, economic necessity forces many workers to be newspaper carriers in the morning, convenience store clerks in the afternoon, and janitors in the evening. Though this is a parody of what Marx imagines, it does suggest that the overcoming of fixed identity is not necessarily an anticapitalist development. Fixed identity is yet another limit that capitalism itself aims to overcome and does.

It is not Marx but Hegel who accurately uncovers the logic of communist society through his analysis of the true infinite. The logic of an egalitarian society is not that there is nothing missing, that society has reached its self-realization. It is not a society of unleashed and unlimited productivity, as it is for Marx. Instead, the egalitarian order involves a recognition of a necessary limit that will not only function as a boundary to its growth but that will simultaneously constitute growth as a possibility. Rather than attempting to overcome this limit—whatever it is— egalitarian society will nurture it as the society's own essence. It would be a society that embraced its obstacle as its very condition of possibility.

The Ends of Capitalism

A PRODUCTIVE SYSTEM OF PRODUCTION

The victory of capitalism over traditional societies is a victory over the ideals of historical continuity and community. In order for capitalism to rule the world, markets and private property are not enough. It requires a new ideal to gain ascendency over the sedimented ideals of traditional societies. This new ideal is productivity and its maximization. As Joyce Appleby points out, capitalism became the ruling economic system at the moment when "the ideal of productivity finally became dominant."[1] Once this ideal takes hold, even capitalism's detractors accept it as their starting point. A capitalist world is a world where productivity is implicitly—and often explicitly—the highest value.

Productivity orients capitalist subjects around an end to be accomplished, and this end promises to exhaust the means used to achieve it. That is, the means are important only for the end that they accomplish. This is a defining capitalist idea, and the devaluing or erasing of means is essential to capitalism. Labor is important not for its own sake but for what it produces—for the capitalist and the consumer. The end may be the realization of profit or the enjoyment of a commodity. But in both cases the actions done to make this end possible lose all importance.

Capitalism's focus on ends spares the subject from the encounter with the trauma of means. The means involve work and the effort that it demands. But the real trauma of means as opposed to ends is that they are never over and done with. When we think in terms of the end product and the accumulation of capital, we don't have to consider the perpetual process required to create the product and the capital. The goal of the end replaces the repetition of the means and enables us to believe in the possibility of concrete and lasting accomplishments that will ultimately deliver us from incessant repetition. Capitalism directs subjects toward ends that they can achieve and obscures means that no amount of productivity will allow them to escape.

At the same time, however, the capitalist system relies on means to accomplish its ends. The capitalist and the worker must devote themselves to the actions that will bring about productivity. The system even requires moments in which the means disrupt productivity in order to reenergize it. Capitalism uses means for the sake of expanding its productive ends, but it never permits subjects to invest themselves in means while remaining in the capitalist universe. Capitalist subjects can think about the goals they want to fulfill without recognizing that they can never really leave the terrain of means, which inheres in subjectivity itself. The degradation of means is central to capitalism's psychic appeal.

In this sense, there seems to be a natural affinity between capitalism and utilitarian philosophy. Though there are prominent utilitarian philosophers (like Peter Singer) who struggle for a more ethical version of capitalism or even for socialism, the philosophy itself, with its focus on ends rather than means, fits the capitalist a priori structure. In other words, the fact that John Stuart Mill is a prominent theorist of both capitalism and utilitarianism should not surprise us. At the beginning of his treatise on utilitarianism, Mill foregrounds the overriding importance of ends. He claims, "All action is for the sake of some end, and rules of action, it seems natural to suppose, must take their whole character and colour from the end to which they are subservient."[2] This idea that the end drives our actions emerges out of capitalism's privileging of productivity.[3]

Of course, the idea that we act to realize ends does not originate with capitalist modernity or with utilitarian philosophy. One finds this emphasis on ends throughout Aristotle's thought, especially when he begins the *Nicomachean Ethics* with the claim that all our actions aim at the realization of some good. But there is a key difference between Aristotle and capitalism. The former views ends as an engine for our actions, but ends don't exhaust our actions or extirpate the means used to attain them. This is what occurs with capitalism. Its emphasis on productivity precludes every attempt to value means on a par with ends. The result is that all affirmations about the intrinsic value of labor have an inherently anticapitalist hue to them.

To put it in the terms of psychoanalysis, capitalism focuses the attention of the subject not on the lost object that causes its desire but on the object that it desires. The capitalist subject is always looking forward to new objects that might attract its desire. In the capitalist universe, objects of desire proliferate and are highly visible. Just walking down the street forces multiple encounters with these objects in the form of advertisements, the cars that people drive, even the clothes that others wear. But the visibility of objects of desire in the capitalist system corresponds to the invisibility of the object that causes our desire.

The object of desire obscures the object-cause of desire or lost object. As we saw in chapter 1, the object of desire is an empirical object, existing in the everyday world, that one can obtain in the form of a new car, a new dress, or a new boyfriend. The lost object that causes desire, however, has no substantial existence and causes the subject's desire only insofar as it is lost. The lost object is loss as such and functions to animate the subject as a being capable of acting in the world. We act—we take an interest in the world—because we begin with loss, with the loss of what we never had. This initial loss defines us as subjects. Thinking about desire in terms of the object of desire makes desire much easier to contemplate. Instead of being doomed to failure, it becomes a worthwhile investment. This realignment of our experience of desire constitutes an essential part of capitalism's charm.

Though capitalism succeeds in deflecting attention from the lost object to the object of desire, it cannot make the object of desire satisfying when the subject obtains it. In fact, capitalism relies on the dissatisfaction that follows from obtaining the object of desire to stimulate consumption. If the commodity proves disappointing, the subject will have to buy another, more improved version. The eighty-inch television will surely provide the satisfaction that the fifty-five-inch one didn't. The older wine will prove more enjoyable than the newer (and cheaper) vintage. But eventually subjects grow wary of this perpetual game of dissatisfaction. Though the commodity always promises a complete satisfaction, it never delivers on this promise. No television can ever be large enough.[4]

Despite the images of satisfaction that float around capitalist society, it is a society structured around the subject's dissatisfaction. If consumption simply satisfied the subject, it would destroy itself and eliminate profit rather than increasing it. A satisfied customer ceases to consume enough to sustain a capitalist economy. The capitalist subject must thus live through a constant struggle between the image of satisfaction that others seem to have and its own perpetual dissatisfaction. Perhaps this contradiction sends them into psychoanalysis.

Psychoanalysis owes its existence to capitalist modernity. It emerges in response to the sense of dissatisfaction that capitalism produces through its incessant focus on the object of desire. Whereas capitalism privileges the object of desire to the exclusion of the lost object, psychoanalysis reverses this valuation and identifies the lost object as the central force within the subject. Psychoanalysis doesn't make existence fully satisfying for the subject by giving it a fully satisfying object. Instead, it turns the subject's attention to the integral role that loss has in its satisfaction and reveals the inexistence of a fully satisfying object.

The psychoanalytic cure involves leading the subject to the point where it can embrace the partial satisfaction that the lost object provides. It is a satisfaction of not having rather than having—and thus radically opposed to capitalist productivity. The idea is not one of accepting the necessity of some dissatisfaction by acceding to the reality principle. Instead, the subject grasps that it already has the satisfaction that it seeks. The partial satisfaction of not having always trumps the illusory total satisfaction associated with having the object of desire. This is the lesson of psychoanalysis in a nutshell.

The combat that psychoanalysis wages against capitalism is not a frontal assault. Instead, it works to transform the subject's attitude toward loss and thus render the subject incapable of investing itself in capitalist productivity and accumulation. Thus, if one leaves psychoanalysis and continues to struggle for enrichment or for accumulating additional commodities, the psychoanalysis has functioned as productive therapy rather than as psychoanalysis. This is the verdict that we can unequivocally render on the analysis that Tony Soprano (James Gandolfini) undergoes in the television series *The Sopranos*. Though it disturbs his ability to continue his accumulation (of money, of women, of power), it never seriously throws this project into question. This represents a perfect image of psychoanalytic failure. Instead of helping subjects like Tony Soprano to accumulate with a good conscience, psychoanalysis aims at creating a recognition that loss is inextricable from satisfaction.

The rarity of psychoanalytic practice actually working to reconcile subjects with the lost object as the source of satisfaction testifies to the triumph of the ideal of productivity within capitalist society even at the site most diametrically opposed to this ideal. By and large, nonproductive psychoanalysis—that is, psychoanalysis as such—becomes productive therapy. Practices that don't accede to the productive ideal either die or quickly transform themselves. The fate of psychoanalysis in capitalist society bespeaks the near omnipotence of this ideal. Despite its emphasis on the nonproductivity of the lost object, psychoanalysis primarily functions as an ideological handmaiden to the productive ideal.

But the victory of the productive ideal is not, for all that, entirely secure. Its vulnerability does not only reside in workers who experience their labor devalued but also in subjects who become dissatisfied with the dissatisfaction necessarily created by the focus on ends. Attention to the means lurking within capitalist ends leads to the possibility of a different economic system. Capitalism depends on an investment in productive ends, but its dependence on means opens the door to the recognition of satisfaction that it cannot tolerate.

THE RECOGNITION OF LABOR

Capitalism creates a strict separation between loss and satisfaction, just as it separates labor from profit. This is what leads to the denigration of labor. Despite the integral role of the worker in the creation of profit, capitalism focuses attention just on the moment where profit becomes realized rather than when it is produced. The end is what matters, and the capitalist does what she or he can to increase profit, even if this means pushing workers past the point of their physical and psychic limits.[5]

In *Modern Times* (Charlie Chaplin, 1936) the image of Charlie Chaplin being sucked into a machine after failing to keep pace with the ever increasing demands of the industry chief captures the indifference of the capitalist to the plight of the worker.[6] Though this is obviously an exaggerated portrait of capitalist production and conditions have improved for most workers today, there are still many unable to keep up with the demands for hyperproductivity, even in supposedly advanced countries. These conditions persist because, for the capitalist, there is no intrinsic relationship between labor and profit. Labor is only a tool to achieve profit, not a part of the profit process. The mistreatment of workers is inextricable from the capitalist conception of the world.

Labor is the means toward the end of profit, and the site of the means is always traumatic. The trauma of means resides in its capacity not to be realized as an end. The means might lead to the end, but it also might not. The means might remain nonproductive, and labor might not realize a profit. Capitalism relies on the means of labor, but it refuses to grant the means any status of its own. There is, in other words, no space for the acknowledgment of pure means—that is, the means that might not realize itself in an end—within the capitalist system. The means is only there to be realized in the end of production.

Capitalism's apotheosis of productivity leads to its disdain for any refusal to actualize the means as an end. The refusal to actualize the means insists on the value of the means independent of the end that it guides it, and this refusal manifests itself most commonly in the strike, which has not become the privileged labor action by accident.[7] The strike confronts the capitalist with a show of the means subtracted from its end. Capitalists abhor strikes not simply because they cut drastically into profits but because they indicate an implicit challenge against the entire capitalist order. When we go on strike, we demonstrate the significance of the means as opposed to the ends. Even when the strike is just a bargaining tool—and thus a means to a clear end—its form belies its function. The idle laborer and the idle machine disturb the universal faith in productivity that rules the capitalist universe. Capitalism demands that all means serve an end. The structure of capitalism is necessarily teleological: it gives priority to the final cause, which would be the realization of value in the sale of the commodity.

In the second book of the *Physics*, Aristotle distinguishes between four forms of causality—the material cause, the formal cause, the efficient cause, and the final cause. Aristotle sees all causes as necessary, but the final cause holds a special place for him because it is determinative in the world. We act, in the last instance, on behalf of the final cause rather than the other three forms of causality. Aristotle says, "that for the sake of which tends to be what is best and the end of the things that lead up to it."[8] Because Aristotle's world is a world of the good in which we act in order to realize certain goods, the final cause necessarily holds sway for him.[9]

Though modern science departs from Aristotle on almost every question, nowhere is its rupture as violent as on the question of causality. Modern science does not permit the researcher to introduce at any point the question of the final cause or the reason why an event occurs. When observing a new species of plant, for instance, we cannot ask why it came into existence, for what purpose.[10] Nature is purposiveness without any ultimate purpose. No scientist would dare make an argument for introducing a final cause. Doing so would testify to a premodern belief in God's divine plan.[11] The rejection of the final cause defines modern science.

Though evolutionary theory seems to embrace a version of the final cause with its conception of adaptation, genuine evolutionary scientists scrupulously distance adaptation from any teleological purposiveness. Evolutionary change occurs through adaptation to the exigencies of the environment, not for the sake of an ultimate external goal (like the ability to see, for instance). The development of a particular organ in a species thus has a completely contingent status. It is always the product of a series of efficient causes that led to the creation and not a final cause. The link between evolutionary science and the final cause is entirely illusory and stems from a basic misunderstanding of this science.

Just after modern science jettisoned the final cause from all its inquiries, Spinoza did the same for philosophy. In the appendix to book 1 of the *Ethics*, Spinoza targets the belief in final causes as an illusion that we must abandon. Because we experience our own ability to realize ends in the world, we assume, Spinoza argues, that God has the same ability on a grander scale. We assume, in other words, that nature follows from God's free will, just as we assume our actions follow from our free will. Both assumptions are faulty because neither we nor God has a free will to guide actions. No final cause guides the natural world, and we do not have the power to direct our action by positing an end toward which they aim. The only cause, for both modern science and Spinoza, is Aristotle's efficient cause. The final cause represents a dream of control that has become untenable in the modern world.

And yet, capitalism, the system that comes into existence alongside modern science, insists on the final cause without any hint of abandoning it. Without the final cause, capitalism would lose itself in the satisfaction of the pure means and fail to actualize all the potential value that it unleashes. The psychic structure of the capitalist subject remains immersed in the final cause as the engine for its actions. The final cause directs capitalists toward the moment of value's realization in the exchange process, and it turns attention away from labor. Means must become ends, and productivity must become the productive act. A system that values productivity above all else must cling to the outdated philosophy of the final cause.[12]

The idea of the final cause has such great staying power not simply because the logic of the capitalist requires it (though it does). It endures by allowing subjects to view themselves, to paraphrase Descartes, as masters and possessors of themselves and their future. The final cause is a conscious plan we lay out and attempt to realize through a series of little efficient causes. The philosophy of the final cause assumes that our conscious plans, our professed intentions, drive our actions. But such a vision misses the extent to which the unconscious generates satisfaction by upsetting these plans.

I may, for instance, begin with the final cause of finding a romantic partner who treats me with more kindness than my previous ones. I consciously choose one who seems to fit the bill. But because I am also an unconscious being, I will, for better or worse, choose someone who appeals to my unconscious desire, even if she appears to serve my final cause. Thus, I end up with a partner who treats me just like my previous partners did, in spite of the studiously conceived plan to avoid this eventuality. Perhaps straightforward aggressiveness now becomes passive aggressiveness. The same lack of kindness repeats itself now under the guise of kindness, but this guise allows me to avoid confronting the trauma of my own repetition. In the same way, we seek respite from the trauma of unconscious repetition by placing our faith in the final cause, and this respite is precisely what capitalism offers us.

The central role played by the final cause in capitalism affects the approach that businesspeople take toward their enterprises. They do not contemplate questions about the significance of what they aim to produce or about the state of the workers who will produce the commodity. Instead, they focus entirely on the end. Great exponent of the free market Ludwig von Mises describes this disposition in detail. He notes,

The businessman, the acting man, is entirely absorbed in one task only: to take best advantage of all the means available for the improvement of future conditions. He does not look at the present state of affairs with the aim of analyzing and comprehending it. In classifying the means for further production and appraising their importance he adopts superficial rules of thumb. He distinguishes three classes of factors of production: the nature-given material factors, the human factor—labor, and capital goods—the intermediary factors produced in the past. He does not analyze the nature of the capital goods. They are in his eyes means of increasing the productivity of labor. Quite naïvely he ascribes to them productive power of their own. He does not trace their instrumentality back to nature and labor. He does not ask how they came into existence. They count only as far as they may contribute to the success of his efforts.[13]

Though von Mises later adds that the economist can't share this single-mindedness of the businessperson, he does correctly insist that it is requisite for success in the marketplace. The capitalist is necessarily a teleological being focused entirely on the goal of creating profit by realizing the potential value created by the production process.[14]

Capitalism and modern science arise at roughly the same point in history and often work in tandem (when capitalists employ scientists to develop new products for them, for instance). But the centrality of the final cause in capitalism and its banishment from modern science reveals an incongruity. In the midst of a modern world where science has stripped away the sense of purpose given by the final cause, capitalism recreates a purpose. Every act within the capitalist universe originates in a purpose: the capitalist's will to create a profit, the consumer's will to find a satisfying commodity, and the worker's will to earn enough to live well. The mastery implicit in the final cause suffuses the capitalist system.

The final cause appears determinative everywhere within the capitalist universe. There is no means that remains just a means. Every means must lead to an end, or else it has no worth at all. Capitalism capitalizes on every means by placing it under the regime of the end, a regime in which the final cause appears to bring everything under its auspices. But the final cause is nothing but capitalism's retrospective illusion. No one acts on behalf of a final cause: no one creates a new commodity in order to realize a future profit; no one plays the lottery in order to purchase a new house; no one goes to church in order to attain eternal salvation. The purpose of the act exists within the satisfaction of the act itself, not in what the act actualizes. This is Spinoza's great insight and the basis for his implicit critique of the incipient capitalist system.[15] But in order to recognize the absence of the final cause and the presence of a series of efficient causes, one must change one's perspective from that of ends to that of means.

THE VIRTUES OF INTERRUPTION

In a number of works dedicated to potentiality, Giorgio Agamben has advocated just this type of change in perspective. He identifies potentiality not with the capacity to realize one's desire but with the satisfaction that comes from the failure to realize it. As he argues in the essay "On Potentiality," "To be potential means: to be one's own lack, *to be in relation to one's own incapacity*. Beings that exist in the mode of potentiality *are capable of their own impotentiality*; and only in this way do they become potential. They *can be* because they are in relation to their own non-Being."[16] Potentiality implies impotentiality and failure, an ability to identify with one's own inability to realize a desire.[17] Potentiality is an immanent alternative that exists within the capitalist system. Despite its insistence on all potentiality realizing itself in actuality, capitalism relies on impotentiality or the interruption of productivity to create new values and to sustain the functioning of the system.

The insistence on impotentiality is not just a protest against capitalism's demand for productive ends. It is also—and perhaps more importantly—an act that contains within it the essence of capitalism's productivity. Impotentiality's refusal blocks the process of capital's actualization, but such refusals are the real source of value. Capitalism relies on subjects of impotentiality even when they destroy potential productivity, because these subjects open up other avenues for productivity. Even though capitalism demands productivity and reduces laborers to instruments of reproduction, it desires and in fact requires an interruption of this pure productivity. The special talent of capitalism lies in its capacity for marshaling the threat of impotentiality in the service of its regime of actuality. This is why the political valence of impotentialty is never cut and dried.

Within the capitalist mode of production, the interruption of productivity becomes a new way of creating surplus value. As Hannah Arendt theorizes it, capitalism—and communism, about which she is equally critical—demands the reduction of all potentially active subjects to laborers. Labor, which is nothing but the reproduction of life itself, becomes the only possible mode of relating to one's existence. Work (which is world creating) and action (which is the realm of the political) cease to be viable concerns within the modern capitalist universe. The dominance of labor and its pure productivity create a world in which there is no value at all, and this destruction of value forms the basis for Arendt's critique of capitalism and communism.[18]

But what Arendt misses is the impossibility of a system continuing to survive just for the sake of surviving.[19] Even when we claim to want only to survive, we must find some satisfaction in this survival or else we wouldn't bother with it. Pure survival simply isn't worth the effort, either for the individual or for the socioeconomic system. Every system needs a source of value, and in order to create it, capitalism relies on the interruption of the pure productivity—or, to put it in Agamben's terms, the interruption of actuality—that it explicitly demands. Pure productivity cannot create value, which is precisely why Marx sees capitalism's production of value infinitely shrinking. This process, for Marx, will ultimately lead to capitalism's decay and overthrow. But capitalism finds new forms of value in those moments when productivity stops and when an interruption manifests itself. This is what Marx fails to anticipate, and his failure is due to his investment in productivity as the fundamental value. Withdrawal from the capitalist system energizes the system by providing it with a new potential that it must work to actualize.

We can see an exemplary case of this in any great modernist work of art. Marcel Duchamp's *Fountain* (1917) is simply a urinal torn from the system of productivity, an interruption of that system. Though Duchamp's work had a scandalous effect at the time of its initial appearance, its interruption of productivity later became the site of immense productivity. Many art historians consider it one of the greatest artworks of the twentieth century, and replicas appear in museums around the world. It now generates revenue through museum admissions, T-shirt sales, and related ventures. Duchamp's work marks a genuine interruption of capitalist productivity, but that productivity uses such interruptions as the fuel that propel it forward.

Even though it is difficult to imagine Duchamp's *Fountain* bringing new life into a decaying capitalist mode of production, this is nonetheless what happens. Duchamp's work is not just resistance but also interruption, and capitalism requires interruption in order to survive. *Fountain* and other similar works force capitalism to change course and begin to do things differently in order to respond to the refusal that they embody. Perhaps Duchamp's subtraction of the urinal from the regime of productivity would create a change in the construction of urinals or of museums, for instance. Perhaps this refusal would lead to the privileging of a wholly new commodity. Insofar as it reduces subjects to beings of pure survival, capitalism would destroy itself, but it can thrive insofar as it can make use of figures such as Duchamp's urinal. What doesn't fit is just as necessary to the perpetuation of capitalism as what does. This applies as much to people as it does to objects.

Nowhere is this reliance on those who don't fit clearer than in the world of fashion. New fashions derive not from insiders but from outsiders, subjects exiled from mainstream society. To take the most obvious example, the style of baggy pants did not emerge in the Upper East Side of New York or from Paris but from street gangs. But it quickly spread to clothing production and provided untold millions in profits for manufacturers who undoubtedly scorned (and didn't socialize with) the gang members who started the trend. The figures that interrupt productivity drive the productivity of the market, even though they receive no monetary benefit for their creative act. They are the exiles from the capitalist system, but they are every bit as integral to it as Donald Trump and Bill Gates.[20]

SLEEPING WITH THE ENEMY

Capitalist society is the first society to live on the interruption of those who opt out of it. In traditional society, opting out represents a mortal danger that occasions exile or the death penalty. This is what occurs in the case of Socrates. He turns away from the law of Athens and listens to his own conscience as the ultimate guide. Athenian society has no way to deal with this act of defiance and thus puts Socrates on trial. In his *Philosophy of World History*, Hegel takes note of the justice of the death penalty that the Athenian people pronounce on Socrates.

Even though Socrates transforms the history of the world by locating truth in the individual subject rather than in external authority, his introduction of this new principle into Athenian life represents a fundamental revolt against that form of life. The people thus have no choice but to try to eliminate the danger. Hegel claims, "On [Socrates'] behalf he had the justification of thought; but for their part the Athenian people were completely in the right too: they must have been deeply aware that respect for the law of the state would be weakened and the Athenian state destroyed by the principle that justification resides in one's own inwardness. Thus it is quite correct that the teaching of Socrates appeared to the people as high treason; accordingly they condemned him to death, and Socrates' death was the highest justice."[21] Despite this act of justice, the contagion of individualism that Socrates birthed had already entered into Athenian society. The society may have killed Socrates, but he destroyed the society by infecting it with individualism. Like every traditional society, Athens had no way to accommodate itself to the refusal of its demands. Every such refusal puts the entire social order at risk.

Capitalism, in contrast, can not only tolerate the refusal of its demands but relies on such refusals—outbursts of nonproductivity—in order to sustain itself. When subjects refuse to enter into the regime of productivity and actualize themselves, they inject new possibilities into the capitalist system and create new values. This doesn't mean that resistance is futile and that nonproductivity changes nothing, only that capitalism can capitalize on it. Whereas the newness Socrates creates in Athenian society destroys that society, capitalism depends on such figures of refusal.

Capitalism's reliance on the outburst of nonproductivity that is politically opposed to the system is manifest in the response to the student movement of the 1960s. For many leftists, the 1960s—and especially May 1968—represent a highpoint in recent political history.[22] In contrast with the apolitical years of the 1980s and 1990s when university students around the world seemed more focused on finding a place within the capitalist economy than on asserting themselves politically, the 1960s were a time of dissatisfaction with this economy, a time when many tried to "turn on, tune in, and drop out."[23] The student radicals took up a position of nonproductivity and refused to comply with capitalist society's demand that they become productive members of this society. They were a group who preferred not to contribute to capitalist relations of production.

The nonproductivity of the student movement became literal in the free speech movement at Berkeley. Led by Mario Savio, Berkeley students began by protesting against, as the name of the movement suggests, university restrictions on speech. When the police arrived to arrest students who occupied university buildings, the students responded in a unique way that indicated their commitment to nonproductivity. Rather than go quietly with the police or resist arrest—what seem to be the only two legitimate options for someone in this situation—they let their bodies go limp so that the police had to drag them from the buildings. When this happens, the resistance against capitalist society and the refusal to go along with the demands of that society confront every viewer of the scene.

The development of this form of resistance represents a brilliant strategy on the part of the free speech movement precisely because it is not just a strategy. The form of the protest is the expression of its content. Fighting back against the police does not simply run the risk of escalating repressive violence. It also involves an assertion of productivity and testifies to an inherent complicity with the capitalist system against which one is struggling. The limp body, in contrast, does not just negate but rather affirms nonproductivity.[24]

Though the authority figures of capitalist society responded to the revolts with displays of force, capitalism as a system found revitalization in them. As Luc Boltanski and Eve Chiapello rightly note in their discussion of May 1968 in France, "it was by recuperating some of the oppositional themes articulated during the May events that capitalism was to disarm critique, regain the initiative, and discover a new dynamism."[25] This final point is the most significant. The assertion of nonproductivity within capitalism's regime of productivity fuels the regime. Capitalism requires the assertion of nonproductivity in order to continue to survive, as nonproductivity renews capitalism by providing it with a limit that it must conquer. In response to the student revolts, it had to realign itself in accordance with the demands that they articulated. New products and professions followed in the wake of these revolts.

The insistence on nonproductivity in the student revolts of the 1960s went beyond limp bodies. It manifested itself in the insistence on sexual liberty, in the refusal to fight in the Vietnam War, in demands for university reform, in advocacy for civil rights, and so on. The nonproductivity of the revolts was the source of new value for capitalist society. This is most clearly the case with the sexual revolution.

The status of sexuality after the student revolts of the 1960s underwent a vast transformation. The idea that sex should be restricted to married life became outmoded and restricted to a nostalgic reaction to sexual liberation. Even if most people did not take up the practice of free love, the relaxation of sexual mores proliferated throughout capitalist society. Though some had the dream that sexual liberation would topple capitalism, the effect was quite the contrary. The movement opened a new market and allowed capitalism to expand into a previously unavailable domain.

After sexual liberation, sex became a new source of value. Businesses began selling more sexy underwear, revealing clothes, and sex toys. The pornography industry began in earnest in the United States in the 1970s, and it opened up a vast field of production to meet an increasing demand. In fact, in 1972 the porn film *Behind the Green Door* (Artie Mitchell and Jim Mitchell) was the fourth highest grossing film of the year in the United States, beating out popular mainstream films such as *Cabaret* (Bob Fosse, 1972) and *The Getaway* (Sam Peckinpah, 1972). And in a more indirect manner, sex became fecund territory for advertisers, as innumerable companies began to appeal to consumers by associating their products with sex. One can now see sexually explicit advertisements that would have been unthinkable in the 1960s. Rather than harming capitalism, sexual liberation helped to save it.

But this should not imply that valuing the means and nonproductivity is a fool's errand, that it simply feeds the society from which it withdraws. The problem lies in the approach that we take to the means. Capitalism requires thinking in terms of the final cause, and prioritizing the means does not fit smoothly in this context. If we recognize capitalism's dependence on the means and insist on the means for its own sake, we undermine the logic that sustains capitalist production. Once the priority of the means becomes apparent, we move beyond the confines of the capitalist system.

The linchpin of a critique of capitalism—and the formation of a workable alternative—rests on valuing the means over the end. Rather than acquiescing to capitalism's use of means for the end of the production of value, rather than submitting the means to the reign of the capitalist final cause, we can turn our attention to the means in itself. Attention to the means is always the revolutionary gesture, even when it ultimately becomes transformed into actuality.

In other words, we must always treat productivity as nonproductivity, as a means that is not necessarily leading anywhere. If we insist on sustaining our focus on the priority of the means rather than its future end, we are already beyond the capitalist system. We can see an example of this in Gabriel García Márquez's *One Hundred Years of Solitude*. In that novel, Márquez depicts a banana manufacturer invading a fictional Colombian town of Macondo. After the company massacres striking workers, a downpour ensues, and the company vows to suspend production until the rain stops. Márquez depicts the rain lasting for four years, which destroys the company's fortunes as it also ruins the town. This depiction of nonproductivity—four years of incessant rain—points the way out of capitalism's need for productivity. We must accept, Márquez implies, the traumatic isolation that comes with the rain if we want to avoid falling back into the trap of capitalist productivity and its insistence on actualizing all potentiality.

If subjects could be reduced entirely to their actuality and thus to their reproductivity, then they would cease to be political or ethical beings. A focus on the means and on nonproductivity frees us from the teleological force of actuality. This is why capitalism now presides over the evanescence of political contestation as such. Within a capitalist economy, the problem is not that potentially political subjects have become satisfied consumers but that all subjects value only ends. In such a system, the political act becomes unthinkable and even absurd. The step toward politicization requires a reorientation of our thinking in the direction of means. As long as we reside on the turf of ends, capitalism retains an advantage that no amount of consciousness raising could overcome. Only the uncovering of our own nonproductivity has the ability to tip the balance away from capitalism's dominance. Any argument of behalf of authentic nonproductivity is inherently a critique of capitalism and an implicit decision for an alternative, but it arrives at that alternative solely out of the implicit logic of the capitalist system itself. The alternative to capitalism lies in the means that capitalism requires and yet cannot avow.

THE IMMANENT ALTERNATIVE

Perhaps the most vexing question for those who challenge capitalist relations of production is the one that asks what system will replace the capitalist one. Communism has been discredited, and those who hold onto the idea of communism, like Alain Badiou and Slavoj Žižek, have no concrete account of what this idea would look like in practice. It is communism as an ideal, as Badiou readily admits, rather than as a concrete historical possibility. Their communism informs their thinking and practice, but it is not a system ready to be imposed. Other champions of communism, like Antonio Negri and Michael Hardt, also fall victim to this inability to envision the communist future in anything other than superficial and ambiguous terms. They are cautious not to invoke any concrete descriptions that might function as rallying cries for a political movement. Still others, like Simon Critchley or Judith Butler, champion resistance to capitalism as an end in itself and offer no sense of an alternative.[26]

Though the political position of unceasing resistance to capitalism and the state seems proximate to a focus on means, one should make an absolute distinction between them. Resistance conspicuously avoids the possibility of taking power. Privileging the means, on the other hand, represents an alternative organization of society, in which productivity and the final cause are no longer determinative. A politics that privileges the means has no problem determining the structure of the social order. In contrast with the proponents of resistance like Butler and Critchley, proponents of the means insist of seizing the reins, even if only indirectly in the manner of the people of Macondo in *One Hundred Years of Solitude*. The champions of the means don't display the caution that proliferates among the partisans of resistance.

This caution is perhaps an effect of the failed communist experiment of the twentieth century. Even Badiou, who is not reluctant to embrace the signifier *communism*, understands that the revolutionary mindset of the twentieth century cannot serve the twenty-first. The revolutionaries of the twentieth century produced tragedies that the revolutionaries of the twenty-first century must avoid.[27] The embrace of the horror of the real leads straight to the gulag, which is the effect of thought attempting to outstrip the act. The catastrophes of the twentieth century, as Badiou sees it, are the result of an effort to think a new system into being rather than to maintain fidelity to the material revolutionary event. The result in the twenty-first century is a philosophical caution, even among the most committed revolutionaries.

In one sense, this philosophical caution about advocating for a new socioeconomic system is warranted. It reflects, on this single issue, the victory of Hegel over Marx. For Marx, the only purpose of philosophical thought consists in its contribution to political practice. As the final thesis on Feuerbach has it, philosophy must forego interpretation in order to commit itself to political transformation. Hegel's ambitions for philosophy are much more modest. He claims that any political ambitions are simply beyond philosophy's province. As he puts it in the preface to *Elements of the Philosophy of Right*, "As far as the individual is concerned, each individual is in any case *a child of his time*; thus philosophy, too, is *its own time comprehended in thoughts.* It is just as foolish to imagine that any philosophy can transcend its contemporary world as that an individual can overleap his own time or leap over Rhodes."[28] According to Hegel, it would seem that philosophy can play no role at all in politics other than identifying the proper questions that our epoch poses and interpreting them. The philosopher cannot theorize a new future.

But even though the philosopher cannot anticipate the future socioeconomic system that might arise after capitalism, she or he can identify how another system already exists implicitly within the current system. This is possible with the category of the means. Though capitalism incessantly transforms means into ends, nothing necessitates this transformation, and in fact, it always occurs with many hiccups. The means are always present along with the end. Thus, privileging the means represents the alternative to capitalism waiting to be discovered. Its discovery depends on a philosophical act on our part.

Usually, theorists cannot take the lead in revolutionary upheavals. When they do, disaster almost inevitably follows. But they can forge an

approach to the world that reveals the unsustainability of the capitalist system and thereby make the alternative readily apparent. This is what
transpires when we abandon the final cause that underwrites capitalist productivity and insist on the means for its own sake and not for
what it will produce. By doing so, we do not magically leap outside the
constraints of our present situation; we do not "jump over Rhodes."
Instead, we show that there is no need to make this jump. The means is
a future that is already present within capitalism, and the task of the
theorist—or even the task of the revolutionary—consists not in creating
a new system but in identifying the implicit presence of this new system
within the existing one.

Privileging the means is an alternative system to capitalism existing
within the capitalist framework. By bringing this system to light, we don't
unleash productive capacity in the way that Marx dreamed. Instead, we
unleash our capacity to pursue means for their own sake, what Agamben calls means without end. We immerse ourselves in the traumatic satisfaction of work that matters more than its goal. The product becomes
a by-product of the means, not the end that the means aims at accomplishing. It is only in such a system of pure means that we can finally
abandon the tyranny of the final cause.

[8]

Exchanging Love for Romance

LOVE FOR SALE

Love seems like a capitalist plot. The prospect of falling in love and the process associated with it form the lifeblood of many corporations—those dedicated to the sale of diamond rings, roses, chocolate truffles, flights to Paris, and so on. The ways of love that redound to benefit of capitalism are not visible only on February 14. It is difficult to look at the array of commodities available in today's world and not see in almost every one some influence of the fantasy of falling in love. Gym memberships, diet soda, mascara, and leather jackets all hold within them the potential to render us worthy of love. Perhaps no one goes to the gym consciously trying to create a lovable body, but keeping oneself in proper shape has some relationship to acquiring and keeping a lover. Those who are fit tend to have much better prospects.[1]

Even if we are unfit and have long odds for acquiring an actual lover, capitalism provides almost infinite opportunities for the fantasy of love. The romance novelist sells love through an impossible fantasy scenario, and even the video game manufacturer promises the social outcast the possibility of heroism that would make this outcast worthy of love. Beer commercials promise love relations if we choose the proper beer, and jewelry advertisements assure us that our proposal will be accepted if we purchase the proper ring.[2] There seems to be no terrain free of the fantasy of love within the capitalist universe. Though love emerges earlier in human history than capitalism, it appears as if capitalism invented love ex nihilo, given how useful it has become for fostering the subject's investment in capitalist relations of production.

The commodity status of love becomes clearest in the case of dating services. The dating service is not simply a refuge for those who fail at falling in love on their own and therefore require assistance. Instead, it provides the paradigm for love in the capitalist system. Its structure is so significant that it is almost impossible to understand how love operates within capitalism without examining the structure of the dating service. One often turns to a dating service out of desperation, and it is this desperation that gives the dating service its revelatory power.

One pays the dating service for the possibility of falling in love. Unlike the gym or the jewelry store, it offers a direct path to love. I sign up in hopes of finding someone with whom I might fall in love without having to go to the trouble of sculpting my body or finding the perfect necklace that would render me worthy of love. The directness of the dating service is the source of the ignominy attached to it. But this direct route provided by the dating service lays bare the commodity status of love under capitalism even more clearly than the advertisements surrounding Valentine's Day. This clarity stems from the way the dating service arranges compatible partners.

The dating service demands that clients list their favorable qualities. When I compile such a list, I portray myself as a desirable and potentially lovable commodity. I offer myself up to the dating service for others to examine, test-drive, and perhaps purchase. To do this, I must transform myself into a series of qualities and preferences that function as an advertisement for myself. The features that render me more appealing as a commodity are necessarily the ones that I emphasize, and I pass over in silence the features that would lessen my exchange value. I highlight my sense of humor and my doctorate in macroeconomics while making no mention of my baldness and chronic bad breath. Even my preferences become part of my commodity status. My love for the outdoors or for watching classic movies helps to render me more appealing. Preferences advertise me as much as qualities do. This mode of self-presentation reveals that one must transform oneself into a commodity when one embarks on the quest for love.

But the dating service doesn't simply require that prospective lovers list their qualities and preferences. They must also choose what they want in their love object. After purchasing an account at the dating service, I must create a profile of my desires, and the service will attempt to match my desires with the appropriate object. For instance, I tell the service that I prefer men in their forties with brown eyes who like to read crime fiction and play chess. Just as I go into a grocery store with a shopping list for the items that I believe will realize my desire, I provide the dating service with a description of the characteristics that I find desirable in a romantic partner. But unlike at the grocery store, I go to the dating service in search of love, not just a carton of ice cream that would provide an inherently fleeting satisfaction for my desire.

The commodity that the dating service sells is much more valuable than those sold by the grocery store because it carries with it the illusion of a complete satisfaction. No one believes that eating a particular kind of ice cream will provide such a lasting satisfaction that I will never desire ice cream again, but many in capitalist society believe that finding one's soul mate will permanently solve the problem of desire for a love object. This difference bespeaks the pivotal role love has within capitalism. It is not just one commodity among many but the central commodity. One might say that all other commodities are modeled on the love object rather than vice versa.[3]

But in addition to exposing the commodity structure of love in the capitalist universe, the dating service enables subjects to bypass the inherently traumatic nature of the love encounter. The list of desirable qualities that I provide the dating service is the key to the service's ideological function. Such a list attempts to remove the trauma of love by eliminating its unforeseen power, its ability to attack the subject at the most inconvenient time and in the most unanticipated form. Though we may have a particular type that we find attractive, the beloved doesn't necessarily fit this type. In fact, we can fall in love with someone because she or he isn't the sort of object that usually appeals to us, not because she or he is. The dating service tries to mask the unexpectedness of love by making it thoroughly predictable. The dating service transforms love from a disruption into a stable structure for one's life.[4]

The permanence attached to the love object is central to the role that love plays within capitalism. Though many people use dating services just to discover temporary sexual partners, the idea of finding a permanent relation looms large for the clients of these services. Even if marriage goes completely out of style, the idea of loving someone else "forever" probably will not. This idea is not purely ideological. It reflects the ability of love to disrupt the course of everyday life and to introduce the eternal into the temporal. But it also reflects the promise inherent in every commodity, the promise of a permanent fulfillment of one's desire that the commodity will never keep.

Like the typical commodity, love always keeps the subject coming back for more. One seeks either to rekindle love with one's partner or to find someone new. In terms of love's connection to the commodity, there is no difference between renewing one's vows, going on a second honeymoon, and leaving one's spouse for a newer model. In each case, the subject experiences the dissatisfaction associated with having the commodity and seeks a new form of the commodity in order to ameliorate that dissatisfaction. Novelty is crucial to keeping love alive within capitalism, even if novelty involves varying relations with the same person. The logic of the commodity rules in the domain of love. One purchase is never enough, despite the claims that the salesperson at the dating service or the priest at the wedding makes.

The existence of the dating service in some form or another is not a recent phenomenon. Though no shadchan had an online presence until recently, the activity of this Jewish matchmaker appears very early in the recorded history of the Jews. But the dating service changes the nature of the office that the matchmaker performs, just as contemporary capitalism changes the nature of love. The dating service is a synecdoche for capitalist society as such. When I go to the dating service, I seek love as an object available for purchase, and this is the form in which love appears throughout the capitalist universe.

Love that one can purchase is no longer love, however. It is romance. Though capitalism appears to rely heavily on love, it necessitates a transformation from love to romance. This is capitalism's ideological operation in the domain of love. By transforming love into romance and thus into a commodity, capitalism provides respite from the trauma of love. Capitalist society loves to talk about love, but even as it does so, it remakes love, which involves an object that we can't have, into romance, which involves an object that we can.

The distinction between love and romance is essential for an analysis of the psychic appeal of capitalism. Romance domesticates the trauma of love, but it doesn't eliminate it altogether. Capitalism gives love such a central place in its workings and encourages subjects to devote so much of their time to it because the trauma of the love encounter enlivens them and keeps them going. Without the traumatic satisfaction that love provides, life often ceases to seem worth living. While it relies on love, capitalism must contain its fundamental disruptiveness and mitigate its trauma so that the capitalist system can continue to function. This is what the transformation from love to romance aims at accomplishing. Though love isn't a capitalist plot, romance is. Romance enables us to touch love's disruptiveness while avoiding its full traumatic ramifications.

OBTAINING WHAT YOU DON'T WANT

Both romance and love begin with desire. The subject sees an other that provokes its desire and hopes that this other will respond by reciprocating this desire. The difference between romance and love is that the former never leaves the terrain of desire. The subject seeking romance sees in the other the possibility of the realization of its desire and thereby reduces the love object to an object of desire. This is why romance inevitably produces disappointment.

Love, though it disturbs the subject, does not disappoint. In love, one can find satisfaction with the love object. But love also removes the subject from the terrain of desire. Though love necessarily begins with desire, it doesn't end there. When one falls in love, one falls for the other's way of enjoying itself, for the other's satisfaction with its own form of failure, its satisfaction with the absence of the object that would realize desire. Love targets the point at which the subject exceeds itself and is not self-identical. According to Joan Copjec, "when one loves something, one loves something in it that is more than itself, its nonidentity to itself."[5] We seek love to escape the constraints of our symbolic identity and to enjoy our nonidentity. In the act of love, one abandons oneself.

When one falls in love, one loses all sense of oneself and one's symbolic coordinates. Love is never a good investment for the subject, and this separates it definitively from romance. This is why capitalism necessitates the transformation of love into romance. This transformation allows us to love on the cheap. Many theorists of love, like Jacques Lacan and Alain Badiou, have remarked on love's inherent disruptiveness. But this is apparent as early as Plato's approach to the question of love.

The first great theorization of love occurs in Plato's *Symposium*. Here Plato recounts seven different versions of love that various characters in the dialogue describe in their speeches. The dialogue takes place at a banquet held in honor of Agathon, who has just won a prize for one of his tragedies. One of the participants, Eryximachus, proposes that instead of the typical entertainment they should each offer a speech in praise of love. Led by Socrates, all of the participants agree, and what follows in the dialogue are six distinct conceptions of the role that love plays in existence. When Alcibiades arrives late and disrupts the proceedings, he adds a seventh contribution after Socrates apparently has the final word.

The structure of the dialogue has occasioned much speculation about where the voice of Plato resides. Unlike more straightforward dialogues that follow a narrative trajectory (like the *Phaedo* or the *Republic*), there is no clear sense of development from one speech to the next. Each speech appears to stand on its own and have an intrinsic validity that the latter speeches do not often directly call into question. It is thus tempting to contend either that Plato is not taking a side or that he sides with Socrates, who is supposed to be the final speaker and often, of course, functions as Plato's stand-in. But the identification of Plato with Socrates is complicated by the role that two other characters play in the dialogue. Alcibiades intrudes and upsets Socrates' position as the source of the last word on love, and, what's more, it is Aristophanes, not Socrates, who offers the most sophisticated and memorable speech about love.[6]

Though many interpreters of Plato have clung to the Socratic discourse that associates love with knowledge, what stands out about the dialogue is not so much its content as its form, which is unique among Plato's dialogues. Through the formal structure, the dialogue offers the key to its content. The idea of love finds expression through disruptions that occur amid the dialogue. The key moments of the dialogue do not occur in any of the speeches but in the interruption of their continuity. By including these interruptions and giving them a prominent role in the dialogue's form, Plato creates an association of love itself with disruption. Love, for Plato, interrupts the everyday life and the stability of the subject. It confronts the subject with what doesn't respond in the way that the subject expects.

The first disruption in the *Symposium* occurs after Pausanias concludes his speech and gives the floor to Aristophanes. The latter is unable to take his proper turn due to a case of the hiccups. The hiccups mark a break within the announced program. Aristophanes must delay and allow to Eryximachus to take his place in the order. The speech of Eryximachus, who is a physician, has the effect (as he himself predicts) of curing Aristophanes of his hiccups, and Aristophanes is able to speak at length after Eryximachus finishes.

The second disruption occurs near the end of the dialogue after Socrates gives what we think will be the final speech. Once he concludes, Plato describes a drunken Alcibiades, shouting outside the house, who comes in to join the party. Eryximachus soon convinces Alcibiades to offer his own speech as the others have. Though he agrees, Alcibiades also changes the terms governing the speeches. He will praise Socrates himself rather than love. This praise of Socrates (which includes a great deal of critique) portrays him, even if Alcibiades is not aware of this, as incapable of love. Plato ends his dialogue about love with an instance of how love can fail.

Alcibiades proclaims his great desire for Socrates throughout his speech, and yet Socrates never responds to this desire with his own desire. What makes Socrates incapable of love, despite all the efforts of Alcibiades to seduce him, is the nature of his desire. As Plato portrays him, Socrates is a figure of purity, and it is his purity that acts as a barrier to love.[7] During his encomium to Socrates, Alcibiades stresses again and again the purity of Socrates. At one point, he claims, "Believe me, it couldn't matter less to him whether a boy is beautiful. You can't imagine how little he cares whether a person is beautiful, or rich, or famous or in any other way that most people admire. He considers all these possessions beneath contempt, and that's exactly how he considers all of us as well."[8] Socrates attaches himself to nothing and refuses the objects that others give themselves over to. As a figure of purity, he avoids succumbing to the disruptiveness of the other, and it is the ability to succumb to this disruptiveness that is the precondition for love.[9]

Plato ends the *Symposium* with Socrates walking off into the sunrise as his interlocutors all drift to sleep. This final image of the dialogue emphasizes the purity of his desire as well as his removal from the terrain of love. While Alcibiades portrays Socrates as incapable of love, his speech emphasizes the power of Socrates to disrupt his everyday life and make life unlivable for him. Though Alcibiades concludes the *Symposium* with an account of the failure of love, he does sustain the emphasis on disruption that manifests itself throughout the dialogue. For Plato, love resides in disruption.

The disruptions that mar the speeches on love occur in the form of the *Symposium*, but the content equally points to the disruption as the crucial ingredient in love. Love is never reducible to the image of harmony for any of Plato's speakers, which is what separates his conception from capitalism's idea of romance. Love emerges out of a disruption, and it lives on through dissymmetry. Even the speech of Aristophanes, which seems like a monument to harmony, actually illustrates the necessary dissymmetry in love. Aristophanes describes love as finding one's other half, which was lost through the cut introduced by Zeus, who found humans too self-satisfied when they were whole. But as Juan Pablo Lucchelli perspicaciously points out, the emphasis in the speech that Aristophanes gives is not on the achievement of perfect complementarity with one's missing half in love (a conception of love as finding one's soul mate) but on the cut that generates the search for the love object. The cut and the dissymmetry that it introduces are essential in Plato's vision of love.

This emphasis on dissymmetry holds not just in the speech of Aristophanes but throughout the dialogue. Though some conception of harmony appears in each speech, the sense of dissymmetry is always more significant. According to Lucchelli, "in the *Symposium*, at no moment is the asymmetry between the beloved and lover completely flattened. The whole dialogue turns around this gap and one could postulate that Plato held to it until the end, when the intervention of Alcibiades pushes this dissymmetry to the extreme."[10] The dissymmetry of love leaves the loving subject in a permanent condition of disruption, and yet this disruption is the source of the satisfaction that love provides. The subject in love enjoys its inability to stabilize its relation with the love object, and this is what Plato makes clear in the *Symposium*. It is the first great treatise of love because it is the first great treatise of disruption.

One can never have the love of the other because one loves what the other doesn't itself have. Even when the other desires us, something in the other remains outside our control. To subdue fully the otherness of the other and master it would effectively eliminate the other as a lovable entity. Thus, a successful love would destroy its object at the exact moment it achieved total success. Love always leaves the subject with a sense of its failure or incompletion, but this incompletion must be experienced as the indication of love's authenticity rather than its absence.

THE TREES OF ROMANCE AND THE FOREST OF LOVE

Though Plato remarkably theorizes the disruptiveness of love, most thinkers in the capitalist world fail to separate love from romance. Even important anticapitalist thinkers often fall into this trap. Though they grasp love's disruptiveness, they nonetheless theorize grasp the satisfaction that the subject finds in love. For such thinkers, love is inherently impossible because it never achieves the harmony that it promises. When we think of love in terms of romance, its failure becomes apparent, though we fail to think of this failure as love's form of success, which is precisely what Plato, in his own way, is able to do.

This problem of love preoccupies Jean-Paul Sartre and receives its most eloquent exposition in his chapter on "Concrete Relations with Others" in *Being and Nothingness*. According to Sartre, love necessarily involves the lover in an intractable contradiction. He claims, "Love is a contradictory effort to surmount the factual negation while preserving the internal negation. I demand that the Other love me and I do everything possible to realize my project; but if the Other loves me, he radically deceives me by his very love. I demanded of him that he should found my being as a privileged object by maintaining himself as pure subjectivity confronting me; and as soon as he loves me he experiences me as subject and is swallowed up in his objectivity confronting my subjectivity."[11] What Sartre diagnoses here is the impossibility of love modeled on the capitalist ideal of the accumulation of commodities. He doesn't see how love might accomplish the impossible and enable the lover to confront the beloved in the form of a loving subject. Love is a contradiction, and yet it occurs. But Sartre can only see it as an ontological impossibility because he imagines love as romance.[12]

Romance eliminates the lost object that predominates in love and replaces it with the object of desire. This flight from the lost object and from loss as such occurs throughout the capitalist universe, but nowhere is it as apparent as in the domain of love. In a love relationship, I cannot have the object but rather love the object through its absence. There is always something missing in love, which is what enables the love relation to endure. In love the subject confronts the incompletion of the beloved object, how this object is fundamentally at odds with itself. When one falls in love, it is precisely this noncoincidence of the beloved object with itself that triggers the fall. The apparently self-identical object, like a contact lens or a blow-up doll, is not an adequate object for love because it lacks the explicit self-division that makes love possible.[13]

Speaking subjects are not capable of love due to their superiority to other beings but due to the way in which language renders the subject's self-division explicit. One loves the failure of the beloved object to achieve self-identity and not any specific trait (except insofar as it embodies this failure). This is why someone genuinely in love cannot give the reasons for the love that she or he feels. Once there are reasons, one has left love and entered into romance. The self-division of the beloved object is the cause of love. This removes the beloved object completely from the terrain of the commodity with its initial promise of plenitude and subsequent disappointing lack. In a romance the object returns to this terrain and becomes obtainable, but, at the same time, it loses the lack that it has in love. Romance transforms the beloved object's self-division into an identifiable, positive trait the dating service can explicate and target for the would-be lover.

The transformation of love into romance attempts to keep love in the field of desire and fantasy. We alternate between these two, but we avoid the trauma of loving. The difference between desire and love concerns the response of the object. As long as we desire without loving, we remain on safe ground. We can pursue the lost object through a series of inadequate replacements and endure the disappointment that follows from each successful acquisition of the object, whether in the sex act or at the shopping mall.

Romance, in contrast to love, doesn't allow the subject to confront the beloved object as such. Once the beloved object has the status of a commodity that the subject can acquire, it paradoxically ceases to be attainable. Like every other commodity, the romantic object promises what it doesn't deliver. Even if one goes to the dating service with an exhaustive list of one's preferences, the commodity one obtains will inevitably be disappointing. In this precise sense, there is no difference between a romantic partner and a vacuum cleaner.

In *Love in the Western World*, Denis de Rougement was the first to theorize the distinction between love and romance. Though Rougement does not discuss romance explicitly as a commodity, his framing of this distinction already anticipates the association of romance with the logic of capitalism. For Rougement, we opt for romance over love in order to keep our desire alive. He notes, "unless the course of love is being hindered there is no 'romance'; and it is romance that we revel in—that is to say, the self-consciousness, intensity, variations, and delays of passion."[14] Romance here is the obstruction of love, the delay in its realization. Romance, as Rougement sees it, allows us to continue to desire and to avoid the act of love. By transforming love into romance, capitalist society allows us to continue desiring. We can treat the love object like any other commodity and thereby escape its exceptional danger.

Though we tend to associate monogamy with the repressive demands of capitalist society, one is almost tempted to call monogamy an anticapitalist practice. In contrast, the subject who moves from object to object in romantic life follows the logic of accumulation. Even if this subject avoids the capitalist fantasy and doesn't believe that any one object will have the final secret, it is often the equally compelling fantasy of quantity that drives this activity. One believes that accumulating a vast quantity of romantic objects will unlock the secret of the ultimate satisfaction, which is exactly the fantasy capitalism proffers.[15] But love, in contrast to romance, doesn't provide anything for the subject to accumulate. Instead of contributing to the subject's wealth, it takes away from it.

THE TRIP BEYOND NARCISSISM

Throughout most of his seminars, Jacques Lacan attacks love as a narcissistic illusion. When the subject loves, it places the other in exactly the same position that the ego occupies in the narcissistic relation. Both narcissism and love enable the subject to short-circuit the relationship with social authority while still remaining within the domain of that authority. One feels free without having to endure the groundlessness of actual freedom. Though he does see the possibility of an exception, Lacan says in a statement representative of his overall attitude, "love is only accessible on the condition that it remains always narrowly narcissistic."[16] While in love with someone else, one loves oneself through this other. No one feels like a narcissist when she or he loves, but this is just the result of love's deception. Nonetheless, narcissism is not the last word on love.

Even though love puts the other in the ego's stead, the relation is always rockier than the narcissistic one. Narcissism is ultimately a disappointing relation that the subject cannot indefinitely sustain, but the love object traumatizes the subject in a way the ego cannot. The ego is just an image, an ideal that the subject has constructed for itself, but in love the image is always incomplete. The other has the capacity to elicit the subject's love insofar as it remains irreducible to its image.

Initially, this irreducibility to the image provokes our desire. We desire what we can't see in the image on the basis of what we can. That is to say, the beloved object does not just remain a desired object. Our desire evokes the desire of the object, and love involves the encounter of these overlapping desires. The encounter with the desire emanating from the beloved object transforms love into an experience different from desire. Desire enables the subject to remain at a distance that love obliterates. Herein lies the radicality of love in relation to desire.

The beloved object's response gives love its disruptiveness. In love, what we can't see reaches back toward us. This is a point that Lacan makes in his seminar devoted to the phenomenon of the transference (and a lengthy reading of Plato's *Symposium*), which includes his most sustained discussion of love. He claims, "love is what passes in this object toward which we hold out our hand through our own desire, and which, at the moment when our desire makes its fire break out, allows for an instant this response to appear to us, this other hand that is held out toward us as the other's desire."[17] Where desire encounters the illusion of an object at the point where it expected something substantial, love encounters what it didn't expect to encounter.[18]

The response from the beloved—"the hand held out toward us"—jolts the subject out of its everyday existence. One cannot predict this moment or work to bring it into being, and it thus appears as a secular miracle. In love the object does not stay in its proper position. The response to desire forces the subject to change its life entirely without any clear guidance as to how it should do so. Inasmuch as it strips away all possibility of an ordinary life, love suffuses the subject with satisfaction. Life no longer just goes on.

Love in an act of proximity. The lover refuses to remain at a safe distance and bombards the subject with its mode of satisfaction, a mode of satisfaction around which the subject must try to orient itself. This satisfaction is what we almost always recoil from, but in the act of love we embrace it. This is why lovers can accompany each other in the most private moments: they can tell each other their most revelatory dreams or allow the other into the bathroom with them. What would alienate or even repulse everyone else becomes integral to the love relation.

We know that someone is in love when the beloved's most repellant qualities undergo a complete reversal of valence. A person's unpleasant smell, slovenly attire, or obnoxious eating habits become appealing quirks rather than reasons for keeping a distance. The lover embraces the most unflattering characteristics of the beloved and treats them as sublime indexes of the beloved's worth. The unpleasant odor resulting from a refusal to shower, for instance, would become an indication of the beloved object's disdain for obsessive daily rituals with which others waste their time. There is no quality so universally negative that it could not undergo this transubstantiation in the act of love: fat can become cuddliness, emaciation can become fitness, bad attire can become idiosyncratic style, and so on. In contrast to desire, love depends on the embrace of what is undesirable in the object.[19]

In *Being and Event* and elsewhere throughout his philosophy, Alain Badiou grants love an evental status, locating it among what he calls the four truth procedures. This inclusion of love seems anomalous. In comparison with the other three truth procedures, love doesn't fit in. When one reads *Being and Event* for the first time, one can't help but feel that the conception of the love event represents a philosophical misstep on Badiou's part, a case where he allowed his own private emotions to have an undue impact on his philosophy. Though Badiou may like the feeling of being in love, this hardly justifies its status as a truth procedure.

Unlike politics, art, and science, love seems to be an isolated phenomenon. A love event—the relationship of Jill and Dave, for instance—doesn't have the same world-historical impact as the French Revolution or the invention of twelve-tone music (examples of the political and artistic event from Badiou). Even a love event that garners great attention, like the affair between Héloïse d'Argenteuil and Peter Abélard, fails to produces the type of substantive changes accomplished by the storming of the Bastille.

But Badiou classifies love alongside the other truth procedures for its disruptiveness of everyday life and—which is in some sense to say the same thing—for its ability to arouse the subject's passion. Love may be an anomalous truth procedure, but perhaps this is because it is the paradigmatic truth procedure. Love's disruption of our everyday life is much more palpable than that of politics, art, or science. The subject in love feels as if it can't exist without the beloved, while even Galileo himself didn't feel this strongly about the scientific event in which he participated. It is much easier to imagine subjects dying for the sake of love than for the sake of the twelve-tone system of modern music. This is because love has a disruptiveness that transcends the other truth procedures.

The cynical approach to love fails to register this disruptiveness. According to Badiou, the cynic contends that "love is only a variant of generalized hedonism," and this cynicism enables one to avoid "every profound and authentic experience of otherness from which love is woven."[20] Dismissing the reality of love—seeing it as just a capitalist plot—is a way of avoiding the transformation that it demands, but it also leaves one's existence bereft of significance.[21] The passion that love arouses impels subjects to continue to go on.

Capitalist society's packaging of love as romance aims at eliminating the disruptiveness of love while sustaining its passion. This is an impossible task, and the love of the capitalist subject is always a diminished love insofar as it's safer. Romance under capitalism is a form of investment, and even a risky investment, as romance sometimes is, remains within the calculus of risk and loss. Love transcends any calculus and forces the subject to abandon its identity entirely, not simply stake its reputation or its fortune.

LEAVING THE NINETY-NINE FOR THE ONE

The risk that occurs in love stems from the status the lover grants to the beloved. The beloved ceases to be just another object that the lover desires and takes the place of social authority itself. When I love the other, I want to count for this other more than any recognition that might come from society at large. I want to matter more than everyone else put together.[22] For the lover, the other must value her or him not just above all else, but she or he must replace all else as the basis for the calculation of value. To put it in the terms of psychoanalysis, love demands that the little other take over the function of the big Other.

As a result of this change, those in love care much less about how others outside of the beloved see them. They are willing to act strangely in public or draw attention to themselves in embarrassing ways because the only recognition that counts is that bestowed by the beloved. Lovers in high school have no problem engaging in officially prohibited public displays of affection because they represent the only real authority for each other. School officials' interdiction of suggestive kissing or touching during school hours bespeaks their recognition that such displays explicitly call their authority into question. The social authority undergoes a radical diminution in its capacity to grant recognition when someone is in love. This transformation grants enormous power to the beloved and, at the same time, lessens the power of the social order over the subject.[23]

This explains the disdain that both Romeo and Juliet show for the most entrenched feeling of their respective families. Even though their love requires them to abandon the hatred their families have preached throughout their entire lives, Romeo and Juliet have no problem taking this step. The family as a figure of social authority becomes simply an external obstacle that they must navigate, not a psychic barrier to their love. This is because, for each, the family simply ceases to matter. Romeo and Juliet will go to any length, including the betrayal of their family traditions, for the love of the other.

Degrading oneself for the sake of the beloved reveals the disruptiveness of the love relation. The person in love agrees to sacrifice social identity for the sake of winning the other's love. When in love, all other considerations disappear before the response of the beloved. This experience of a complete loss of one's usual coordinates is at once the appeal and the trauma of love. Though we tend to think of love as a pleasant experience, it actually produces much more suffering than pleasure. We feel pleasure when our lives move along smoothly and with relative security, but love is always rocky and insecure. As we fall in love, we can never be sure if the other truly loves us in return, and we spend our time worrying about what the other is doing. This is why it is easy to picture the lover phoning a beloved an abundance of times when there is no answer. The lover experiences of the trauma of love with each unrequited phone call.[24] Life no longer just goes on when we love. Instead, it bombards us with a series of traumatic jolts that preclude any peace of mind. Our very symbolic identity loses its stable coordinates.

But in the ideology of romance this loss of identity becomes an investment that one makes in the future secure possession of the romantic object. Romance promises that the initial trauma will lead to a stable relation, and it offers the lover a new symbolic identity. One can become a husband or a wife or a spouse: in each case, the subject gains recognition from the romantic attachment. Rather than sustaining the disruption, we turn it into an investment and move on to the possession of the object.

Not only does romance transform love into an investment, but it plays a crucial role in the development of capitalism by suggesting to consumers that they can find the perfect commodity, the commodity that will create wholeness for them. Every act of consumption has its basis in an attempt to access the lost object, to find the perfect commodity that would provide an ultimate and lasting satisfaction. Although this fantasy underlies every purchase of a commodity, with most commodities we see easily through the illusion. Very few buy a roll of toilet paper thinking that they've found their lost object once and for all. With a Twinkie, the fantasy becomes more tenable. But with a romantic object, one can fully invest oneself in the promise of the object. Romance immerses subjects in the capitalist fantasy of the perfectly satisfying commodity, and this commodity has a precise name—the soul mate.

When we talk about finding or having found our soul mate (if we do), we do not believe ourselves to be immersed in the capitalist economy. But this is an even more important terrain for capitalism than the convenience store where we buy a soda and candy bar or the stock exchange floor where companies are financed. The idea of the soul mate plays a crucial role in the promulgation of consumption. If I believe that a perfect commodity exists in the romantic field, this changes my relationship to all commodities. Commodities become more attractive insofar as each one stands in for the perfect partner. Though a hammer at the hardware store most likely cannot function as my soul mate, I will find more pleasure in purchasing it with the idea of an ideal commodity informing the purchase, and this is what the soul mate provides. That is to say, the idea of the soul mate underwrites all consumption within the capitalist universe.

The soul mate is the commodity in the form of the subject's complement. This is why the idea of the soul mate has such importance for capitalism. The subject experiences itself as lacking whenever it desires, and no object can fill this lack. But the promise of the soul mate is the promise of completion, an object that would complement the lacking subject perfectly and thereby ameliorate its lack. No such complement exists outside of ideological fantasies, but capitalism requires subjects who invest themselves in such fantasies.[25]

ROMANTIC COMEDIES AND LOVE COMEDIES

The romantic comedy genre is constructed around the idea that love is a good investment, that love is reducible to romance and the acquisition of the soul mate. Though such films often show love to be inconvenient, difficult, or disruptive, they always conclude with a sense that love helps one turn a profit in terms of social (and often financial) status. It is almost impossible for love to cost someone either social recognition or economic well-being within the universe of the romantic comedy. Romantic comedies play with the traumatic impact of love, but they almost inevitably conclude by eliminating this trauma for the sake of a romantic bargain.[26]

The attitude that the romantic comedy takes toward love—its romanticization of love or transformation of love into a commodity—manifests itself in the montage sequences that populate almost every entry in the genre.[27] Typically, the montage shows the couple just after the relationship begins as they are starting to fall in love. We see them walking in the park, eating in a restaurant, feeding each other ice cream, going to the movies, or even having sex. What is striking about these montage sequences is that they elide the part of the relationship that is the most exciting—the act of falling in love itself. They show the couple falling in love, but they do so in a montage that minimizes rather than extends the time that this takes. If Hollywood usually takes seriously Alfred Hitchcock's legendary claim that "movies are real life with the boring parts cut out," then the elision of the initial stages of relationships seems shocking. As anyone who has fallen in love knows, the beginning is not the boring part.

Romantic comedies sacrifice this initial excitement in order to pass quickly over the traumatic disturbance that occurs when couples fall in love. The act of falling in love disrupts every aspect of one's life. Even the quotidian details of one's life become charged with anticipation and concern. By compressing this traumatic time in a montage sequence, the romantic comedy assures us that love can take place without any traumatic disruption. Love can simply be romance.[28]

If we look at the most famous romantic comedy starring Julia Roberts, we can examine the romanticization of love in an almost pure form. *Pretty Woman* (Garry Marshall, 1990) depicts Roberts in her breakout role as prostitute Vivian Ward who falls in love with a rich client, Edward Lewis (Richard Gere). Initially, the recently single multimillionaire Edward hires Vivian to accompany him rather than have sex with him, and they subsequently fall in love during a week together. The film ends, as this genre almost always does, with their romantic union. Though Edward's friends balk at his relationship with a prostitute, and his commitment to her flags at times during the film, he decides in the end to become her partner rather than her client. The relationship has the effect of pulling Vivian out of her working-class position as a prostitute and into the upper class. Falling in love doesn't disrupt her social identity and class status but dramatically lifts both. Love, for Vivian, is a good investment.

Of course, Edward falls in love with Vivian because she doesn't seem to be looking to him for social advancement. Despite his suspicions at one point, she doesn't value him for his social utility but simply falls in love with him. The film insists on the authenticity of Vivian's love for Edward, but at the same time, it does depict her receiving clear monetary and social rewards for this love. Edward forces store employees to treat her like a wealthy client rather than a working-class prostitute, and he also takes her to dine in fine restaurants. When he comes for her at the end of the film, he does so in a limousine. Even though Vivian is not trying to profit from love, she does, and this is the point that the film highlights. Within the dictates of capitalism, love becomes profitable even when we don't enter it looking for a profit. The logic of capitalism permeates the disruptiveness of love and transforms it into romance.

But *Pretty Woman* cannot entirely avoid a depiction of love's disruptiveness and remain an enjoyable film. If love were only romance in the film, it would not remain one of the most appreciated romantic comedies in the history of Hollywood. There must be a kernel of authentic love in even the most ideological romances, or else they would fail entirely. These fragments of authenticity are evident when we see Edward's friend Philip Stuckey (Jason Alexander) make sexual advances on Vivian when he learns of her occupation. Though Vivian rebuffs him, his action eventually forces Edward to abandon him as a friend. Edward's love for Vivian has the same effect on her: she loses her connection with her best friend and roommate Kit (Laura San Giacomo) because of her relationship with Edward. Though the film minimizes these disruptions, it nonetheless includes them as indications of the effect of love. Love is primarily romance in *Pretty Woman*, but there are points at which love manifests itself.

If *Pretty Woman* establishes Julia Roberts as a Hollywood star, *Notting Hill* (Roger Michell, 1999) makes use of this status. Unlike the earlier film, it emphasizes the persistence of the love object even where it appears most evidently to be a romantic commodity. Whereas *Pretty Woman* depicts Roberts as an inexpensive commodity in the form of a prostitute, in *Notting Hill* she is Anna Scott, the most famous actress in the world, and she meets William (Hugh Grant) when she walks into his London bookshop. In the same way that Edward is a good investment for Vivian, Anna is a good investment for William, and this seems a driving force of his attraction to her. But *Notting Hill* makes clear that love disrupts the lives of both subjects involved and isn't such a good investment after all.

William commits himself to Anna completely, but he continually discovers what he doesn't expect to find. Even though Anna is a fantasy object for William and the other characters in the film, she doesn't fit smoothly into his daily life. Whenever their relationship seems to gain a foothold, she abandons him or inadvertently reminds him of his lesser social status. For instance, when she invites him to visit her hotel, he comes expecting to spend time alone with her. But he arrives amid press interviews for Anna's new film, and he must talk to her in the guise of a journalist interviewing a film star. When Anna finally professes her love for William, he has her earlier abandonments in mind and rejects her, not wanting to submit himself to another trauma. Though he eventually tracks Anna down and makes it clear to her that he has changed his mind, this first rejection reveals the danger associated with Anna's love for William.

For her part, love with William forces Anna to endure public exposure: the legions of reporters that follow her see her leaving William's apartment, and this creates a huge scandal. The film concludes with her implicit declaration of love for him at a press conference. Throughout the film, Anna seeks privacy and refuge from the public, but in order to love William, she must abandon herself to the public's look. She has to give up her insistence on having a private life removed from the public world. To be in love is to be seen in a way that we don't want to be seen, and nowhere is this clearer than in the case of Anna Scott in *Notting Hill*. In this sense, she represents the counterpart of Vivian in *Pretty Woman*, who concludes the film being seen just as she wants to be.

The romantic comedy may be the most ideological genre that Hollywood produces, but it also has its moments where authentic love breaks through. Love works against the logic of acquisition that dominates the capitalist universe, and if acquisition of the object takes place at the conclusion of almost every romantic comedy, there are also occasions when characters must confront the other's lack along with their own. When this happens, the romantic comedy becomes a love comedy and ceases to be the ideological handmaiden of the capitalist universe that produced it.

The replacement of love with romance reduces the danger involved with love. Though one still replaces the social authority with an individual other, this other, within the logic of romance, has the endorsement of the social authority. Thus transformed, love can make the lover feel better about her or his social status while in love, while authentic love should render the question of social status insignificant. The subject in love abandons the recognition of the Other or social authority for the recognition of the love object. Romance dilutes this act by replacing the love object with a socially authorized object. The result is an impoverished form of love—love without the traumatic core that makes love worth experiencing.[29]

It is easy to see how the capitalist system uses love as a marketing strategy and as a model for all accumulation. In the midst of this transformation of love into romance, it is difficult to keep sight of love's disruptiveness. Capitalism delivers us from it while simultaneously permitting us to believe that we remain within the orbit of love. But in the process, it robs us of the events that make our life worth living. Opting for romance instead of love is the profitable choice, but it costs us everything.

[9]

Abundance and Scarcity

THE CAPITALIST SINE QUA NON

Though within the capitalist universe we tend to think of scarcity as the natural condition of humanity, many societies have existed on the earth without this threat constantly hanging over them. The original form of human society—the hunting and gathering society—was a society of abundance that dealt with only occasional bouts of scarcity rather than the constant threat that haunts us today.[1] The ease of finding food and shelter often allowed for a degree of abundance absent among all but the extremely wealthy within capitalism. But once capitalism arises, the threat of scarcity becomes the background against which exchange takes place.

Capitalism doesn't require that scarcity is real—that there isn't enough for everyone to have what they need to survive and find satisfaction—but it does demand that the threat of scarcity be credible. If subjects know that they can find an enjoyable life without capitalist relations of production, they will have no incentive to enter into these relations. Capitalism depends on the subject's sense of insecurity and on the belief that an absence of plentiful resources looms just around the corner. Living under capitalism means living with this constant threat and thus in perpetual unease about tomorrow. This is one of the lures with which capitalism seduces its subjects.

Though we imagine that scarcity and insecurity are what we seek to avoid, they actually provide an integral part of capitalism's appeal. When we exist in a state of perpetual insecurity or scarcity, we can posit an external obstacle—the source of our insecurity—as the barrier to our satisfaction. In this way, we avoid confronting the internal obstacle that prevents complete satisfaction. By ensconcing us in scarcity, capitalism enables us to avoid the trauma of an always partial satisfaction.

One of the principal justifications for a capitalist economy is the limited quantity of natural resources. The inequalities generated by the market offer a way of dividing up the resources that the natural world provides without recourse to physical violence.[2] If the natural world were abundant, there would be no need for capitalism's unflagging effort to squeeze the maximum productivity out of labor for the least possible cost. There would be no need for competition. This is why all proponents of capitalism presuppose scarcity. Without this presupposition, the desire to accumulate would undergo a radical transformation.[3]

The role that scarcity plays in capitalism becomes evident as capitalist economists work out the variegations of the market. In his *Principles of Political Economy and Taxation*, David Ricardo develops his version of a labor theory of value and theorizes profit within the contours of this theory. As he does so, he includes the assumption that "the laws of nature . . . have limited the productive powers of the land."[4] Ricardo never develops a proof for natural scarcity, but simply asserts it as a given. He refuses to countenance the possibility that the productive powers of humanity might increase to such an extent that this natural scarcity, even if it exists now, might be overcome. For him, natural scarcity must have the status of an immutable law. This is a presupposition that he shares with every other defender of capitalism. There are no exceptions.[5]

In fact, economics as a science only develops on the basis of scarcity. It doesn't exist prior to the capitalist epoch, and its calculations about human behavior depend on the idea that the world is not abundant or plentiful.[6] Economists can make mathematical calculations about the functioning of markets because they know that there are a limited number of resources that society must distribute. If these resources were unlimited, economic equations would become instantly incalculable. It would be as if one placed a zero in the denominator of a fraction: division of resources only makes sense as long as we have a finite amount to divide.

Capitalist economist Lionel Robbins, for one, claims straightforwardly that scarcity is the sine qua non of economic science. He says, "Everywhere we turn, if we choose one thing we must relinquish others which, in different circumstances, we would not wish to have relinquished. Scarcity of means to satisfy ends of varying importance is an almost ubiquitous condition of human behaviour."[7] If nature provided abundance or society achieved it, there would be no struggle to allocate resources and no need to distribute them unevenly. Capitalism would have no place in the abundant world. In other words, if scarcity didn't exist, capitalism would have to invent it. And when scarcity begins to disappear, capitalism does embark on the task of reinventing it over and over again. Arguing on behalf of capitalism requires an investment in the inevitability of scarcity as an article of the faith.[8]

But just as the defenders of capitalism cling to scarcity as an absolute presupposition of existence, they also present capitalism as a solution to scarcity. If we stick to its demands, capitalism will lead us out of the desert of scarcity to the promised land of abundance. As a solution to scarcity, capitalism's investment in the promise becomes clear. It is the promise of a better future with no possibility for the fulfillment of that promise. As far into the future as we can plan, resources will be scarce, though we can imagine a time when they won't be.

This contradiction besets every attempt to champion the capitalist future, but nowhere does it become as clear as in the thought of Deirdre McCloskey.[9] McCloskey's project champions the virtues that capitalism produces along with material wealth. In contrast to those who lament capitalism's deleterious effect on morality, McCloskey highlights its moral benefits and sees the malfeasance of investment bankers as a betrayal of the capitalist ethic rather than its expression. Like Ricardo, she emphasizes that "scarcity in your own life seems essential for a real human life."[10] Without scarcity, we would cease to strive and thereby cease to be virtuous.

But this belief in the necessity of scarcity doesn't prevent McCloskey from speculating on what would happen if we simply left people alone "to buy low and sell high."[11] The result would be not just "material abundance" but also "the scope to flourish in higher things" and a society of virtue. She proclaims, "We can have . . . a spiritual life untrammeled by need, a clean planet, long and happy lives. By the standards typical since Adam's curse we can have by the year 2100 another Eden."[12] Though McCloskey admits the dangerous utopian tenor of these remarks, their presence within her book, along with the statement about the necessary role of scarcity in human existence, exposes the intricate relation between scarcity and abundance that capitalism necessitates. One must have an untrammeled belief in natural scarcity and an equally powerful faith in the market's capacity for ameliorating that scarcity in a far-off future. McCloskey is not simply an ideologue trying to advance a doctrine that she knows to be at odds with itself. Instead, she gives voice to a position that emanates from the contradictions of the capitalist system.

Though McCloskey describes a brief account of the capitalist utopia, her main interest lies in exploring the virtues produced by the demands that scarcity places on us. Scarcity is the justification for capitalism, and capitalism makes us hardworking and virtuous. What she doesn't explain—and what no polemicist for capitalism explains—is why this image of the human condition wins adherents. When compared with the idea of shared abundance that most versions of communism or socialism proffer, capitalism appears to be a less appealing economic system. Who would opt for a philosophy of scarcity when they might have instead a philosophy of abundance? The answer would seem to be that people have simply found the former to fit reality in a way the latter does not. But this implies that adherents choose their philosophies based on their correspondence to reality and not on the satisfaction that they offer. It is my contention, however, that the psychic attraction that capitalism exerts stems in large part from the essential role scarcity plays within its theorization. We are drawn to capitalism in large part because it enables us to avoid thinking about the horror of abundance or postscarcity. Scarcity might be physically frightening, but it is not inherently traumatic. Scarcity is a psychically appealing presupposition, and the fact that capitalism requires this presupposition is part of its attraction for us.

Though we typically associate trauma with scarcity, there is nothing inherently traumatic for the psyche about not having enough. Trauma is not a category of survival. If I don't have enough to eat and almost starve to death or if I don't have any shelter from the cold and almost freeze to death, these are not inherently traumatic experiences. In each case, I suffer from not having needs fulfilled, but this suffering can take place without trauma, though of course it usually doesn't. It is necessary to make a fundamental distinction between physical suffering and psychic trauma. Though they often accompany each other, we cannot reduce trauma to physical suffering. Doing so plays directly into the hands of capitalist ideology, which posits us as beings pursuing our survival and advancing our self-interest.

Though we associate scarcity with trauma and obviously experience trauma in certain times of scarcity, it is the hidden excess in the situation of scarcity that is the real source of the trauma. We experience trauma not just when we are hungry but when someone deprives us of food, not just when we are cold but when we cannot pay the heating bill. No one experiences trauma in complete isolation, but only in relation to others, even if these others are only fantasy objects, and this is why it is not the result of some ontological scarcity that rules as the natural state of things. Trauma depends on a psychic experience of excess, not a lived experience of scarcity.[13]

The groundbreaking insight of psychoanalysis lies in its association of trauma with excess rather than with scarcity. Prior to Freud, thinkers for the most part pictured human life as a struggle with scarcity. But Freud entered the scene and showed how excess—specifically, excessive sexuality—disturbs the psyche in a way that scarcity doesn't. All of Freud's patients experienced an overabundance of sexual stimulus that they couldn't integrate into their psychic lives. These encounters with abundance initially led Freud to the development of the seduction theory, but he soon abandoned this theory when he understood that the encounter with abundance was psychic rather than physical and thus could occur purely on the level of fantasy.[14] For psychoanalysis, the terrain of the battle shifts: we don't fight over limited resources but struggle over how to deal with the trauma of abundance. Unlike psychoanalysis, capitalism provides an avenue for escaping the trauma of overabundance by assuring us that scarcity is the intractable background against which we act. But the idea of natural scarcity is ideological.

TOO MUCH IS REALLY TOO MUCH

In a time of abundance, it is no longer possible to sustain the illusion of an ultimate satisfaction. The benefit of scarcity lies in the justification that it provides: if it weren't for the scarcity, we believe, we could access the ultimate satisfaction, and we can anticipate it when we overcome scarcity. In this sense, scarcity functions in relation to abundance just like prohibition works in relation to impossibility. The lost object is impossible—if we obtain it, we find that we have missed it—and yet the law bars access to this object. In exactly the same way, scarcity hides the impossibility of an ultimate enjoyment that becomes evident through abundance. The barrier to this enjoyment is internal rather than external, which is why it is impossible, no matter how securely we have the object. The idea of scarcity allows us to continue to see ourselves as externally limited rather than internally limited subjects.

In addition to hiding our satisfaction from us, scarcity also obscures the nature of that satisfaction, translating it from the subject's relation to its lost object into a relation with the other. In a world governed by scarcity, the other becomes a mortal threat to my satisfaction. That is to say, scarcity produces envy. I see the cause of my lack in the other's excess. I envy the other's enjoyment and believe that this enjoyment comes at my expense. But I also see my excess as the cause of the other's lack. I enjoy myself insofar as the other does not. The connection that scarcity produces is not a positive connection through a shared object but a negative one. Even though the other appears as a threat to my enjoyment, we connect through our mutual envy. The firefighter envies the riches of the stockbroker, who, in turn, envies the celebrity of the rock star. This circle of envy knows no end in the world of scarcity, but it links subjects to each other and creates an intimate concern with the other's mode of satisfaction. An abundant world precludes this mode of satisfaction and leaves us on our own.

Ironically, abundance isolates us psychically in a way that scarcity does not. Though utopians tend to imagine a future of abundance would make true community possible, scarcity is the glue that holds a social order together, and a world of abundance would have no such societal glue.[15] The lack that scarcity produces in subjects focuses their attention and their desire on what others seem to have, and this creates the social link. Without this sense of lack and with a sense of abundance, there would be no reason to turn toward the other.

When I have enough to achieve self-satisfaction, I no longer look to the other with envy; I don't imagine that the other's satisfaction comes at my expense. I can coexist alongside the trauma of the other's enjoyment because I can accept that this satisfaction and mine are not mutually exclusive. The idea of abundance holds an enormous appeal for us. Almost every vision of the afterlife focuses on the abundance awaiting the believer. Whether it is gardens of flowing streams or streets of gold, the afterlife has abundance as its necessary condition. This is an index of our mode of fantasizing. Our fantasies include the possibility of having more than enough of what we desire. But abundance isn't as desirable as we imagine it to be, which is why visions of the afterlife always remain bizarrely vague—the Qur'an, for instance, never goes beyond the image of everlasting life in gardens of flowing streams accompanied by pure wives—and why our fantasies never present abundance in an unalloyed form, that is, without a corresponding vision of scarcity.[16]

It is impossible for us to fantasize pure abundance. We can produce a fleeting image of it, as the Qur'an does, but fantasy requires the staging of lack alongside abundance in order to render it palatable. Fantasy doesn't simply stage loss in order to present its transformation into abundance, but loss provides the source of the satisfaction that the subject finds in the fantasy scenario. The scenario often depicts the loss and recovery of the object, but the illusion is attached to the loss itself, which implies that the subject once had the lost object. Fantasy creates an image of abundance prior to scarcity, and this allows it to fulfill its fundamental task.

The task of fantasy is envisioning the possibility of a complete satisfaction that the subject can never experience. As Juan-David Nasio notes, "The function of the fantasy is to substitute for an impossible real satisfaction a possible fantasized satisfaction."[17] Outside of fantasy, the subject never overcomes loss because loss constitutes the subject as a subject. Overcoming loss would require the powers of Baron von Munchausen, not those of a mere subject. The subject experiences satisfaction through the mediation of the constitutive loss that makes both the subject and its satisfaction possible. But fantasy shows the subject moving from loss to satisfaction and from satisfaction to loss, allowing the subject to believe in the possibility of getting rid of loss once and for all (even as it relies on loss to depict this possibility).

Capitalism does not just employ fantasy in order to seduce subjects into investing themselves in the capitalist system. The relationship is isomorphic. As a socioeconomic system, capitalism shares the formal structure of fantasy: it introduces a cause for scarcity (the natural competition for resources) that retroactively creates the illusion of a lost original abundance, and then it provides a solution (unbridled capitalist accumulation) that will lead to future abundance. As with fantasy, the structure deceives us concerning the location of the satisfaction. We believe that we work toward a future abundance that equates with unalloyed satisfaction, but the satisfaction capitalism produces occurs during the time of supposed scarcity.

It is none other than Adam Smith who lays bare the deception involved in capitalism's ideal of future satisfaction associated with abundance. As I noted earlier in the discussion of the invisible hand in Smith's work, Smith claims, in *The Theory of Moral Sentiments*, that nature deceives us about the rewards of wealth. We look at the wealthy, and we think that they find pleasure in their wealth. But they don't find much "real satisfaction" at all but are instead mired in a situation that is "in the highest degree contemptible and trifling."[18] Despite the contempt that Smith feels for the lives of the wealthy, he sees the deception concerning this lifestyle as a necessary and productive one. He contends that this illusion "rouses and keeps in continual motion the industry of mankind."[19] Though individual capitalists may consciously believe that they invest for the sake of future wealth, the enjoyment that this wealth promises is just a lie. Smith has no theory of the unconscious, but what he describes is essentially an unconscious process. Individual capitalists act without knowing what they're doing, and the system survives and prospers on the basis of this ignorance.

As individuals invested in the capitalist system, we may believe that we are doggedly in pursuit of future abundance as we endure the present scarcity, but it is actually the struggle with scarcity that appeals to us. We find unconscious satisfaction in scarcity, while our conscious thoughts focus on abundance. We need to presuppose both the existence of this scarcity and the possibility of its future elimination for us in order to continue to struggle within the determinants of the capitalist system. If we give up the fantasy of either present scarcity or the illusion of future abundance, we give up capitalism as such.

But capitalism does not have a monopoly on the ability to access the fantasy structure. We can see evidence of a similar proclivity among the partisans of socialism and communism. Socialism and communism have oscillated between the direct promise of abundance from figures like Charles Fourier and Robert Owen and the appeal for enduring a time of scarcity for a future of abundance. This is the position that V. I. Lenin and Rosa Luxemburg, among many others in the twentieth century, take up. Ironically, it is when proponents of communism call for direct access to abundance that they fail to produce an adequate fantasy scenario. Lenin's adherents require the alibi of a future classless society, but this image of abundance is not the nodal point of the Leninist fantasy. The follower of Lenin identifies with struggle that occurs in the scarcity of the present. The satisfaction one derives from being a Leninist derives from this struggle, not from the abundance promised in the future. Because scarcity had a role in the fantasy that Lenin proffered, he could mobilize people to struggle for abundance.[20]

Utopian socialists like Fourier and Owen don't offer their followers a fantasy path toward enjoying the abundance that they promise. By portraying abundance as accessible apart from scarcity, they destroy the possibility for finding abundance satisfying. This is the reason for the abject failure of every utopian project: such projects fail to include the struggle with lack into their conception of abundance. A world in which one can have whatever one wants crashes on the very way that the subject achieves its satisfaction. If subjects lack any lack, they will create it in order to carve out a path to satisfaction. The subject's self-destructiveness—its proclivity for ruinous acts when life is going well—stems from an unconscious recognition of the stultifying nature of abundance.[21] We don't engage in self-destructive acts because we are stupid but because such self-destruction enables us to enjoy our loss by reinstalling or reaffirming this loss. We will do whatever it takes to avoid a situation of abundance, which is what all the utopian projects of the nineteenth century failed to take into account. Even the rivalries that develop between members of a commune bespeak the subject's effort to introduce loss and scarcity into plenitude.[22]

It is the creation of scarcity in times of abundance that leads to the revolutionary turn in Freud's thought in 1920. Freud comes to recognize that the subject cannot endure abundance, that it does not simply obey the dictates of the pleasure principle. When things are going well and we are experiencing pleasure, we sabotage ourselves and reintroduce loss into the situation. Freud finds this dynamic at work in analysis itself: when patients come to the brink of a successful cure, they find a way to derail the analysis and delay the cure. This "negative therapeutic reaction" is not the result of an inability to recognize therapy's success but an unconscious awareness that success stifles us and failure enables us to continue.

Capitalism as an economic system thrives on the essential role played by failure in the subject's satisfaction. Without our enjoyment of failure and our constitutive allergy to success, capitalism would never have developed. Although champions of the capitalist system preach success and the system's most fervent defenders are the successful rather than the downtrodden, their professions of success mask the key role that failure has in the system. Just on a psychic level, a sense of failure or dissatisfaction drives the capitalist to create new products or find new markets for existing products, and it prompts the consumer to purchase new commodities. The system itself expands because failure functions as an economic engine for individual capitalist and consumers. Even those who are successful find motivation in the fear of future failure. Scarcity is always just around the corner.

Though they consciously seek economic success or a fully satisfying commodity, the actions of both capitalists and consumers, like the actions of Freud's patients, give the lie to this conscious impulse. In every case an unconscious desire trumps the conscious will. The capitalist continues to produce to the point of failure, and the consumer continues to purchase commodities that never bring a complete satisfaction. Whenever we flirt with abundance, we find our way back to scarcity. Scarcity isn't natural but is, nonetheless, a necessity for the subject.

THE DIFFICULTIES OF SUSTAINING SCARCITY

The desire for sustaining scarcity becomes most evident when we consider the phenomenon of the economic crisis. The theorists of capitalism—both apologists and critics alike—run into their gravest difficulties when they try to explain the business cycle. As Paul Krugman notes, it triggers "many of them to produce their worst work."[23] Within Marxism, the problem of the business cycle has proven a notorious sticking point, as Marxist theorists move from the business cycle to the demise of capitalism without explaining the possibility of recovery that leaves capitalism healthier than it was before. Though there are many

Marxist explanations for the business cycle, they tend to have difficulty accounting for the productive burst that occurs from amid recession and depression because they most often theorize the measures that capitalism takes to deal with downturns as rearguard actions.[24]

Capitalism doesn't recover from economic downturns just by meagerly limping along in a degraded state. Downturns often lead to tremendous outbursts of unprecedented productivity, which is what occurred in the aftermath of the Great Depression. Just at the moment when capitalism seemed in its death throes, it rebounded with an unforeseen vigor. This phenomenon demonstrated conclusively that the business cycle itself would not destroy capitalism and thus necessitated a revaluation of orthodox Marxist thinking about capitalist development.[25] But the business cycle is no easier for non-Marxists to explain.

Both John Maynard Keynes and Milton Friedman offer competing accounts of the business cycle that have attracted numerous devotees, but in each case the description of how the cycle actually begins remains cloudy. For Keynes, the downturn in the business cycle stems from a dimming of what he calls the "animal spirits," that is, our tendency to passionately engage in the world with hope for the future. He claims, "if the animal spirits are dimmed and the spontaneous optimism falters, leaving us to depend on nothing but a mathematical expectation, enterprise will fade and die;—though fears of loss may have a basis no more reasonable than hopes of profit had before."[26] Our animal spirits gain their spiritedness from witnessing the passions of others engaged in acts of production. Thus, these spirits wane when we see others beginning to save rather than invest.

Our productivity depends, according to Keynes, not just on a belief that we will profit from our investment but also from witnessing others engaged in the activity of producing. It is as if production requires subjects to act against their own spontaneous inclination, and the motivation for this action comes from the encounter with a certain image of others. Without this image, nothing would spur the business cycle out of its downward spiral. As Keynes sees it, sociality itself revives capitalism, while the failure to witness others moved by their animal spirits inevitably produces crises. But this still leaves unexplained why the first investor decides to withdraw her or his capital from circulation, the act that begins the catastrophe.[27]

Milton Friedman offers a tidier account. The economic crisis, according to Friedman, is always a monetary crisis. Recessions and depressions develop because the money supply fails to grow. His explanation of the Great Depression centers around the creation of the Federal Reserve, whose mismanagement of the money supply, as he views it, caused the Great Depression when the economy should have just experienced a simple down cycle. But even as Friedman claims that a failed monetary policy is responsible for the extent of the downturn, he acknowledges that it is not to blame for the business cycle itself. Without a moribund monetary policy, we would still have to endure the vagaries of the business cycle, though the economy would never dip into depression. To the extent that Friedman begs the essential question, Keynes provides an ultimately more satisfying answer, and it points to capitalism's categorical refusal of abundance.

As the capitalist economy approaches a state of abundance in which most workers have jobs and most businesses are operating at capacity, the system begins to suffocate on its own effectiveness. Individuals, business owners, and investors begin to draw money out of the system out of fear that a crisis will come, and this act itself produces the crisis. The crisis results from a loss of faith in the economy, but the loss of faith stems from the nearing abundance. As production approaches a state of abundance, producers and investors begin to fear that the markets for their products will disappear. They believe that an absence of scarcity will discourage consumption. And the closer the capitalist system comes to true abundance, the greater sway that fear about the future has over the capitalist. Depression or recession results when individual capitalists see others withdrawing their capital from the system. If I see someone else start to save rather than invest, I will follow suit because I don't want to be the last one left with an investment that will not provide any return as a result of the upcoming scarcity. I believe that the other has an insight into this scarcity that I do not. The cascading withdrawal of capital from the system derives from an initial sense that abundance has become a real possibility, and this triggers a return to great scarcity in the form of recession or depression. If Friedman is correct—and I don't think that he is—then the mismanagement of the monetary system might be at fault for the severity of the renewed scarcity, but it will not be entirely to blame.

The economic crisis spirals out of control because of the subject's investment in the desire of the Other. Individual capitalist subjects do not simply mind their own business. Instead, they constantly examine what others do in order to know what they should do. This logic operates both on the stock market and in the shopping mall. We invest where others invest, and we buy what others buy. But even the power of the Other's desire fails to explain why the first subject begins to lose confidence and save rather than invest, the action that begins the economic crisis. This loss of confidence, this failure of the animal spirits, occurs when the subject confronts the possibility of abundance.

The recoil from abundance is not just a result of capitalist ideology or the demands of the capitalist system. It is rather the inherent response of the subject, whose desire depends on the inaccessibility of the object. The subject will engage in acts of self-sabotage at the moment when it approaches too closely its lost object. This self-sabotage derives from an unconscious recognition of the necessity of sustaining the object as absent.

The subject's satisfaction depends on sustaining a relation to loss. This satisfaction functions on the basis of the object's absence. When we obtain the object—when we achieve abundance—the emptiness of the object manifests itself, and we must confront the traumatic connection between loss and satisfaction, as well as the impossibility of ever obtaining satisfaction without loss or complete satisfaction. It is impossible to obtain the object, and the subject satisfies itself through this impossibility. The prominence of loss in our subjectivity becomes apparent with abundance, which enables us to see that we can never have the object. The trauma of abundance is at once the trauma of subjectivity itself. For this reason, scarcity is not traumatic psychically for the subject in the way that abundance is. We retreat into scarcity to avoid the recognition that we require the object to be lost in order to enjoy it.

But capitalism plays on appeal of scarcity and sustains the scarcity that it requires through the subject's response to abundance. The unconscious investment individual capitalist subjects have in scarcity props up the capitalist system, which cannot survive with the image of an abundance of resources. Abundance would undermine all justifications for capitalist relations of production, and yet capitalism itself has brought the world to the brink of this abundance.[28] By bringing up to the edge of abundance, capitalism paves the way for its own overthrow.

THE NEW GRAVEDIGGERS

The idea that capitalism would produce its own self-destruction is as old as Marx. Marx identifies the proletariat as the gravediggers of capitalism, and he sees them as a product of the capitalist system. Capitalism produced the class that would inaugurate its downfall. But it turned out that the proletariat was ultimately unable, as a class, to overthrow capitalism. Though capitalism creates the conditions of its own overcoming, it also creates a psychic investment in its survival among the working class and all others. We greet the possibility of abundance with flight rather than with open arms. Capitalism has paved the way for abundance, but in order for us to access it, a psychic revolution is necessary.

The proletarian revolution didn't fail because of a lack of class consciousness or because of capitalism's ideological victory over the proletariat or even because of its capacity for integrating subversive challenges to the system into the system. No revolution successfully displaced capitalism due primarily to the capitalist economy's ability to keep the trauma of abundance at bay. Though capitalism promises abundance for those invested in it, this is always a dream deferred. It delivers scarcity in lieu of abundance, and this scarcity is satisfying for us as subjects. It protects us from the trauma of abundance.

Critics of capitalism often point out that its productive capacity has developed to such an extent that it could now easily provide basic necessities for the entire population of the world. The barrier to this possibility is not inadequate distribution or the callousness of the wealthy. It is instead the horror that abundance arouses in the capitalist subject. The producer looks at abundance and sees the disappearance of demand and thus the elimination of profit. Restaurants prefer to throw away their excess stock rather than give it to homeless shelters because the latter activity has the effect of suppressing demand. If one hears of the possibility of obtaining French fries for free, one becomes instantly reluctant to pay for them. The capitalist thinks, along the lines of sexist parents advising their daughter to refrain from sexual activity, that "if they can get the milk for free, then they won't buy the cow." And in this line of thought, the capitalist (unlike sexist parents) is not incorrect: charitable acts like donating excess food to homeless shelters do potentially erode the value of the commodity and make subjects reluctant to pay for it.

The horror of abundance stems from the radical break that we sustain between it and scarcity. In psychoanalytic thought, lack and excess both have a central role, but they cannot be clearly divided from each other. The subject's lack is correlative to an excessive satisfaction that defines it. Because the subject lacks, it cannot find satisfaction in the way that other living beings do. Instead, it enjoys too much, and its every act is marked by this excessive satisfaction. As a result of the damage done by the signifier to the human animal, it becomes a figure of monstrous excess.[29]

Both capitalism and socialism as traditionally conceived insist on the radical separation of scarcity and abundance. We exist now in a state of scarcity, and if we adopt the proper politics, we will accede to a state of abundance. This separation derives from the structure of fantasy, which presents abundance as a fully satisfying solution to the problem of scarcity. But the satisfaction that abundance provides is not removed from the lack associated with scarcity. We can enjoy having too much because we experience it through the mediation of loss.

The point is not simply that we will remember our former state of scarcity when we arrive at abundance but that any future abundance must include scarcity within it. Even when we have enough for everyone, lack will continue to structure our subjectivity. We will still experience ourselves as lacking subjects in an abundant world because no amount of abundance will provide the missing lost object. Abundance would make the psychic necessity of scarcity abundantly clear.

Even in abundance we will not lose scarcity. The mediation of loss will continue to inform our existence. But we will lose the image of a future enjoyment associated with abundance. That is to say, real abundance will take from us the illusion of future abundance, which is why we are constantly subverting the possibility of creating a society of abundance or postscarcity. Giving up this illusion is a political act in a world of enforced scarcity; giving it up entails abandoning the capitalist ground under our feet. A path toward this political act is illuminated by the landmarks of modernist literature.

Modernism is most often associated with absence—absence of ground, absence of center, absence of God. If there are times of fulfillment, like Lily Briscoe's artistic epiphany at the conclusion of *To the Lighthouse*, they are necessarily fleeting and incapable of any duration. The modernist world is one of scarcity, where it is not uncommon to encounter emptiness everywhere. The barren landscape of Samuel Beckett's *Endgame* is typical of this world in which characters endure complete alienation from their object. They exist in a state of heightened lack as a result of the distance separating them from the object. It may be visible or present, but it tends to end up utterly inaccessible.

There is, however, a reverse side to modernism, a world of abundance in which the object is not absent but overpresent. In this world, characters have no trouble accessing their object and suffer from its proximity. It is a suffocating world like that depicted in Jean-Paul Sartre's *No Exit*, where characters cannot get away from each and do not even have the hope of dying as a respite. The difference between these two modernist worlds manifests itself in the opposition between Ernest Hemingway and William Faulkner. Their personal rivalry was a disguised expression of this philosophical contrast.

Hemingway's first two major novels are explorations of the suffering produced by a world of scarcity. In *The Sun Also Rises*, World War I has contributed to the ontological scarcity of the world and left characters either psychically or physically damaged. The novel's hero, Jake Barnes, loves Brett Ashley, but a war wound leaves him unable to consummate the relationship during the novel. At the end of the novel, Brett laments the missed possibility for satisfaction, but Jake corrects her in one of the most celebrated concluding lines in American literature. He asks rhetorically, "Isn't it pretty to think so?"[30] This question makes clear that ontological scarcity would have proved a barrier to their complete satisfaction, even without the devastation of the war. This sense of ontological scarcity continues in Hemingway's second novel, *Farewell to Arms*, where the love of Catherine and Frederic ends with the former's death during childbirth. Hemingway's modernism is the modernism of absence and thus of dissatisfaction.[31] The case is altogether different with William Faulkner, despite their historical proximity.

The difference between Hemingway's world and Faulkner's is that in the former the reader experiences an external barrier to complete satisfaction in the form of Jake's war wound or Catherine's death. Even if the scarcity is ontological, these depictions nonetheless enable us to avoid seeing the satisfaction produced by the lost object. Hemingway's dissatisfaction, like that of many modernists, creates an image of possible satisfaction that we miss rather than highlighting the satisfaction that we can't escape. The rain that falls on Frederic at the end of *Farewell to Arms* suggests the possibility of sunshine, even if the world of the novel can never provide it. Hemingway's world is disappointing, but the very absence of the object indicates another, more complete satisfaction associated with its possible presence.

In Faulkner's world the situation is entirely reversed. In Faulkner's two greatest novels, *The Sound and the Fury* and *Absalom, Absalom!*, the fundamental problem is not scarcity but abundance, and this radically alters the situation for the subject. In the former, Caddy Compson, the sister whom everyone desires, is not missing for the reader and the other characters but overpresent. Her sexuality suffuses the narrative, and Faulkner uses the narrative device of the mentally deficient brother Benjy in order to capture her overwhelming proximity, which even defies the distance of temporality. Though Quentin, another brother, tries to take refuge in temporality itself and its evanescence, he cannot escape Caddy and kills himself to find relief.[32] In *Absalom, Absalom!*, it is not Caddy but Quentin's entire history that burdens him. It is a history populated by overpresent objects: the incestuous relations make any type of distance impossible. Here the reader sees the suffering that access to the object produces.

The difference between scarcity and abundance, between Hemingway's universe and Faulkner's, is the difference between dissatisfaction and satisfaction. The idea of scarcity sustains us in our dissatisfaction, while the idea of abundance makes us aware of the satisfaction that we find in the lost object. When lack appears in a positive form, the traumatic nature of our satisfaction confronts us with full force. Satisfaction ceases to be a goal that we desire and becomes an experience to be recognized. The overpresence of the object signals the impossibility of continuing to believe in our dissatisfaction. We avoid abundance in order to avoid this recognition, but it becomes clear in Faulkner's version of modernism.

Both Hemingway's and Faulkner's modernism refuse the absolute separation of scarcity and abundance that capitalism promulgates. We don't endure one in order to some day magically attain the other. Instead, the problem of scarcity confronts us with that of abundance, and vice versa. But it is Faulkner, the writer whose novels give priority to abundance, who speaks more poignantly today. The problem, he shows, is how we deal with abundance. Though both scarcity and abundance are ontological problems—being is both insufficient and excessive, which is why speaking beings emerge out of it—the problem of abundance is the more intractable problem. Scarcity allows us to imagine abundance as a form of escape; abundance permits no such respite. Satisfaction is always more traumatic than dissatisfaction.

As long as the political and economic discussion remains on the terrain of scarcity, capitalism has the home field advantage. Even more than this, it has already paid off the referees and assured its victory in the game. When the question turns to abundance, however, the situation undergoes a complete reversal. The defenders of capitalism have no possible response to the problem of abundance except to transform it into a new version of the problem of scarcity. This is why Molly Rothenberg proclaims, "The revolution starts at the point of excess."[33] The recognition that we have too much and not not enough marks the opening and yet decisive stage in the battle.

But the problem with previous attempts to theorize a postscarcity economy is that they view abundance as a solution rather than as a problem.[34] Abundance does not remedy the pain of scarcity; instead, it is scarcity that protects us from abundance. With the recognition of abundance, we must take up the burden of our satisfaction and abandon the refuge of dissatisfaction. Though capitalism militates against it, we have the capacity to recognize the necessary role trauma plays in our enjoyment and to confront the problem of abundance without retreating into the logic of scarcity. Confronting abundance without respite demands an infinite courage, the courage of a genuine partisan of emancipation. In a world of abundance, we can no longer hope for something more. It is only with the ceding of this hope that we leave the logic of capitalism.

[10]

The Market's Fetishistic Sublime

A LIFE WORTH LIVING

Every society makes use of sublimity. The sublime serves as the engine for social organization and for individual activity within that organization. Without some indication of the sublime, a society would become idle and cease even to reproduce itself. The sublime gives the subject the capacity for enjoyment by convincing it that its life is not simply a series of empty physical processes. The subject's capacity for satisfaction emerges along with the idea of the sublime and can't endure without this idea. The end of the sublime would mark the end of subjectivity itself in addition to the social order in which the subject exists. As subjects of the signifier, we need a reason to go on, and sublimity provides that reason for us.

The act of sublimation occurs when the subject creates an object that is out of reach, but it is precisely the status of being out of reach that serves to animate the subject. If we did not have an object that we could not obtain, we would cease to be active subjects because we would find ourselves with no incentive to act. Everything would be attainable, and nothing would be worth attaining. Sublimation provides a way for the subject to fail, and the subject satisfies itself by repeating a necessary failure. It produces satisfaction for the subject, but this satisfaction is never that of obtaining the object.[1]

Traditional society based on rigid social hierarchies and capitalist society are radically distinct. But both share the need for the sublime. If capitalism simply eliminated the sublimity of traditional society, it would not be able to provide any enjoyment for its subjects, and they would never invest themselves in its perpetuation. Because there are people devoted to capitalist society, we know that it has not eliminated sublimity altogether. And yet, the situation with regard to the sublime is not what it once was. The site of sublimity has undergone a transformation, and in the process, our understanding of the sublime has shifted as well.

In traditional societies, gods, leaders, or priests bore sublimity. People followed their commands because these commands emanated from a site that transcended the brute material world and gave significance to that world. Though some people continue to treat political or religious leaders as sublime figures today, this status has for the most part been lost in the epoch of capitalist modernity. A popular music star or famous athlete is more likely to appear sublime than a president or a priest, but this type of sublimity is contingent and confined to a limited number of fans. Capitalism allows for the beheading of kings, the mockery of presidents, the critique of popes, and the denunciation of preachers. All of traditional society's bastions of sublimity find themselves exposed to desecration under capitalism. Capitalist society appears to function without the necessary ingredient for social reproduction. But sublimity doesn't disappear under capitalism, even though it seems like it does.

The transformation in the sublime that capitalism effectuates creates a more palatable version of sublimity for the subject. Just as capitalism gives us love in the less traumatic form of romance, it gives us the sublime without the awe-inspiring and terrorizing figure that we must obey. Capitalism sustains sublimity, but it subtracts the traumatic figure in which subjects experience this sublimity. Even though capitalist sublimity lacks the power to produce the extreme versions of satisfaction produced by the traditional sublime, it gives it to us in a more tolerable package. This is the bargain the capitalist subject accepts: a less terrifying sublime in exchange for a lessened satisfaction that derives from the sublime.

Capitalism's transformation of the sublime is not self-evident, even though everyone can see that we no longer live in a world of kings or priests. But a seeming contradiction in Marx's thought reveals the complex operation that capitalism performs in regard to the sublime. To grasp the nature of the capitalist sublime—that is, to see why people invest themselves to profoundly in the self-destructiveness of the capitalist system—one must confront this point at which Marx speaks against himself. The tradition of this type of reading of Marx begins with Louis Althusser, but we must take it in a new direction.

MARX CONTRA MARX

In an effort to reconcile contradictory directions within Marx's thought and render Marx's critique of capitalism more cogent, Althusser conceives of an epistemological break during Marx's career. There is no other way, as Althusser sees it, to rid Marx of the humanism that besets his early work and cripples its political efficacy. In *For Marx*, he articulates this idea of a radical break, and he marks 1845 as the year when humanistic concepts disappear from Marx's thought.[2] The problem of revolution at this point undergoes a radical change. After 1845, according to Althusser, Marx develops a science that enables him to analyze the functioning of capitalism without the concept of alienation that would transform revolution into a reclaiming of a lost humanity. But the gap between the humanism of the young Marx and the sophisticated economic analysis that appears in *Capital* is not the point at which Marx appears most at odds with himself. This point of seemingly irreconcilable self-contradiction occurs after 1845, when Marx talks about the transformation wrought by the commodity and its logic.

The contradiction occurs in two of the most famous passages from Marx's work: his description of the effects of the commodity in *The Communist Manifesto* and the "Commodity Fetishism" section from the first volume of *Capital*. The difficulty here is that this doesn't reflect a case of Marx changing his mind or a case of his position evolving. That is, we cannot make the claim that an epistemological break transpires between Marx's analysis of the commodity in *The Communist Manifesto* and in *Capital*, even though almost twenty years elapse between the two works. The fact that the first work is a polemic and the second a detailed theoretical exploration is also insufficient for explaining the vast transformation that the figure of the commodity undergoes. Between these two passages, Marx remains in the same conceptual universe, but his emphasis in that universe shifts. In the earlier work, he points out the desublimating effect of capital, and in the later, he draws attention to the sublimity of the commodity, its tendency to give social relations a theological hue.

There is, nonetheless, a way of reconciling the radically different direction that Marx takes in the two passages, and this consists in reading them in a causal relationship. In other words, capitalism destroys the traditional form of sublimation in order to prepare the ground for the new form it would usher in. Initially, the desublimating effect of capital removes any transcendent place from the social terrain and thus enacts an unprecedented social upheaval. As Marx and Engels describe this process in *The Communist Manifesto*, "All that is solid melts into air, all that is holy is profaned, and man is at last compelled to face with sober senses, his real conditions of life, and his relations with his kind."[3] Capitalism portends the end of the sacred or sublime location that could continue to reside outside of the system of exchange. Everything becomes secular and quotidian because everything can be exchanged for the right price.[4] This is the universe we continue to inhabit today, a universe in which value is reducible to exchange value and in which nothing transcends the gravitational pull of exchange—not honor, not loyalty, not even love.

Sublimity depends on the transcendence of the everyday. In this sense, the body of the king or the vastness of space has a sublime status due to the impossibility of encountering them in one's daily life. But the onset of capitalism transforms these sublime impossibilities into commercial possibilities. With enough money, anyone could dine with a nation's leader or hire a rocket to fly into space. Capitalism introduces a chain of equivalences that destroys all sublime transcendence. With capitalism, the stars fall down to Earth

But the elimination of the space for the sublime and the process of universal commodification have a magical effect. This process transforms ordinary objects into commodities, which are mystical entities endowed with sublime properties. In what is probably his most important philosophical and political discussion, Marx analyzes this transformation in the "Fetishism of Commodities" section of the first volume of *Capital*. Here he says, "A commodity appears at first sight an extremely obvious, trivial thing. But its analysis brings out that it is a very strange thing, abounding in metaphysical subtleties and theological niceties."[5] Though the exchangeability of the commodity eliminates the transcendent sublime, the effectiveness of the commodity depends on the reintroduction of the sublime on another level, internal to the system of exchange—an immanent sublime.[6]

The idea that capitalism produces sublime objects is not one of Marx's most controversial claims. But perhaps it should be. The sublime, as Kant defines it in the *Critique of the Power of Judgment*, necessarily transcends all sensible presentation and involves instead the ideas of reason. In this sense, the commodity is most often a material object and cannot be sublime: we can grasp through our senses even the most sophisticated commodities. But there is another sense in which the term *sublime* fits the commodity perfectly.

In our encounter with the sublimity of the natural world, Kant insists that this sublimity derives not from the awesome power of nature but rather from our capacity to regard our own self-interest as insignificant. The sublime object enables us to recognize our self-transcendence, our victory over utility. When confronted with a sublime object, we exhibit more concern for the object than for our own situation. Sublimity proves, for Kant, that we are not simply natural beings or beings confined entirely to a plane of pure immanence. This is why the conception of an immanent sublime, like what Marx proposes in his discussion of commodity fetishism, seems at first glance oxymoronic.

Capitalism appears irreconcilable with sublimity not solely through its destruction of all transcendence but also through its insistence that all capitalist subjects must operate as self-interested entities. The sublime marks the point at which the subject abandons its self-interest, and capitalism refuses to recognize any such point. The logic of capitalism and of its ideological defenders is that self-interest is always, in the last instance, determinative, and this amounts to a rejection of the sublime as a possible category. In contrast, this is the only source of Kant's philosophical concern for the sublime.

Kant sees the sublime as the bridge to morality because it attests to our capacity to break the chain of natural causes and to dismiss the significance of our own good. A natural being would not be capable of such an act, nor would the perfect subject of capitalism, which attests to the strained relationship that capitalism has with sublimity. Kant argues, "in our aesthetic judgment nature is judged as sublime not insofar as it arouses fear, but rather because it calls forth our power (which is not part of nature) to regard those things about which we are concerned (goods, health and life) as trivial, and hence to regard its power (to which we are, to be sure, subjected in regard to those things) as not the sort of domination over ourselves and our authority to which we would have to bow if it came down to our highest principles and their affirmation or abandonment."[7] Unlike other animals, subjects can abandon their everyday concerns and devote themselves to a transcendent cause.

Like the natural world, capitalism doesn't offer a transcendent cause to which subjects might pledge their fidelity. It is impossible to imagine someone fighting a war in the name of capitalism, which isn't to say that this doesn't happen under other guises, like freedom or democracy.[8] Capitalism itself is not a repository of sublimity and offers none of the transcendence that Christianity or the Roman Empire does. But capitalism does provide a different form of transcendence—one that inspires satisfaction and devotion, even if only to a lesser degree than the sublime figures of traditional society. It is this transcendence that comes to the fore when the capitalist subject confronts the commodity.

Many commodities are useful. Paper towels clean spills, and watches indicate the time. But the sublimity of the commodity resides in its fundamental disdain for utility and the disdain that it reflects in the subject. The commodity implies a thoroughgoing transformation away from use value, which is why Marx himself claims that exchange value is value as such. Once the commodity emerges, there is no contrast between use value and exchange value but only exchange value, and the sublime resides in the abandonment of use value. The utility of the commodity is not only secondary; it is necessarily marginalized through the creation of exchange value.

Just as our experience of the sublime in nature, according to Kant, enables us to marginalize our self-interest and adhere instead to the moral law, the experience of the sublime commodity allows us to set aside our concern for how the commodity might be useful to us and serve our self-interest. This is what Marx sees as the theological dimension of the commodity. It provides the subject an enjoyment through its lack of utility, like the enjoyment that religious worship offers. We enjoy it not in spite of its uselessness but actually because it serves no practical purpose.

When we look around at our dwellings at the end of our lives and survey all the commodities that we have accumulated, we often come to the insight that they amount to nothing but a heap of worthless junk. Like most insights that come as one approaches the end, this one is entirely misleading. The fact that the commodities were worthless junk from the beginning is what gave them their sublimity and what gave us enjoyment in accumulating them. No one values accumulating useful things. The collector, who is a derivation of the capitalist bent on total accumulation, always collects items with no use value—old stamps, empty beer cans, baseball trading cards, and so on.[9] One doesn't collect useful items because there is no enjoyment attached to their accumulation. Though capitalism preaches self-interest, the enjoyment that it offers—the enjoyment of the sublime commodity—is an enjoyment that depends on the absence of self-interest.

Capitalist subjects value commodities for their transcendence of utility, and this transcendence produces their sublimity. It is not even possible to escape the commodity's disdain for utility and purchase commodities purely for their usefulness. Within the capitalist universe, usefulness itself becomes a form of inutility, as the fashion for apparently useful products like blue jeans or SUVs attests. The utility of these products disappears beneath their fetishistic sublimity. One buys a useful commodity in order to present oneself as a subject concerned only with utility, not because one is concerned only with utility. One buys the SUV for its sublimity even as one insists on its usefulness for hauling things. Every consumer and producer within capitalism falls victim to the sublimity of the commodity that derives from the commodity's inutility. There is no path back to pure use. Though capitalism presents itself as a regime dominated by utility, the capitalist sublime depends on a thoroughgoing break from this utility.

The commodity is sublime both for the producer and for the consumer. The producer experiences it as a magical entity that creates value out of nothing, and the buyer sees in it the power to inject a moment of transcendence into daily life. The invisibility of the labor that produces the commodity is integral to its sublime status. If the excess productivity of the labor becomes visible, then the commodity loses its sublimity and becomes an ordinary object to be bought and sold. Because it is an effect of the transformative power of an invisible labor, capitalism's immanent sublime is difficult to recognize, unlike the transcendent sublime (that predominates in religious experience, for example). But it accounts for the interest that the producer and the consumer sustain for the commodity.

THEOLOGICAL COMMODITIES

The sublimity of the commodity for the producer emerges when the commodity realizes the creation of value. As the capitalist sees it, a miracle takes place; something emerges out of nothing. The passing of time and the laws of supply and demand enable the capitalist to transform an object, the commodity, into profit. As Deirdre McCloskey puts it without any trace of irony in *The Bourgeois Virtues*, "It's the Bourgeois Deal: leave me alone to buy low and sell high, and in the long run I'll make *you* rich."[10] When presented like this, the deal that McCloskey offers seems hard to pass up. It reflects an investment in the sublime status that the commodity has for the producer. The creation of value is a miracle because it depends solely on the time lag between buying and selling.

Even the more complex theories of value, like the labor theory developed by Adam Smith and David Ricardo, promulgate the miraculous dimension of the commodity. For them, labor creates value that becomes profit. But neither of them explains—and this is the lacuna that Marx takes as his point of departure—how the capitalist is able to profit on the commodity while paying the market price for labor. Every exchange is fair and balanced, as they see it, which logically eliminates any point at which value might enter into the structure. This theorizing is not simply a historical accident: in order to function effectively, capitalism must obscure the moment of value creation. If we can see value emerge, the commodity loses its sublime ability to turn nothing into something, and capitalism loses its true believers who put their capital to work for the sake of profit.[11]

Capitalist producers rely on the sublimity of the commodity to continue doing what they do, but they also pass on this sublimity to consumers. The sublimity of the commodity acts as the hidden source of satisfaction for both producers and consumers in the capitalist system. Though the producer parts with the commodity and the consumer acquires it, it accomplishes the same thing for both. The commodity makes the producer richer and the consumer poorer. But the transaction allows both parties to truck with sublimity, which is why both keep returning to transactions. The way that capitalists present commodities for sale highlights their sublimity. Without this, there would be no buyers.

The commodity form is sublime, not the particular content of the commodity. Just as the act of production renders the creation of sublimity obscure and vague, the sale of the commodity disguises the formal nature of the sublime and identifies it with the commodity's content. If consumers recognized that the commodity's sublimity was purely formal, the commodity would lose its sublime status. The sublimation of the commodity is a formal operation that emerges out of the basic structure of capitalist exchange: this exchanges carries with it the power of sublimation. No particular commodity, whatever its content might be, can have an inherent sublimity.

No seller can avow that the commodity owes its sublimity to form rather than content. Instead, the seller emphasizes that the Mercedes Benz or even the Ford Focus is a car without equal, that only this particular content can provide the sublimity the consumer seeks. If the car dealer proclaimed that any car would suffice because the commodity form itself produces the sublimity, the sublimity would disappear. It survives only in masked form.

The sublime inheres in the promise of something extra that the commodity offers to both producer and consumer. This is the purely formal quality of its sublimity. Most commodities are everyday empirical substances with clear material limits, like the package that contains them. The empirical package of the product serves as a vehicle for the sublimity inherent in every commodity. But the form of the package is not just a vessel for the sublime content. Every commodity requires a package, whether it is a physical one or an imaginary one. This package provides a barrier to the enjoyment of the commodity, but it is this barrier that ensures the commodity's sublimity for the consumer and thereby enables the consumer to enjoyment the commodity. Without the barrier and its sublimating effect, commodities would appear to us as worthless junk.

When I buy a new iPhone, I don't immediately have access to the iPhone itself. Instead, I must navigate the packaging and disentangle the commodity that I want from the inessential form that I don't. This act of unpacking focuses my attention on the content and obscures the production of sublimity, which occurs through the form of the packaging. The package creates the promise of more, and even commodities that arrive without any packaging at all carry this promise. In this sense, the excessive packaging of the commodity has an ontological necessity.[12] As we search for a knife to cut through the annoying packaging, we ask ourselves in the midst of cursing the producer why we must always navigate this excess. We never take this question seriously, but we should. The excessive packaging provides the form that invigorates the commodity with the sublimity that renders it desirable. As we cut through the packaging, we perform an act akin to that of the mystical saint's moment of communion with God, but we do so without the trauma of the mystical rupture. The commodity embodies the promise of an ultimate satisfaction or enjoyment that would transport the consumer beyond the secular world, a promise that no commodity will ever fulfill.

With the packaging of the commodity, capitalism reveals that it has adopted a key lesson of psychoanalysis—the distinction between the object that causes our desire (the lost object that can never become present) and the object of desire (the empirical object that we can obtain). What causes our desire is the barrier or obstacle that presents itself to the subject. The recalcitrant packaging is the object-cause of our desire, just like the glass window of the auto showroom that separates us from a new Porsche. The object of desire is the content hidden by this formal barrier, and in itself the content has no value. The form of the object-cause of desire creates whatever value the object of desire has, which is why obtaining objects of desire inevitably leaves us disappointed or even depressed.[13]

The sublime satisfaction that the commodity promises becomes visible in advertisements, which try to imagine what this sublime satisfaction might look like. Advertisements show certain clothes worn by celebrities or a driver with a car going through a picturesque countryside at high speed. No one advertises a commodity by showing how it will anchor one in the drudgery of daily life. This is true even for the products that sustain daily life. Advertisers present soap, laundry detergent, and even toilet bowl cleaners as if they have the capacity for creating transcendence out of everyday tedium. Rather than simply cleaning the remnants of urine and feces from the toilet, I will transform the much used toilet into a shining embodiment of purity and cleanliness if I have the correct cleaner. Instead of just removing the dirt from my body in the shower, I will experience a complete bodily and spiritual renewal if I use the proper soap. The advertisement for even the basest commodity invokes the sublime and promises it to the future consumer.

The failure of commodities to live up to the promise of their advertisements in no way lessens the power of the advertisements over us. In fact, it augments their power. When a commodity fails to deliver the promised transcendence, we search even more diligently for another product—perhaps a new and improved version of the same one—that will come through for us. This is the logic behind someone buying a videocassette of a film, then a DVD of the same film, a Blu-ray DVD of it, and finally a digital copy.[14] In each case, the advertisement promises a transcendent filmic experience that never arrives, but the new version renews the promise. This promise's vitality depends on the commodity's failure to deliver on it.

Within capitalism, the advertisement is more important than the product. Though we often find advertisements annoying and try to avoid them (by changing the channel of the television or turning the page of the magazine), they are actually the site of our satisfaction with the commodities we consume. We enjoy through the advertisement, even when we try our best to ignore it. We believe that the commodity must redeem the promise of sublimity that the advertisement makes, but the advertisement is the source of that sublimity. The commodity never fulfills the promise, but the act of promising itself has a creative power. The advertiser in the capitalist universe is the forger of sublimity. The satisfaction that we derive from commodities is the product of advertising, not the commodities themselves.

By invoking the sublime, advertisements enable capitalist subjects to come close to the transcendence eliminated by capitalism's emergence. The transformation Marx and Engels document in *The Communist Manifesto* demands the creation of a new type of sublime, and this is what the advertisement specializes in. It is a much less satisfying sublime than that associated with kings and priests, but, at the same time, it is a sublime that mitigates the trauma inherent in all sublimity. The commodity disguises its sublime transcendence, and as a result, no consumers feel as if they are touching the hand of God when they buy a new car. Though the act of buying a new car approximates the sublimity that existed before capitalism, it also spares us some of the sublime's capacity for producing enjoyment. The satisfaction of the commodity pales in comparison with the satisfaction found in God.

DRIVING THE CAR OFF THE LOT

By aligning sublimity with the always deferred future of the commodity, capitalism exploits the nature of the subject's desire. As Georg Simmel explains in his treatise on money, desire relies on distance. He notes, "We desire objects only if they are not immediately given to us for our use and enjoyment; that is, to the extent that they resist our desire. The content of our desire becomes an object as soon as it is opposed to us, not only in the sense of being impervious to us, but also in terms of its distance as something not-yet-enjoyed, the subjective aspect of this condition being desire."[15] The commodity form has this distance, and it endows the commodity with its sublimity. Once we traverse the distance and acquire the commodity, we experience the profound disappointment, to repeat the formulation of *The Communist Manifesto,* of all that is solid becoming air, of the sublime becoming quotidian.

Even capitalist economists display an insight into this point when they analyze the utility that a commodity has. Marginal utility theory does not address the actual satisfaction that a commodity provides for the consumer. It is the anticipated satisfaction that, according to this theory, functions as the basis for the decision concerning what to consume. The capitalist economy takes anticipated rather than realized satisfaction as the motor for the decisions that occur within it. Even if the jeans I bought are too tight or the apple is rotten to the core, the utility of these commodities, for the purposes of calculation, lies in my expectations. The commodity's sublimity is futural.[16]

The prospect of consumption is always more gratifying than the act of consumption. We love to go shopping for the commodities we desire because in the act of looking at several possibilities we tarry with the sublime. The joy of shopping lies in the interaction with a seemingly infinite number of promises of future satisfaction. Before we purchase an object, it has a transcendent quality, akin to a religious icon from the Middle Ages. After the purchase, the sublimity rushes out of it, and we are left with an ordinary object that falls far short of our expectations.

Theorists of capitalism chronicle the desublimation of the commodity through the terminology they employ to describe the process of consumption. In his *Principles of Economics*, for instance, Carl Menger reserves the word *commodity* for an object in the production and circulation process, while using the word *consumption good* for the object after its final purchase. This phraseology bespeaks an implicit understanding of the transformation that purchases enact. He says, "from the possession of the first into the possession of the last owner, we call them '*commodities*,' but as soon as they have reached their economic destination (that is, as soon as they are in the hands of the ultimate consumer) they obviously cease to be commodities and become '*consumption goods*' in the narrow sense in which this term is opposed to the concept of '*commodity*.'"[17] Though Menger doesn't comment on the commodity as a sublime object, his desire to bar the term for the object after the consumer has it suggests an association of the commodity with future sublimity. Once one has the commodity, however, this sublimity evaporates, and one must go to extreme lengths to recover it.

The objective correlative of this dramatic shift occurs with the purchase of a new car. While looking around the lot for the right car to buy, one is choosing among a series of sublime objects. But immediately after buying the car, it ceases to be sublime, even if one is relatively content with one's choice. The fact that the new car loses significant value from the moment one leaves the dealership testifies to the loss of sublimity. The religious experience of seeking the commodity becomes immediately secular after one has it. This emphasis on the future promise inheres in our conception of the sublime, and capitalism utilizes, though it does not create, this association.

In order to forestall this secularization of the commodity at the moment one buys it, the consumer must resort to drastic measures that would recreate the distance that existed prior to the purchase. One tack toward this end is to create an aura of insecurity around the object. If I believe that a criminal might steal my new car at any moment, it retains some of the sublimity that the act of attaining it eliminated. Arming my car with a car alarm, locking the doors, and putting it in a secure garage represent efforts to restore the lost sublimity of the newly acquired commodity.

There are, needless to say, actual threats to our commodities. There are criminals who would steal what we own. But security systems are not designed to prevent theft or deter criminals, though this is their secondary function. The primary function of the security system is to restore the sense of sublimity that the purchase of the commodity destroyed. This is why people often employ security systems for items that no decent criminal would think of stealing. The annoyance of the car alarm that one must constantly disengage (or that goes off inadvertently) reminds one that even the little compact car is a sublime object.

Threats to the object render possession insecure and produce a psychic distance that nourishes the future sublime, which is the only form of the sublime that exists in the capitalist universe. Commodities are sublime—they abound "in metaphysical subtleties and theological niceties"—because we see them through the shop window. Capitalism brings the sublime down from the transcendent, but it remains at a distance in the field of immanence.

Even though capitalism locates the sublime within the field of immanence (which distinguishes it from traditional societies), it always imagines the sublime in the future. The capitalist subject never experiences the sublime here and now but only in the promise that the commodity embodies. It is in this sense that capitalism holds the sublime at a distance while rendering it immanent. By leaving sublimity always in the future, capitalism obscures our actual experience of the sublime. It does so in the way that Kant's morality obscures the sublimity of the moral law by depicting it as a future act to be accomplished rather than an act already done. Hegel's critique of Kantian morality thus functions as an implicit critique of capitalism's futural sublime. When we think of the sublime in the future, we fails to see how this future has already manifested itself and made possible our act of conceiving it. The turn from Kant to Hegel is the turn from a future sublime to a present sublime. It is the turn from capitalism to an egalitarian society.

HEGEL'S CONTRIBUTION TO THE CRITIQUE OF COMMODITY FETISHISM

The great philosopher of the sublime, Immanuel Kant, eliminates the external distance that separates the subject from sublimity with his conception of the moral law. The location of the sublime undergoes a dramatic transformation. Even though Kant's most sustained discussion of the sublime occurs in the third *Critique*, the *Critique of the Faculty of Judgment*, it is at the conclusion of the second *Critique* where Kant's relocation of the sublime takes place. In a stunning passage that relates two apparently disparate phenomena, Kant claims, "Two things fill the mind with ever new and increasing admiration and reverence, the more often and more steadily one reflects on them: *the starry heavens above me and the moral law within me*."[18] Through the equation of the starry heavens above and the moral law within, Kant manages to conceive an immanent form of transcendence. The sublime continues to transcend the everyday, but it exists in the midst of the everyday that it transcends. It is not just above us but also within us and our subjectivity. In this sense, Kant repeats the revolution perpetuated by the commodity, which replaces external transcendence with the commodity's transcendence of itself.[19]

This is not to say that Kantian morality is in any way reducible to capitalism or capitalist morality but rather that Kant accomplishes a parallel transformation of the sublime. Both capitalism and Kant bring the sublime into the field of immanence—for capitalism it moves from the king to the commodity and for Kant from the stars above to the moral law within—but neither goes far enough in this revolutionary act. The sublime, in each case, remains futural and thus reproduces the distance from the sublime that exists in traditional societies. It would fall to Hegel to rectify Kant's error and to a future egalitarian society to rectify the parallel error of capitalism.[20]

Hegel finds Kant's theorization of the moral law his greatest philosophical achievement, and yet, he recognizes a blind spot that detracts from the conceptual insight. The recognition of this blind spot allows Hegel to point the way past the commodity's determination of the sublime while still retaining an immanent sublimity. Though the moral law represents an internalization of sublimity so that the figure of the sublime no longer appears in the natural world, Kant actually retains the distance that separates the subject from the sublime in the way that he formulates the moral law. For Kant, the moral law addresses the subject as an imperative. It presents the subject with a duty that the subject ought to accomplish. This ought (or *Sollen*) marks the point at which Hegel takes issue with Kant's invocation of the moral law.

As long as morality remains a sublime possibility that we ought to attain, a distance between the subject and the sublime remains, and morality continues to function like the commodity, promising a sublimity that it will never deliver. Instead, we must conceive morality as something already attained and accomplished. As Hegel puts it in his critique of Kant in *The Phenomenology of Spirit*, "Consciousness starts from the idea that, *for it*, morality and reality do not harmonize; but it is not in earnest about this, for in the deed the presence of this harmony becomes *explicit for it*."[21] Hegel privileges the moral deed rather than the moral imperative to act in the future. According to this way of thinking, we should conceive morality as sublime and yet also as already accomplished.

Hegel's vision of the moral law is Kant's vision with the future subtracted from it. The moral law lifts us out of the everyday, but it does this when we accomplish moral deeds, not when we experience the moral imperative (as it does for Kant). Morality is not a sublime duty that we ought to accomplish but a sublime duty that we have accomplished and continue to accomplish. Hegel's transformation of Kantian morality away from the ought or the future accepts Kant's basic premise—that the moral law is sublime—while rejecting its link with capitalism—its emphasis on the future. Hegel's morality preserves the radicality of the Kantian revolution while discarding its accommodationist structure. The Hegelian form of morality is thus antithetical to the form proposed by capitalism.

Capitalism accommodates itself well to morality. One might even discover within capitalism a moral code, as Milton Friedman does, that will enable one to combat various forms of discrimination. According to Friedman, capitalism charges us for our prejudices—if we refuse to buy from members of another race, for instance, we end up paying more—and thereby works to eliminate them. This sort of morality remains within the bounds of utility and has nothing sublime about it. But the Kantian moral law rejects any claim to utility and thus disrupts the process of accumulation. Kantian morality is sublime rather than useful. Unlike Freidman's morality, it is not a good investment.[22]

Due to its rejection of interest, Kantian morality is quite distinct from any capitalist morality. And yet, Kant does not go far enough because his morality retains the furtural dimension of the capitalist sublime. This is what Hegel discards in his reformulation of Kantian morality. This is also what the emancipation from capitalist society must do in order to break fully from the capitalist universe.

When we conceive of the Kantian moral law as already accomplished, as Hegel enjoins us to do, the location and temporality of the sublime undergo a shift. The sublime is no longer a future event but a present one. It is no longer the promise of satisfaction but the attainment of it. This change in understanding the sublimity of the moral law can be translated into the theorization of the commodity's sublimity. Though we attach the commodity's sublimity to a future possibility, the sublime exists in the commodity form itself as already realized. The promise is already its fulfillment. This shift of perspective, which removes sublimity from the future, destroys the commodity's power over us. One finds satisfaction in commodities, but one ceases to expect any more satisfaction. The Hegelian relation to the commodity demands the abandonment of one's claims to dissatisfaction with the content because it locates satisfaction in the commodity form itself irrespective of the content.

A SATISFIED ORIENTALISM

We can see the contrast between the dissatisfied relation to the commodity and the satisfied relation in the West's relationship to the Far East. That is to say, we can see the difference between capitalism's futural sublime of the commodity and socialism's already accomplished sublime by examining the trajectory from orientalism to Sofia Coppola's antiorientalism developed in her *Lost in Translation* (2003). Since the beginnings of capitalism, the East or the Orient has had a sublime status for the West. Orientalism transforms the East into a site of mysterious wisdom, holding secrets that remain ever out of reach. It is both the location of exotic commodities and itself one. As Edward Said points out when he identifies the problem in *Orientalism*, this attitude toward the East functions as the engine for colonial exploration that seeks the Orient qua commodity.

Like the love object, the Orient is a paradigmatic commodity. It embodies mystery for the capitalist West and is difficult to attain. One must traverse thousands of miles, learn foreign languages, fight wars, and investigate unfamiliar customs. And even with all this probing, the Orient seems to resist all efforts to know it fully. One is always trying to know it but never achieving any epistemic mastery.

When Said theorizes the problem of orientalism, he begins with an epigraph from Marx's *18th Brumaire of Louis Bonaparte*. The epigraph does not announce any critique of capitalism but Marx's own dismissal of the political efficacy of the lumpenproletariat and this class's need for someone to represent its interests. Though Said is not a champion of the lumpenproletariat, he includes this line in order to show Marx's dismissive attitude toward otherness.[23] Within the book itself, Said sees Marx as symptomatic of orientalism rather than as one who fights against it. Despite this discussion of Marx, Said avoids any mention of capitalism as the system that produces orientalism, even though all his examples of the orientalist mindset come from the capitalist epoch.[24]

For Said, orientalism is basically an instance where knowledge functions as the justification for power.[25] Orientalists domesticate the otherness of the Orient and transform it into a comprehensible object. But the important gesture does not occur with this transformation into an object of knowledge but in the very constitution of the Orient as a mystery to be known. Said approaches this point when he notes, "The relation between Orientalist and Orient was essentially hermeneutical: standing before a distant, barely intelligible civilization or cultural monument, the Orientalist scholar reduced the obscurity by translating, sympathetically portraying, inwardly grasping the hard-to-reach object."[26] The key phrase in Said's account is the last one: the oriental object is hard-to-reach and thus sublime, which is why it arouses the desire of the orientalist.

Though orientalism may be, as Said claims, the impetus for the colonial project rather than its a posteriori justification, it is nonetheless the case that orientalism is a product of capitalism. Prior to the capitalist epoch, one might conquer or destroy the other, but one would not view the other through the prism of the commodity's sublimity. Once capitalism arrives on the scene, everything changes, and orientalism doesn't just become possible but entirely necessary. One cannot imagine capitalism without some form of orientalism, some mode of transforming the other into a figure of sublimity that must be explored. The exoticism of the other is the extension of the fetishism of the commodity, and it remains the prevailing attitude toward the other today. The only way to counter this attitude is to show that the other or the commodity doesn't have a secret that the future might reveal.

When Sofia Coppola's *Lost in Translation* appeared in theaters, critics and spectators greeted it with much acclaim, and it earned Coppola an Oscar nomination for best director, recognition that only three other women in the history of the Oscars have received. But it also occasioned a virulent opposition for its investment in orientalism. For many critics, Coppola's film exemplifies a typically racist mode of thinking about Japan: it never tries to depict an authentic Japan but remains satisfied with a view from two Westerners.

There seem to be just two possible responses to the predominance of orientalism. One can either perpetuate it with images of exotic otherness or debunk it with images of the authentic other, thereby desublimating the East. Critics indicted Coppola for doing the former and failing at the latter. The objections to the film went so far as to gel into a campaign against the film entitled "Lost-in-Racism" that encouraged Academy Award voters to eschew any support for it. One of the film's critics, Peter Brunette, summarizes the argument against the film when he states, "the characters take cab rides through the brightly-lighted Ginza area of Tokyo, where a rainbow of neon plays on their faces, go to nightclubs and hang out with strange people, stare respectfully at Buddhist ceremonies, watch a flower-arranging class, go golfing at the foot of Mt. Fuji, and never, ever get even one millimeter below the surface of this apparently impenetrable Other and these Kodak moments."[27] For Brunette and other critics of Coppola, there is no real Japanese particularity in Coppola's Japan, and this is the indication of Coppola's orientalism.

But it is this absence of an authentic Japan that comprises the antiorientalist core of *Lost in Translation* and the film's challenge to the sublimity of the commodity. Coppola neither perpetuates the orientalist image of Japan as an exotic other nor does she present spectators with the real Japan. As Coppola conceives it in the film, the essence of Japan is not a sublime mystery that one can penetrate or just another desublimated object. Its sublimity resides in the encounter that the Western visitors have with it, and in the film, Coppola shows that what makes Japan appear sublime is the perspective taken up toward it. This does not eliminate the sublimity but does remove it from its entanglement with the commodity. The sublime is in our act of sublimation, not in the commodity that promises a sublime future.

The film depicts the relationship that develops between Bob (Bill Murray) and Charlotte (Scarlett Johansson) while he is in Tokyo filming a television commercial and she is there visiting with her spouse. Unlike other films in which Asia serves as the backdrop for the growth of Western characters, Japan does not function in Coppola's film as a site of mystery or wisdom. There are no oriental secrets waiting to be discovered in the film. Instead, we see Bob and Charlotte having an experience of the sublime through their own way of relating to Japan. The fact that they don't probe beneath the surface of the country, far from being an indication of the film's racism, suggests a refusal of the logic of the commodity that infuses orientalism.

Even when the film seems to employ the most obvious cultural stereotypes, it uses them to illustrate where the sublimity actually resides. At one point in the film, Charlotte asks Bob, "Why do they switch the *r*s and the *l*s here?" This question indicates the possibility of a hidden particularity within the Japanese approach to English, but Bob's response bespeaks the absence of any such secret. He says, "For yucks, you know, just to mix it up. They have to amuse themselves because we're not making them laugh." Bob's offhand answer suggests that the question itself is completely wrongheaded: there is no secret to find in the Japanese pronunciation. It is produced for the Western audience and in relation to this audience.

The film's destruction of oriental mystery becomes clearest in its depiction of the role that America plays in the exoticism of Tokyo. When one looks for the hidden particularity of Japan in *Lost in Translation*, one finds American culture rather than any authentic otherness. This is apparent from the film's opening scene. Bob stares out at the excesses of the Tokyo nightscape, and Coppola cuts from these images of excess to the awestruck look on his face. But subsequently we see a large billboard image of Bob himself amid the nightscape. Later in the film, Coppola shoots Bob and Charlotte running through Tokyo at night while the city background remains out of focus. When part of this background does come into focus, it is the billboard of Bob's face. In the heart of Tokyo, the spectator finds the figure from the West rather than the secret identifying Japanese otherness.

The fundamental idea of *Lost in Translation* is that the sublimity of Japan is sublimity for Bob and Charlotte, that there is no secret to Japan that might be lost in translation. This revelation invalidates Japan as a commodity, and it represents a key to transcending orientalism, which is the zero level of the commodity's sublime effects. One can no longer relate to the other as a sublime commodity when one recognizes that the sublime is not a goal to be achieved but an absence already discovered. This is the transition from Kant to Hegel.[28]

The Hegelian form of sublimity that manifests itself in the commodity results in two ever present possibilities accompanying capitalism—the threat of the fundamentalist reaction and the promise of revolutionary emancipation. These two possibilities inhere within the commodity's sublimity. The former is the result of the dissatisfaction that follows the experience of the sublime. One turns to fundamentalism not because capitalism fails to deliver the sublime but because it does, and fledgling fundamentalist subject refuses to accept that the sublime can actually be experienced. The would-be revolutionary subject, in contrast, grasps that it has really touched the sky in the act of acquiring the commodity and thus can divest from the capitalist project of accumulation. The satisfaction that derives from the commodity can exhaust the desire for the accumulation of commodities.

THOSE FOR WHOM CAPITALISM IS NOT SUBLIME ENOUGH

Capitalism's failure to deliver on the promise of sublimity most often produces fundamentalists rather than revolutionaries. This is because the revolutionary must accept that the sublime we can actually have is the only possible sublime, that there is no more sublime future out there somewhere, whereas the fundamentalist is able to retain the promise of an ultimate enjoyment attached to a transcendent sublime. The appeal of the fundamentalist is inextricable from the broken promises of the commodity. It is a reaction that remains within the system that it purportedly rejects. Fundamentalism simply demands that capitalism keep the promises inherent in the commodity. It is the internal effect that the capitalist economic system produces, not a foreign enemy seeking to destroy it from the outside.

Even though he is a defender of capitalism, Joseph Schumpeter recognizes that the new form of sublimity that capitalism offers has deficiencies in comparison with the religious sublime that it replaces. According to Schumpeter, "the stock exchange is a poor substitute for the Holy Grail."[29] Schumpeter believes that the immanent sublime created by capitalism is not genuinely sublime. The result will often be a revolt against the leveling process and an attempt to restore the lost sublimity of religion. But the problem with the sublimity of the commodity is not that the commodity fails to be sublime. It is that the sublime can actually be attained. Unlike traditional societies that always keep the sublime at a transcendent level, capitalism brings the sublime down to Earth and paves the way to disappointment. When he recognizes the potential disappointment of this version of the sublime, Schumpeter anticipates the fundamentalist reaction to the commodity, though he himself sustained his faith in the commodity and avoided this seduction.

Fundamentalism is a product of capitalist modernity. It is a revolt against the form of sublimity that the commodity provides. The fundamentalist is not someone who fails to experience the satisfaction that capitalism offers but someone, instead, who experiences it fully. This satisfaction is dissatisfying for the fledgling fundamentalist because it doesn't live up to the promise that capitalism makes. No commodity is the equal of its advertisement, and this gap is the source of the fundamentalist's disappointment. For most of us, the gap leads to distrust in advertisements or to an unending search for better commodities. This is because, unlike the fundamentalist, we remain within the field of consumption. But the fundamentalist is a disaffected consumer, one who turns away from consumption like a scorned lover.

The structure of fundamentalism—its status as a response to the failures of capitalism—explains why so many suicide bombers come from middle-class families and have ample experience of Western life. Even Islamic fundamentalism is an internal rejection of capitalism for its failure to keep its promises rather than an external attack. This is not to say that the United States was responsible for the 2001 attack on the World Trade Center or that France was responsible for the 2015 attack on Paris, a thesis that denies all agency to the attackers. But it is to say that those attackers were not outsiders. Their differences in religious belief from the majority of American or French capitalists were simply contingent and their attack stemmed from a profound desublimation that affects other non-Islamic fundamentalists as well, as the case of Timothy McVeigh, another fundamentalist bomber, reveals.

The fundamentalist doesn't translate the disappointing experience of consumption into a verdict on the sublime itself but seeks out a genuine sublime in the form of religious belief, nationalism, or something of the sort. This is to fall under the spell of capitalism even more than the avid consumer. The fundamentalist accepts the logic of the promised sublimity of the advertisement, though she or he seeks the fulfillment of this promise in what she or he views as the ultimate commodity—a return to the solid ground of genuine belief that capitalism has eradicated.

In the contemporary world, it seems as if the only alternatives are investment in the sublimity of the commodity and fundamentalist revolt against this form of the sublime. But there is another possibility: confrontation with the failure of the commodity to deliver the ultimate satisfaction it promises can lead one to a new understanding of the sublime. Rather than seeking out a genuine sublime by joining a militia or wearing a burka, one can recognize that the commodity form of the sublime reveals the true nature of the sublime.

The commodity doesn't promise a false sublime and then fail to deliver an authentic version. No, its form of promise and failure constitutes the nature of the sublime. The sublime exists in our failures, not in our successes, and this is what we take pains not to confront. In this sense, capitalism lays bare the sublime that earlier epochs employed while simultaneously rendering it obscure. The task today is to be adequate to what capitalism reveals, to confront the sublime in its inevitable failure rather than to seek respite in the promise of its future realization. That is to say, when it comes to the sublime, we must be Hegelian rather than Kantian. We must follow the logic of the commodity to its end point in order to unlock the secret of sublimity.

The failure of the commodity's promise to deliver the ultimate satisfaction is at once the failure of the sublime as well. The point is not that we inhabit a completely secular world with no traces of the sublime.[30] The sublime exists, but it is not located in a future moment of transcendence. It is present in the capacity for transcendence, for the creation of something out of nothing, in everyday life. Once we can see through the promise of the commodity, we can change the way that we view the sublime. Though capitalism cannot itself accommodate this leap, its transformation of the sublime from transcendence to immanence makes it possible. This is its great achievement, one that we should not cease to applaud.

Marx was entirely correct to claim that capitalism is necessary for the development of the egalitarian system that would replace it, but this necessity is psychic as much as it is economic. We can only make this psychic step if we pay attention to the lesson that the commodity teaches us about sublimity. Our disappointment with the new car that we just purchased is not the moment of the failure of the capitalist sublime but the moment when its truth is revealed. Without capitalism and the commodity, we couldn't see that we already have what the commodity promises for tomorrow. But once we do see that we already have what the commodity promises, we emancipate ourselves from the strictures and the obfuscations of the capitalist system. Capitalism is the ladder to a new understanding of the sublime that we must kick away if we are genuinely to achieve that understanding.

Conclusion

Enjoy, Don't Accumulate

Capitalism bombards us with the image of our dissatisfaction. Challenging capitalism today doesn't depend on focusing subjects on how dissatisfied they are with capitalist relations of production. This type of response plays into the hands of the capitalist system and the promise of a better future that it employs. This is the response that manifested itself in the nineteenth-century critique of capitalism's injustice and in the twentieth-century critique of capitalism's repressiveness. Despite the vast differences between these two lines of critique, they share an emphasis on the dissatisfaction that capitalism produces, and this line of attack does fully uncover capitalism's real psychic appeal.

Though dissatisfaction with capitalism seems necessary for any critique of the system, dissatisfaction as such inheres within the capitalist economy. Capitalist subjects remain capitalist subjects because they see themselves as dissatisfied beings in pursuit of satisfaction and thereby misrecognize the satisfaction they have found. The critique of capitalism must begin out of our satisfaction with capitalism and not our dissatisfaction with it. But the capitalist system never avows this satisfaction. Recognizing it requires the most radical act today—that of interpretation.

It is important never to take a system at its word. This is especially true in the case of an economic or political system, in which the workings of the system aren't self-evident to anyone. Even when leaders are caught revealing the machinations that take place behind the scenes, we should not assume that they are giving away the keys to the kingdom.

Freud's discovery of the unconscious implies that the subject knows what it's doing but cannot articulate this knowledge. As a result, others, from the perspective of interpretation, have more insight into the subject's designs than the subject itself. This is just as true for an economic or political system.

The secrets of every system are present in what the system says about itself, but these statements require interpretation. They cannot be taken at face value. This imperative to interpret exists for the analysts of capitalism, despite the system's apparent obviousness. Capitalism deceives us as to its structure and appeal by laying its cards on the table. The proponents of capitalism readily avow that it speaks to our baser instincts, to human selfishness, and to the desire for more. The most extreme of these proponents translate selfishness into a virtue, but even those who don't see how an inducement to selfishness among individuals might create a more prosperous and thus happier collective. Greedy individuals produce a wealthy and secure social order.

This interpretation of capitalism fails because it never interprets. It simply accepts how capitalists characterize themselves and how the laws of the system explicitly structure the economy. Within the capitalist system, self-interest seems pervasive, and the benefits of the pursuit of self-interest are plain for everyone to see. But the act of interpretation requires seeing what is hidden amid obviousness. What seems self-evident must itself become subject to interpretation, and this is what Marx does in the move from the first volume of *Capital* to the second.

In the first volume of *Capital*, Marx explores how capitalism views itself. He famously points out that capitalism operates according to a single imperative. In the place of any religious duty or Kant's categorical imperative, capitalism proclaims, "Accumulate, accumulate! That is Moses and the prophets!"[1] Even manual laborers who are just trying to survive must, according to this transcendental imperative, concern themselves with accumulation in order to survive and possibly prosper in the future. Capitalist subjects cannot get by simply by getting by but must always concern themselves with tomorrow. One always accumulates with an eye to future prosperity, but this capitalist imperative has a superegoic dimension to it, which means that one can never accumulate enough. The imperative to accumulate doesn't permit capitalist subjects to feel as if they no longer have any need to accumulate. According to the morality of capitalism, too much is never enough.[2]

The first volume of *Capital* is an exploration of the dynamics of a system in which everyone tries to obey the imperative to accumulate. Though Marx is critical of this imperative, he doesn't articulate an alternative. In this sense, he remains proximate to the defenders of capitalism. For the defenders of capitalism, accumulation is the first and last word. There is no other motivation for our action than accumulation or the advancement of self-interest. The structure of the capitalist economy itself seems to reveal the accuracy of this claim: it rewards those who try to accumulate and punishes those who refuse to engage in this activity.

But accumulation is only what capitalism and its defenders claim moves the system. It is not the real engine driving capitalism. It functions ideologically to blind us to the role that satisfaction has in structuring our subjectivity. Even when we are fully bent on accumulating, it is satisfaction that provides the basis for our accumulation. Capitalism survives because we find our accumulation satisfying, but our focus on accumulation at the expense of satisfaction short-circuits the recognition of this satisfaction. The political task today is to wrench satisfaction from the hold of accumulation by exposing the deception involved with accumulation.

The problem with the model of accumulation is that it hides its own manner of producing satisfaction. While the accumulating subject aims at obtaining the ultimate satisfaction in the future, this subject satisfies itself in the present through the sacrifices that it makes to obtain the object it seeks. Accumulation serves as a cover for sacrifice—the sacrifice of time, of energy, of resources, of freedom, and so on. In doing so, it obscures the role that loss plays in all satisfaction. We don't find satisfaction in having or obtaining a privileged object through acts of accumulation but rather enjoy the object in its loss or absence. The sacrifice that accumulation demands provides satisfaction because it recreates our experience of loss, but no one who is bent on accumulation can recognize the role that loss plays.

Capitalism's privileging of accumulation obscures the role that traumatic loss plays in our satisfaction. There is no satisfaction without loss. Or to put it in other terms, we are not subjects who might obtain a satisfying object but subjects who can find satisfaction only through the necessity of the object's loss. Even when we are right next to someone we love, we enjoy what is absent in the beloved, not what is present: that part of the beloved that we can't decipher. Capitalism's success derives from shielding our psyches from this necessary loss and its intrinsic connection to our satisfaction. But we can recognize the disappointment that accompanies accumulation.

Whenever we accumulate enough to obtain what we desire, we inevitably find that this is not what we desire. This transformation of the object that occurs when we obtain it derives from the difference between the lost object that animates our desire and the actual objects of desire. No object of desire can ever be the lost object (which exists only insofar as it is lost), but we nonetheless inscribe this lost object within a series of empirical objects of desire that we pursue. Obtaining the object reveals the difference and thus produces disappointment and renewed pursuit of a new object of desire.

The functioning of capitalism depends on our mistaking the object of desire for the lost object. This inability to see the central role of the lost object in our desire creates subjects of accumulation who believe in the promises of the logic of accumulation. We invest ourselves psychically (and financially) in new commodities with the hope that they will provide the satisfaction that the previous commodity failed to provide, but no commodity can embody the lost object. Every object of desire and every commodity will fail. Capitalism thrives on this failure, and we can never escape its perpetual crises without recognizing this link. Only the turn from the logic of accumulation to the logic of satisfaction—with an acceptance of the lost status of the object—can move us beyond the crisis of capitalism.

Capitalism is not the worst economic system that the world has produced, and it is not the cause of all our woes. Its effects are not universally doleful. Capitalism has provided the economic background for a widespread easing in the struggle to survive, the creation of vast material wealth, the political emancipation of women, the elimination of serfdom, and so on. But its triumphs have exacted an incredible toll that we do not have to continue to pay.

The turn from accumulation to satisfaction portends the abolition of capitalism. Of course, the end of capitalism requires a political act, but a change in the psyche must inform this act. Satisfaction is traumatic, but the attempt to avoid this trauma merely results in its diffusion in the form of a crisis, not in its evasion. The attempt to bypass trauma inevitably leads back to it. The more we enrich ourselves in order to escape trauma, the more crises we produce.

This way of understanding the turn from accumulation to satisfaction finds support in an unexpected location, a place where Marx writes a single sentence that conveys the foundation of capitalism and the possibility for emancipation from it. In all of Marx's writing on capitalism, there are innumerable insights into how capitalism plays on the psyche of those who fall under its spell. Marx hopes, of course, to break this spell, especially as it infects the proletariat. But Marx's greatest insight into capitalism and its continued survival lies buried in an obscure part of his work, as if he wanted to enact formally the point he makes: it is through the banality of the everyday, not in the promised satisfaction of the future, that one discovers the sublime.

The second volume of *Capital* is not a page-turner. It lacks the narrative-like structure of the first volume and the astonishing theory of surplus value and profit developed in the third volume. The aridity of the work makes it impossible to anticipate the fact that this volume contains Marx's most important formulation. The distance from the first volume of *Capital* to the second is immense because in the second Marx turns away from capitalism's ideological self-conception that privileges accumulation. He comes to see that subjects do not act as they do in order to accumulate but in order to satisfy themselves.

With this insight, Marx uncovers the key to the third form of the critique of capitalism. The critique of capitalism begins with its injustice and moves to its repressiveness. But the decisive problem with capitalism is not the injustice that it produces or its repressiveness. It is our inability within the capitalist dynamic to recognize how we obtain satisfaction. As long as we remain capitalist subjects, we see ourselves as dissatisfied beings pursuing a future satisfaction. This satisfaction is embodied in the promise of the commodity.

In the second volume of *Capital*, Marx makes a statement that summarizes capitalism and the possibility of undermining it. It is a statement worthy of Freud after 1920, and yet he made it roughly fifty years in advance of Freud writing *Beyond the Pleasure Principle*. Marx says,

"For capitalism is already essentially abolished once we assume that it is enjoyment that is the driving motive and not enrichment itself."[3] Here Marx understands that capitalism depends on a psychic investment in the promise of the future and that a sense of one's satisfaction is incompatible with the continued survival of capitalism. This is his most profound statement and his most important legacy. Until we accept that the satisfaction of loss is our driving motive, we will remain the hostages of an economy of enrichment.

Notes

INTRODUCTION: AFTER INJUSTICE AND REPRESSION

1. Though we often think of Aristotle as the more democratic thinker because he foregrounds political struggle in his philosophy and thereby confines economy to the household in a way that Plato does not, he cannot conceive of a society without slaves, whereas Plato can. This is undoubtedly why Alain Badiou decided to produce a modern version of the *Republic* and not the *Politics*.

2. Karl Marx, *The Economic and Philosophic Manuscripts of 1844*, trans. Martin Milligan (New York: International, 1964), 107.

3. Michel Onfray, *Le crépuscule d'une idole: l'affabulation freudienne* (Paris: Grasset, 2010), 479.

4. Thinkers often tried to find a constitutive link between the thought of Marx and Freud. Here Erich Fromm provides a representative example. He claims, "Freud was a liberal reformer; Marx, a radical revolutionist. Different as they were, they have in common an uncompromising will to liberate man, an equally uncompromising faith in truth as the instrument of liberation and the belief that the condition for this liberation lies in man's capacity to break the chain of illusion." Erich Fromm, *Beyond the Chains of Illusion: My Encounter with Marx and Freud* (New York: Continuum, 2009), 18.

5. Theodor W. Adorno, *Minima Moralia: Reflections from Damaged Life*, trans. E. F. N. Jephcott (New York: Verso, 1978), 102–3.

6. Adorno, *Minima Moralia*, 103.

7. Otto Gross, "Zur funktionellen Geistesbildung des Revolutionärs," in *Werke 1901–20* (Hamilton, NY: Mindpiece, 2009), 355–56.

8. In David Cronenberg's *Dangerous Method* (2011), Otto Gross (Vincent Cassel) plays a prominent role in convincing Carl Jung (Michael Fassbinder) to

have sex with his patient Sabina Spielrein (Keira Knightley). Though the film seems to take up a critical view of Freud (Vigo Mortensen) and offer a positive portrayal of Jung (and Gross, to a lesser extent), the denouement of the film reveals that Freud's emphasis on the uncontrollable distortion that sexuality produces on subjects trumps both Gross's claims for free love and Jung's belief in a balance of competing drives.

9. The key works are Wilhelm Reich, *The Sexual Revolution: Toward a Self-Governing Character Structure*, trans. Theodore P. Wolfe (New York: Farrar, Straus and Giroux, 1963) and Wilhelm Reich, *The Mass Psychology of Fascism*, trans. Vincent Carfagno (New York: Farrar, Straus and Giroux, 1980).

10. Reich's importance as a figure for the countercultural movement in the 1960s seems to follow implicitly from the original German title of his book *The Sexual Revolution: Die Sexualität im Kulturkampf.*

11. The allusion here is, of course, to Marcuse's *One-Dimensional Man*, a treatise, like Adorno's *Minima Moralia*, that inveighs against the capitalist elimination of difference through enforced equality.

12. Herbert Marcuse, *Eros and Civilization: A Philosophical Inquiry Into Freud* (New York: Routledge, 1987), 46.

13. Throughout his work, Freud insists on the fundamental difference between sublimation and repression, even though both seem to share the same structure. He champions sublimation as fiercely as he critiques repression. The former enables subjects to find satisfaction and the latter leaves them dissatisfied with the satisfaction they find. The distinction becomes clearest in Freud's essay on Leonardo da Vinci, who achieves sublimation and escapes the trap of repression, despite the absence of any sexual activity in his life.

14. Michel Foucault, *The History of Sexuality, volume 1: An Introduction*, trans. Robert Hurley (New York: Random House, 1978), 5.

15. In Alfred Hitchcock's *Psycho* (1960), Tom Cassidy (Frank Albertson) tells Marion Crane (Janet Leigh) that he is spending $40,000 for a house for his daughter's wedding present not as a way of "buying happiness" but instead of "buying off unhappiness." This puts the promise in negative terms, and the inversion attests to the ubiquity of the promise within the capitalist domain.

16. Jacques Derrida, *Specters of Marx: The State of Debt, the Work of Mourning, and the New International*, trans. Peggy Kamuf (New York: Routledge, 1994), 73.

17. Joseph Breuer and Sigmund Freud, *Studies on Hysteria*, trans. James Strachey, in *The Complete Psychological Works of Sigmund Freud*, 24 vols. (London: Hogarth, 1955), 2:7

18. Theodor W. Adorno, "The Stars Down to Earth," in *The Stars Down to Earth and Other Essays on the Irrational in Culture*, ed. Stephen Cook (New York: Routledge, 1994), 49.

1. THE SUBJECT OF DESIRE AND THE SUBJECT OF CAPITALISM

1. This is the position of Allan Meltzer, who claims, "Capitalist systems are not rigid, nor are they all the same. Capitalism is unique in permitting change and adaptation, so difference societies tend to develop different rules and processes, often reflecting cultural requirements." Allan H. Meltzer, *Why Capitalism?* (Oxford: Oxford University Press, 2012), 3. Meltzer, like other defenders of capitalism, applauds its adaptability to cultural difference, and in this way he makes clear the compatibility of capitalism with the insistence on a multicultural perspective. There is nothing about cultural difference that threatens the logic of capitalism because capitalism thrives on the introduction of differences.

2. Guy Debord, *Society of the Spectacle*, trans. Donald Nicholson-Smith (New York: Zone, 1995), 29.

3. The rise of capitalism appears necessary rather than contingent simply because we observe it retroactively from the perspective of its historical victory. A key lesson of Hegel's philosophy of history is that this perspective—and thus the impression of necessity—is inescapable. The retroactive perspective erects a barrier to distinguishing between the necessity and contingency of past events.

4. The great philosopher of mediation is Hegel, who wrote, improbably enough, before the rise of modern linguistics. Hegel contends that it is not even possible for us to identify the most basic element before us—to say "here" or "now"—without implying layers of a complex system of mediation that the philosopher must take the pain and time to work through. He nonetheless sees how easily we fall into the trap of failing to see these layers of mediation and thereby believing in our immediate access to what we perceive. The privileging of immediacy that occurs in philosophy after Hegel (with, for example, Kierkegaard) represents a case of thinkers succumbing to precisely the illusion that a prior thinker (namely, Hegel himself) warned against throughout his work.

5. The company Apple understands that this particular object doesn't coincide with itself and that this noncoincidence creates an excess that subjects desire. The simplicity of the object hides its excess and enables subjects to enjoy this excess without recognizing the relationship between their enjoyment and the divided status of the object. Apple suggests to its clients that its brand name connotes wholeness while making possible an enjoyment of the excess attached to the name.

6. Jacques Lacan explains the distinction between need and desire in terms of the effect of the signifier. See Jacques Lacan, "The Signification of the Phallus,"

in *Écrits: The First Complete Edition in English*, trans. Bruce Fink (New York: Norton, 2006), 575–84.

7. Kant's distinction between thing as it appears and the thing in itself is a way of articulating the difference that Saussure identifies. On the basis of the division introduced by the signifier, we can posit a thing in itself existing beyond the world of appearances. Though the division is not an illusion, the existence of the thing in itself is, which is why the subsequent German idealists (Fichte, Schelling, Hegel) work to expel this concept from Kant's philosophy.

8. Ferdinand de Saussure, *Course in General Linguistics*, ed. Charles Bally and Albert Sechehaye, trans. Wade Baskin (New York: Philosophical Library, 1959), 112.

9. Onomatopoeia seems to eliminate the gap between signifier and signified, but a comparison of the onomatopoeic words from different languages reveals that even these words emerge through a socially motivated estimation of the signified rather than an actual identity. Saussure points out that "they are only approximate and more or less conventional imitations of certain sounds." Saussure, *Course in General Linguistics*, 69. It is as if onomatopoeia exists only to enable us to disavow the gap between signifier and signified.

10. It would be incorrect to align the emergence of absence with the introduction of the signifier. Though the signifier makes our confrontation with absence evident, absence or negativity makes signification possible. That is to say, without some absence or negativity within being itself, we could never begin to speak and thereby render absence present to us. This is what leads Hegel in the famous opening of *The Science of Logic* to assert that being and nothing are identical. He claims, "Being, the indeterminate immediate is in fact *nothing*, and neither more nor less than nothing." G. W. F. Hegel, *The Science of Logic*, trans. George di Giovanni (Cambridge: Cambridge University Press, 2010), 59. Without positing nothing within pure being, Hegel argues, we could not account for our capacity to speak, since speech requires the interruption of pure being with negativity. In other words, we can formulate an ontological claim about the relation between being and nothing or presence and absence on the basis of the foundational role that nothing plays within signification. If nothing did not inhere in pure being, we couldn't have casual conversations about the weather. The role that nothing plays in signification attests to the role that it has in being itself. But signification effectively brings absence to the fore and confronts us with its ubiquity.

11. Psychoanalysts often make the error of addressing themselves to frustration (the loss of a real object due to the exigencies of the social order) rather than castration (the constitutive loss of an imaginary object). Frustration is loss produced by injustice, but castration is the loss of nothing or of the object that embodies nothing, a loss that is not unjust but necessary for subjectivity itself. Psychoanalysis can do nothing about frustration. Instead, it must

focus on the subject's relation to its castration and to the subject's efforts to retrieve what it never had in the first place. For more on this important distinction, see Jacques Lacan, *Le Séminaire XII: Problèmes cruciaux pour la psychanalyse, 1964–1965*, unpublished seminar, especially the sessions of March 3, 1965, and March 10, 1965.

12. W. R. D. Fairbairn, "Object-Relationships and Dynamic Structure," in *Psychoanalytic Studies of the Personality* (New York: Routledge, 1990), 138.

13. In the case of Melanie Klein (to whom Jacques Lacan owes an enormous debt), a similar sense of dealing with actual objects that are lost occurs. The child is not dealing with a constitutively lost object but with empirically good and bad objects. As Klein notes, "The development of the infant is governed by the mechanisms of introjection and projection. From the beginning the ego introjects objects 'good' and 'bad,' for both of which its mother's breast is the prototype—for good objects when the child obtains it and for bad when it fails him." Melanie Klein, "A Contribution to the Psychogenesis of Manic-Depressive States," in *The Selected Melanie Klein*, ed. Juliet Mitchell (New York: Free Press, 1986), 116.

14. The recognition of foundational status of loss for the subject can lead either to a severe depression or a sense of genuine freedom. The necessity of unending loss might prompt one to end one's life or view each empirical loss with complete equanimity.

15. Jacques Lacan, *The Four Fundamental Concepts of Psycho-Analysis*, ed. Jacques-Alain Miller, trans. Alan Sheridan (New York: Norton, 1978), 179.

16. Recently, several voices championing Alfred Hitchcock's *Vertigo* (1958) as cinema's greatest achievement, even surpassing *Citizen Kane*, have arisen. For instance, in the *Sight and Sound* poll of 2012, *Vertigo* took over the top spot as the greatest film from *Kane*. Like *Kane*, *Vertigo* also explores the contrast between the lost object and its replacement. Scottie (James Stewart) begins the film desiring Madeleine (Kim Novak), and her death only increases his desire as she becomes an inaccessible object. When she reappears as Judy (Kim Novak), he lives out the fantasy of obtaining the lost object. The discovery that Madeleine never existed, that she was just Judy playing the part of Madeleine, deprives both Scottie and the spectator of the fantasy of obtaining the lost object by making clear that the lost object exists only as lost. The superiority of *Kane*, however, consists in its formal rendering of the distinction between the satisfying lost object and the dissatisfying replacements, while Hitchcock plays out the difference primarily in the film's content.

17. The conflict between psychoanalysis and deconstruction takes place precisely over the terms of the relationship between metaphor and metonymy. For psychoanalysis, metaphor has primacy over metonymy. The metonymic movement from object to object obscures the loss that transpires during metaphoric substitution. Deconstruction, in contrast, views the

movement within signification as primary and the marking of a foundational loss as a secondary attempt to arrest this movement.

18. Though *Citizen Kane* relies on a final twist—"Rosebud" is the sled—it is not what Hugh Manon (Clark University) calls a spoilerfilm, that is, a film that one can destroy for a first-time viewer simply by revealing the twist. Many of M. Night Shyamalan's films fit into this category, but what saves *Citizen Kane* from it is that the object presented in the final twist is just the embodiment of nothing, an absence that has been present throughout the film. One can freely give away the ending and inform the neophyte viewer of *Citizen Kane* that Rosebud is the sled without ruining the film.

19. In the early *Economic and Philosophic Manuscripts*, Marx first advances the idea that capitalism works through the production of new needs, which he links to the ruin of the subject who acquires these new needs. He notes, "every person speculates on creating a new *need* in another, so as to drive him to a fresh sacrifice, to place him in a new dependence and to seduce him into a new mode of *gratification* and therefore economic ruin." Karl Marx, *The Economic and Philosophic Manuscripts of 1844*, trans. Martin Milligan (New York: International, 1964), 147.

20. Karl Marx, *Capital: A Critique of Political Economy*, vol. 3, trans. David Fernbach (New York: Penguin, 1981), 347.

21. Karl Marx, *Grundrisse*, trans. Martin Nicolaus (New York: Penguin, 1993), 334.

22. The fact that *Grenze* is not just a term for boundary but also the word for the border between nations lends even more importance to Marx's claim. The national border is never a border for capital. As Marx himself points out, capitalism was global capitalism from the beginning.

23. Martin Heidegger's name for the Other is *das Man* or "the they." *Das Man* manipulates us into an inauthentic relation to Being and to death by stripping away the uniqueness or individuality of that relation. The problem with Heidegger's formulation is that the escape from *das Man* and its demand for conformity enables one to access a successful being toward death, while for psychoanalysis proper the escape from the Other leads only to the confrontation with the necessity of failure.

24. The idea that the Other does not exist is precisely what Hegel is aiming at when he says in the opening of the *Phenomenology of Spirit* that "everything turns on grasping and expressing the True, not only as *Substance*, but equally as *Subject*." G. W. F. Hegel, *The Phenomenology of Spirit*, trans. A. V. Miller (Oxford: Oxford University Press, 1977). 10. We believe in substance and take it as foundational, while subject is at odds with itself and completely uncertain. Hegel's contention here is that even what seems most foundational, even the surest form of the Other, must assume the status of subject

for the philosopher and thus must prove to be ultimately unreliable. The point of this statement is not some type of subjectivism but rather an assertion of the groundlessness of our existence. No existentialist could push the idea of groundlessness any further than Hegel does at this moment.

25. Of course, all fashion trends seem strange and even idiotic in retrospect. Henry David Thoreau offers the definitive account of our relation to past fashions when he notes that we mock those of the past while slavishly following those of the present.

26. Jacques Lacan, *Le Séminaire XIV: La logique du fantasme, 1966–1967*, unpublished manuscript, session of June 14, 1967.

27. The existence of secret societies like Skull and Bones functions as a site for societal disavowal. When we encounter a secret society, we implicitly fail to see that society as such operates according to the logic of the secret society. Secret societies thus permit us to disavow the fantasmatic entrance requirement for the social order itself.

28. The description that Claude Lévi-Strauss provides of marriage rules in *The Elementary Structures of Kinship* shows how these rules regulate social activity, but it is less clear how these strict rules affect the desire of the subject. Desire can gain a measure of freedom amid strict social rules, a freedom not available under the regime of capitalism. See Claude Lévi-Strauss, *The Elementary Structures of Kinship*, trans. James Harle Bell, John Richard von Sturmer, and Rodney Needham (Boston: Beacon, 1969).

29. In *Debt*, David Graeber offers a representative statement of the role that faith plays in sustaining the value of money. He notes, "a gold coin is not actually useful in itself. One only accepts it because one assumes that other people will." David Graeber, *Debt: The First 5,000 Years* (New York: Melville House, 2011), 47.

30. Georg Simmel, *The Philosophy of Money*, 2d ed., trans. Tom Bottomore and David Frisby (New York: Routledge, 1990), 179.

31. Milton Friedman states this directly. He notes, "I know of no example in time or place of a society that has been marked by a large measure of political freedom, and that has not also used something comparable to the free market to organize the bulk of economic activity." Milton Friedman, *Capitalism and Freedom* (Chicago: University of Chicago Press, 2002), 9.

32. Gilles Deleuze and Félix Guattari, *Anti-Oedipus: Capitalism and Schizophrenia*, trans. Robert Hurley, Mark Seem, and Helen Lane (Minneapolis: University of Minnesota Press, 1985), 257.

33. Sigmund Freud, *Beyond the Pleasure Principle*, trans. James Strachey, in *The Standard Edition of the Complete Psychological Works of Sigmund Freud*, 24 vols. (London: Hogarth, 1955), 18:63.

2. THE PSYCHIC CONSTITUTION OF PRIVATE SPACE

1. Jean-Jacques Rousseau, *The Social Contract*, in *The Social Contract and Other Later Political Writings*, ed. Victor Gourevitch (Cambridge: Cambridge University Press, 1997), 113.

2. The danger that any public institution poses to capitalism becomes visible whenever a reformer introduces a new public program in a capitalist nation. One can see this clearly in the history of the United States. With Franklin Roosevelt's introduction of Social Security, Lyndon Johnson's creation of Medicare, and Barack Obama's passage of universal health care, opponents consistently brought up the specter of socialism or communism, even when the program, like Obama's health care law, had its basis in the market. The construction of a new public program opens up the question of privacy as such, which is why the partisans of capitalism rightly see such a grave danger in this act.

3. Saul A. Kripke, *Wittgenstein on Rules and Private Language: An Elementary Exposition* (Cambridge: Harvard University Press, 1982), 89.

4. See Hannah Arendt, *The Human Condition*, 2d ed. (Chicago: University of Chicago Press, 1998).

5. Arendt devalues the pure reproductivity of labor not out of a simple hostility to capitalism but because her ontology grants priority to the act of creation. Giving birth to the new represents, for Arendt, the essence of humanity, and the reduction of humans to laborers alienates them from this essence. In her eyes, communism is as much guilty of this reduction as capitalism.

6. Despite their joint critique of the turn away from the *citoyen*, there are significant disputes between Agamben and Rancière. According to Rancière, Agamben, following Arendt, desires a pure politics, a politics uncontaminated by any private concerns, and this is part of the evisceration of the political realm rather than part of the critique of that evisceration. Though he mentions only Arendt in the following passage, it is clear that Agamben is also a target: "the radical suspension of politics in the exception of bare life is actually the ultimate consequence of Arendt's archi-political position, that is, of the attempt to preserve the political from contamination by the private, the social or a-political life." Jacques Rancière, *Dissensus: On Politics and Aesthetics*, trans. Steven Corcoran (New York: Continuum, 2010), 66.

7. Giorgio Agamben, *Means Without Ends: Notes on Politics*, trans. Vincenzo Binetti and Cesare Casarino (Minneapolis: University of Minnesota Press, 2000), 138–39.

8. Adam Smith, *An Inquiry Into the Nature and Causes of the Wealth of Nations* (Hamburg: Management Laboratory Press, 2008), 21–22. The morality that Smith develops in his other famous treatise, *The Theory of Moral Senti-*

ments, appears initially at odds with his inability to theorize a public world in *The Wealth of Nations.* In the former (and earlier) work, Smith argues for the sacrifice of private interest for the sake of the public. He claims, "The wise and virtuous man is at all times willing that his own private interest should be sacrificed to the public interest of his own particular order or society." Adam Smith, *The Theory of Moral Sentiments* (New York: Penguin, 2009), 277. But even here, the ruling presupposition is that the private world and private interest come prior to the public, even if private interest must ultimately be sacrificed. The ontological priority of the private remains the same through Smith's intellectual career and separates him from thinkers like Hegel and Marx.

9. Carl Menger, *Principles of Economics* (New York: New York University Press, 1981), 97. Because economics as a field takes private self-interest as an indisputable first principle, it is able to achieve a level of predictive accuracy that the other human sciences cannot. This is the contention of Alfred Marshall in his classic study *Principles of Economics,* where he claims, "the motive is supplied by a definite amount of money: and it is this definite end and exact money measurement of the steadiest of motives in business life, which has enabled economics far to outrun every other branch of the study of man." Alfred Marshall, *Principles of Economics,* 9th ed. (New York: Macmillan, 1961), 14.

10. Richard H. Thaler, *The Winner's Curse: Paradoxes and Anomalies of Economic Life* (New York: Free Press, 1992), 198.

11. Barack Obama's passage of the health care act was, in contrast to his underfunded stimulus package, a genuine political act. Against a recalcitrant opposition, he managed to lay the groundwork for a future public health care system in the United States, and, in this sense, Vice President Joe Biden was correct tell Obama, as he signed the bill, that it was a "big fucking deal." But that said, Obama had to accomplish it by expanding the market for private insurance companies, which is why many leftists view Obama's great victory as a pyrrhic one.

12. Habermas views modernity as an unfinished project because there are still those left out of the public sphere, but the project of modernity is itself, for him, one of universal inclusion. If the public sphere became truly universal, we would reach the point at which communicative rationality—the basis for the ethical system that Habermas develops in his later works—would be realized. This is the connection between the young Habermas who theorizes the decline of the public sphere and the mature Habermas who champions communicative rationality.

13. Jürgen Habermas, *The Structural Transformation of the Public Sphere: An Inquiry Into a Category of Bourgeois Society,* trans. Thomas Burger with Frederick Lawrence (Cambridge: MIT Press, 1989), 160.

14. Marx points out that what appear to capitalists themselves as purely private acts of exchange are always public as well because capitalists relate to their workers not as individuals but as part of a whole. The universal relation mediates the particular one. In the third volume of *Capital,* Marx notes, "each particular capital should be viewed simply as a fragment of the total capital and each capitalist in fact as a shareholder in the whole social enterprise, partaking in the overall profit in proportion to the size of his share of capital." Karl Marx, *Capital: A Critique of Political Economy,* vol. 3, trans. David Fernbach (New York: Penguin, 1981), 312. By explaining the universal dimension of every particular capitalist relationship with the worker, Marx hopes to show that what passes for a private exchange is actually thoroughly involved with the public. Or, for Marx, there is no private exchange.

15. The problem with the private police force came to a head in a gated community in Sanford, Florida, in March 2012, where George Zimmerman shot and killed Trayvon Martin. Zimmerman, part of a neighborhood watch group organized as a form of private police, confronted Martin for what he deemed suspicious behavior. The fact that Martin was black was clearly the basis of the suspicious behavior, and Zimmerman's shooting of him can be traced to his paranoid reaction to Martin's skin color. But the equally dramatic cause is the private community itself and its private neighborhood watch group. No matter how abusive (or even deadly) a public police force becomes, it is always preferable to the private version. Of course, the public police force is never free from the intrusion of privacy (most often today in the form of racist violence), but because it is public it is easier for subjects to seek redress. A public entity is almost always more accountable than a private one.

16. Robert D. Putnam, *Bowling Alone: The Collapse and Revival of American Community* (New York: Simon and Schuster, 2000), 228.

17. Christopher Lasch, *The Culture of Narcissism: American Life in An Age of Diminishing Expectations* (New York: Norton, 1991), 72.

18. This is why we can imagine the idea of enjoying one's symptom as a radical political strategy. When one identifies with and enjoys one's symptom, one sides with the part of oneself that resists ideological interpellation, even though this resistance implies suffering.

19. Sigmund Freud, *Civilization and Its Discontents,* trans. James Strachey, in *The Standard Edition of the Complete Psychological Works of Sigmund Freud,* 24 vols. (London: Hogarth Press, 1961), 21:140.

20. As Freud points out in *The Psychopathology of Everyday Life,* "It can in fact be said quite generally that everyone is continually practising psychical analysis on his neighbours and consequently learns to know them better than they know themselves." Sigmund Freud, *The Psychopathology of Everyday Life,* trans. James Strachey, in *The Standard Edition of the Complete Psychological Works of Sigmund Freud,* 24 vols. (London: Hogarth, 1953), 6:211.

21. Throughout the course of his intellectual career, Lacan's understanding of the relationship between the analyst and the public changed dramatically. Early on, he believed that the analyst should identify with the public itself or the Other, but in the late 1950s this idea underwent a shift. He came to see identification with the *objet a* or desire of the Other, not the Other itself, as the essence of psychoanalytic practice.

22. Molly Rothenberg makes clear how the internal disjunction of the subject has an inextricable connection to the social field. She claims, "In producing the social subject, extimate causality also leaves a remainder or indeterminacy, so that every subject bears some unspecifiable excess within the social field." Molly Anne Rothenberg, *The Excessive Subject: A New Theory of Social Change* (Malden, MA: Polity, 2010), 10.

23. The great advance in Jacques Lacan's thought occurs in his seminar on anxiety (*Seminar X*) when he definitively privileges what he calls the *objet a* over the object of desire. There are hints of this distinction in his *Seminar VI* on desire, but at this earlier epoch in his thought Lacan also fails to sustain the distinction at certain points, as he labels the *objet a* the object of desire. See Jacques Lacan, *Le Séminaire, livre X: L'angoisse, 1962–1963*, ed. Jacques-Alain Miller (Paris: Seuil, 2004) and Jacques Lacan, *Le Séminaire, livre VI: Le désir et son interprétation, 1958–1959*, ed. Jacques-Alain Miller (Paris: Martinière, 2004).

24. As anyone who has ever drank Coke knows, a single can of Coke, despite its small size, provides infinitely more satisfaction than a two-liter bottle, even if one drinks the whole bottle oneself. One enjoys the limit the can creates. In this sense, the advertising cliché that the packaging counts more than the product is absolutely true. The package as a limit gives the product a sublimity that it otherwise doesn't have.

25. Unfortunately, in the four sequels to *Les quartre cents coups*, Doinel returns to the form of capitalist subjectivity and seeks an object that would provide him the ultimate satisfaction. These films count among Truffaut's failures because they fail to grapple with the insight he arrives at at the end of his first feature. In contrast, many of Truffaut's other films—*Tirez sur le pianiste* (*Shoot the Piano Player*, 1960), *Fahrenheit 451* (1966), *La mariée était en noir* (*The Bride Wore Black*, 1968), and his masterpiece *La sirène du Mississippi* (*Mississippi Mermaid*, 1969), to name just the most important—reveal that he had the ability to integrate the perspective of the necessity of the obstacle into his filmmaking project even after his first feature. The return to Doinel was a temptation that Truffaut should have thoroughly rejected.

26. Hannah Arendt, *The Origins of Totalitarianism* (New York: Harcourt, 1968), 338.

27. The role that surveillance plays in changing the way that subjects think of themselves requires that everyone knows that surveillance is occurring.

Though governments prosecute whistle-blowers who expose clandestine surveillance activity, this exposure plays a crucial part in the elimination of the public world.

3. SHIELDING OUR EYES FROM THE GAZE

1. Baudelaire says this in his prose poem "Le joueur généreux." He writes, "la plus belle des ruses du diable est de vous persuader qu'il n'existe pas" ("the devil's most beautiful trick is to persuade you that he doesn't exist"). Charles Baudelaire, "Le joueur généreux," *Le spleen de Paris*, in *Oeuvres Complètes* (Paris: Robert Laffont, 1980), 191.
2. Jacques Rancière, *Dissensus: On Politics and Aesthetics*, trans. Steven Corcoran (New York: Continuum, 2010), 139.
3. Another thinker who attacks the prevailing depoliticization, Agamben, tries to bring economy to bear on his call for politicization in *The Kingdom and the Glory*. In this work, Agamben examines how economic thinking came to prevail over political thinking in the realm of theology. An economic theology paved the way, as Agamben sees it, for today's triumph of the economy over politics. See Giorgio Agamben, *The Kingdom and the Glory: For a Theological Genealogy of Economy and Government*, trans. Lorenzo Chiesa with Matteo Mandarini (Stanford: Stanford University Press, 2011).
4. Marx's error with regard to the possibility of revolution does not consist, as so many opponents of Marxism claim, in underestimating human selfishness. It lies rather in the opposite direction. Because Marx hadn't read Freud, he mistakenly viewed subjects as inherently self-interested beings and assumed that they could come together to seize the forces of production when it became clear that the contradiction with the relations of production impeded the social and individual good. If Marx is wrong, it is because subjects are not self-interested enough.
5. Joseph Breuer and Sigmund Freud, *Studies on Hysteria*, trans. James Strachey, in *The Complete Psychological Works of Sigmund Freud*, 24 vols. (London: Hogarth, 1955), 2:305.
6. Ayn Rand turned to fiction as a vehicle for her economic thinking because she understood that this form would have the effect of further naturalizing the capitalist system that she defended. It is no accident that Rand is far more well known for her fictional works like *Atlas Shrugged* and *The Fountainhead* than for her economic treatises like *The Virture of Selfishness* or *Capitalism: The Unknown Ideal*.
7. Ayn Rand, *Atlas Shrugged* (New York: Penguin, 1999), 411.
8. Rand repeatedly invokes Aristotle as her only philosophical master, but this is disingenuous on two counts. It requires an absurd reading of Aristotle that obliterates his insistence on the primacy of political contestation and his

corresponding thoroughgoing denunciation of economy, which he associates with the subhuman (slaves and women) and the household. This claim also obscures Rand's profound debt to Nietzsche and his vitalistic celebration of the master's pure productivity. Though Rand recoils from Nietzsche's irrationalism, he is her true intellectual parent figure, not Aristotle.

9. In *History and Class Consciousness*, Georg Lukács takes the journalist as the model for capitalist reification. The journalist who pretends to report objectively fails to see the acceptance of capitalism's rules of the game that undergird this objectivity. The point is not that all journalism is subjective, but that its objectivity depends on a political decision. One can either avow this decision or obscure it. See Georg Lukács, *History and Class Consciousness: Studies in Marxist Dialectics*, trans. Rodney Livingstone (Cambridge: MIT Press, 1971).

10. Even Adam Smith notes that humanity is not simply a more developed form of animality, but qualitatively different. This difference consists in what Freud would call humanity's premature birth—the human individual's fundamental dependence on its fellow humans. This dependence renders the human an unnatural being. As Smith describes, "In almost every other race of animals, each individual, when it is grown up to maturity, is entirely independent, and in its natural state has occasion for the assistance of no other living creature. But man has almost constant occasion for the help of his brethren, and it is in vain for him to expect it from their benevolence only. He will be more likely to prevail if he can interest their self-love in his favour, and shew them that it is for their own advantage to do for him what he requires of them." Adam Smith, *An Inquiry Into the Nature and Causes of the Wealth of Nations* (Hamburg: Management Laboratory Press, 2008), 21. Smith moves quickly here from human difference to an ideological justification for capitalist relations of production, but nothing necessitates such a turn.

11. Alain Badiou, *The Meaning of Sarkozy*, trans. David Fernbach (New York: Verso, 2008), 100 (translation modified).

12. For a discussion of the nefarious effects of this reading of the gaze, see Todd McGowan, *The Real Gaze: Film Theory After Lacan* (Albany: SUNY Press, 2007).

13. As Lacan puts it, "as subjects, we are literally called into the picture, and represented there as caught." Jacques Lacan, *The Seminar of Jacques Lacan, Book XI: The Four Fundamental Concepts of Psycho-Analysis*, ed. Jacques-Alain Miller, trans. Alan Sheridan (New York: Norton, 1977), 92.

14. Joan Copjec, *Read My Desire: Lacan Against the Historicists* (Cambridge: MIT Press, 1994), 35.

15. The difference between the gaze understood as a mastering look and the gaze understood as a traumatic object is perhaps most clearly manifested in

the opposing interpretations of Alfred Hitchcock's *Rear Window* (1954). For the former position, the gaze is either the voyeuristic look of Jeff (James Stewart) on the courtyard behind his apartment or the threatening return look across the courtyard that Lars Thorwald (Raymond Burr) gives to Jeff when he realizes that Jeff has discovered that Thorwald has murdered his wife. For the latter position, the gaze manifests itself in Thorwald's window insofar as this window arouses Jeff's desire and thereby colors the entire visual field of the courtyard. As Miran Božovič notes, "Thorwald's window gazes back at him differently from any other because Jeff sees it in a different way: in it, there is something that intrigues him, something that all other windows lack, something that is 'in the window more than the window itself' and has always been of some concern to him—in short, the object-cause of his desire. *Faced with the window, Jeff can see himself only as the subject of desire.*" Miran Božovič, "The Man Behind His Own Retina," in *Everything You Always Wanted to Know About Lacan (But Were Afraid to Ask Hitchcock)*, ed. Slavoj Žižek (New York: Verso, 1992), 169. The gaze distorts the visual field by showing us how the entire field constructs itself around our desire. The gaze is always present as a founding absence, but it only appears to the subject when the visual field loses its stability.

16. One might interpret the difference between *The Searchers* and *Drive* as the result of the historical distance between the two films. The change in positioning of the camera—from inside to outside, from shelter against the gaze to identification with it—would represent an increasing refusal of prohibition and an attempt to inhabit directly the promise of enjoyment embodied in the gaze.

17. Though gold does occur in nature and appears to have a substantial value, its value is every bit as contingent as that of paper currency. One could have all the gold in Fort Knox, but if everyone ceased believing that gold had a value, this gold would instantly become worthless. But gold seems more secure than paper currency because it permits a fetishistic disavowal of its dependence on collective belief for its value.

18. Jodi Dean stresses that the main achievement of the Occupy movement consists in politicizing the economy and in bringing social antagonism to the fore. See Jodi Dean, *The Communist Horizon* (London: Verso, 2012).

19. For those who couldn't afford to buy a vacant house, the housing crisis is a crisis of scarcity rather than one of overproduction. But in almost every case within the capitalist economy it is overproduction that leads to scarcity.

20. David Harvey, *The Enigma of Capital and the Crisis of Capitalism* (Oxford: Oxford University Press, 2011, 5.

21. Karl Marx, *Grundrisse*, trans. Martin Nicolaus (New York: Penguin, 1993), 374.

22. Emancipatory politics has the advantage of promising subjects equality, but fascism has the far more valuable advantage of promising them an external enemy on which they can blame their lack of equality. The figure of the external enemy gives the fascist leader an appeal that is often decisive. If the emancipatory leader resorts to evoking an external enemy, this leader immediately cedes the terrain of emancipation. There is no emancipation that relies on an external enemy to constitute itself.

4. THE PERSISTENCE OF SACRIFICE AFTER ITS OBSOLESCENCE

1. Joseph A. Schumpeter, *Capitalism, Socialism, and Democracy* (New York: Harper, 2008), 83.
2. The fact that Schumpeter is not really theorizing the role of sacrifice in capitalism is evident in the emphasis that he places on creation in the act of creative destruction. It is not as if the system, as Schumpeter sees it, produces satisfaction through destruction but rather that the destruction is necessary for the process of creation, which is the real aim of the capitalist system. Within capitalism, overt sacrifice, when it exists, must occur for the sake of future growth.
3. The realm of the sacred doesn't simply exist. The act of sacrifice constitutes the sacred, which is why every religion, even the most lenient, demands some form of sacrificial act, even if it is just sacrificing one's time for the socially useless endeavor of worship. Through the act of sacrifice, we create an absence that serves as a placeholder for the beyond or the sacred.
4. See G. W. F. Hegel, *The Phenomenology of Spirit*, trans. A. V. Miller (Oxford: Oxford University Press, 1977), 329–49.
5. I accept the shared belief of Sigmund Freud, René Girard, and Marcel Mauss that society cannot sustain itself without sacrifice, but this sacrifice does not necessarily have to remain openly acknowledged. In modernity the obfuscation of sacrifice is a necessary condition for it.
6. As Richard Boothby puts it, "sacrifice serves to constitute the very matrix of desire." Richard Boothby, *Freud as Philosopher: Metapsychology After Lacan* (New York: Routledge, 2001), 189.
7. The essential role that vitalist thought plays in the defense of capitalism renders it incapable of playing any part at all in constituting an alternative. This is the problem with the political thought that comes from Gilles Deleuze and his followers (like Michael Hardt and Antonio Negri). When they begin with a vitalist belief that life has an inherent value, they have already bought into a philosophy that justifies capitalist relations of production. Their objection to capitalism—and this is always the case if one examines works

like *Anti-Oedipus* or *Commonwealth*—can only be that capitalism hasn't gone far enough. Hence, they will say, capitalism deterritorializes, but we need more deterritorialization; capitalism breaks down borders, but we need to break them down more thoroughly; capitalism produces hybrid identity, but we need more hybridity; and so on.

8. Hannah Arendt, *The Human Condition*, 2d ed. (Chicago: University of Chicago Press, 1998), 84.

9. Both Martin Heidegger and Giorgio Agamben make a point of noting that the Greeks had two distinct words for life—*bios* and *zoē*. The latter designates the life that humans share with animals, while the former applies specifically to the capacity for political acts.

10. Entrance into the system of signification constitutes the first act of human sacrifice. The human animal gives up a part of itself in order to enjoy through the signifier, which constitutes a system of absences. But in this act of sacrifice the subject individual sacrifices what it never had and only comes to have retrospectively after having lost it.

11. The inability to see sacrifice as inherently enjoyable runs through the Marxist tradition, beginning with Marx himself. He cannot imagine that workers would continue to invest themselves in the capitalist system when the system simply demanded sacrifice from them without any recompense. Marx doesn't grasp that the very irrationality of the sacrifice can constitute the source of its appeal.

12. Lionel Robbins, *An Essay on the Nature and Significance of Economic Science*, 3d ed. (New York: New York University Press, 1984), 15.

13. Even the most conscientious companies, like Levi Strauss, must succumb to outsourcing their labor and using workers who earn in a week what former American workers used to earn in an hour. If Levi Strauss had failed to take this step out of concern for their workers, no one would be wearing Levi's today. For a personalized account of this trajectory, see Kelsey Timmerman, *Where Am I Wearing? A Global Tour to the Countries, Factories, and People That Make Our Clothes* (Hoboken, NJ: Wiley, 2009), 126–29.

14. Friedrich Engels, *The Condition of the Working Class in England* (Oxford: Oxford University Press, 1993), 200.

15. Public perception of Apple, like public perception of Google, has undergone a shift. The trajectory is always the same. Companies begin by presenting themselves as conscientious producers and eventually transform into firms that act just like the manufacturers in Manchester in the nineteenth century. We should not look at this transformation as the loss of founding ideals but as the inevitable trajectory that capitalism demands. Apple must become Microsoft, and if it doesn't, it will disappear.

16. For more on Apple's relationship to mining in the Congo, see the Enough Project at http://www.enoughproject.org/.

17. For an account of some of the horrors associated with the mines in the Congo, see Lydia Polgreen, "Congo's Riches, Looted by Renegade Troups," *New York Times*, November 15, 2008, http://www.nytimes.com/2008/11/16 /world/africa/16congo.html?pagewanted=all&_r=0.

18. David Renton, David Seddon, and Leo Zeilig, *The Congo: Plunder and Resistance* (London: Zed, 2007), 208.

19. Ironically, the attempt to avoid entirely minerals from the Congo has had the effect of worsening the situation there for the impoverished. With no one to buy the minerals that they mine, workers suddenly found themselves even more destitute than they were when they were working indirectly for Apple. The consumer of the iPhone can feel better now that the product most likely no longer contains conflict minerals, but the Congolese are worse off.

20. Charles Duhigg and David Barboza, "In China, Human Costs Are Built Into an iPad," *New York Times*, January 25, 2012, http://www.nytimes.com/2012 /01/26/business/ieconomy-apples-ipad-and-the-human-costs-for-workers -in-china.html?pagewanted=all.

21. Duhigg and Barboza conclude their article on the manufacturing of iPads in China by citing an anonymous Apple executive who makes the situation perfectly clear. He claims, "You can either manufacture in comfortable, worker-friendly factories, or you can reinvent the product every year, and make it better and faster and cheaper, which requires factories that seem harsh by American standards." Duhigg and Barboza, "In China."

22. Modernity begins with the critique of unnecessary sacrifices that premodern society demands, sacrifices that most often include the sacrifice of knowledge. The Inquisition burned Giordano Bruno in 1600 as the embodiment of knowledge that it had to sacrifice in order to sustain the structure of traditional society. But even though he died, time was in fact on Bruno's side.

23. The fetishistic disavowal at work in consumption becomes especially evident during holiday sales. Consumers can say that they awaken at 3 AM and stand in line for hours in order to save money, but the situation is actually the reverse. The alibi of saving money enables them to enjoy sacrificing their sleep and free time standing in line for products that they might not even desire otherwise.

24. It is no accident that Supreme Court Justice Antonin Scalia compared President Obama's mandate to purchase health care (part of the 2009 Affordable Heath Care Act) to a demand that citizens eat broccoli. Scalia and other conservatives objected to the forced expenditure because of its association with utility rather than with enjoyment and sacrifice. If Obama had proposed a mandate that everyone purchase a handgun for sport hunting, one can guess that Scalia might have found this compulsion justifiable.

25. Marxist economist Ernest Mandel believes that capitalism's excessive waste renders it existentially untenable as a system. In *Late Capitalism*, he claims, "The dynamic of the wastage and destruction of the potential development that is henceforward involved in the actual development of the forces of production, is so great that the sole alternative to the self-destruction of the system, or even of all civilization, is a higher form of society." Ernest Mandel, *Late Capitalism*, trans. Joris De Bres (New York: Verso, 1978), 222. Mandel's mistake here lies in his failure to recognize the enjoyment associated with waste. The "wastage and destruction" of capitalism is not an argument against the system, but an argument for it.

26. Werner Sombart, *The Quintessence of Capitalism: A Study of the History and Psychology of the Modern Business Man*, ed. and trans. M. Epstein (New York: Howard Fertig, 1967), 351.

27. The negative effect of future abundance on investment drives companies to constantly invent new products. The new product, at least temporarily, avoids the trap of future abundance that inheres in every commodity. But the invention of the new must take place at a rapid enough pace to outstrip not just the realization of abundance but even the envisioning of it. This is necessary to counteract a negative impact on investment in the company.

28. John Maynard Keynes, *The General Theory of Employment, Interest, and Money* (New York: Harcourt, 1964), 105.

29. Paul Baran and Paul Sweezy make this point about useless military spending from a more critical perspective in their *Monopoly Capitalism*. Despite its age and the inaccuracy of some of its analyses, their work retains value for its insights into capitalism's necessary destructiveness. See Paul A. Baran and Paul M. Sweezy, *Monopoly Capital: An Essay on the American Economic and Social Order* (New York: Monthly Review Press, 1966).

30. Keynes, *The General Theory of Employment*, 131.

31. Contemporary conservative economists who attack Keynes and Franklin Roosevelt by arguing that it was World War II, not the New Deal, that rescued the American economy fail to realize exactly what this statement indicates about the essence of capitalism. While they defend capitalism as an inherently just and moral system (that rewards the hardworking and punishes the lazy), the claim that the senseless sacrifice involved in war was necessary for economic recovery gives the lie to any pretense of an ethical capitalism.

32. Léon Walras, *Elements of Pure Economics, or the Theory of Social Wealth*, trans. William Jaffé (London: George Allen and Unwin, 1954), 73.

33. This profound limitation of the capitalist economist becomes evident in what seems like an uncontroversial statement by Lionel Robbins. In the midst of arguing that economics does not import moral valuations into the objects of its study, he proceeds to do so and consequently display capital-

ism's profound aversion to unnecessary sacrifice. He says, "it is not legitimate to say that going to war is uneconomical, if, having regard to all the
issues and all the sacrifices necessarily involved, it is decided that the anticipated result is worth the sacrifice. It is only legitimate so to describe it if
it is attempted to secure this end with an unnecessary degree of sacrifice."
Robbins, *An Essay on the Nature and Significance of Economic Science*, 144.
Robbins's claim that capitalist economics can allow for sacrifice when it is
necessary and worth the price represents a complete misunderstanding of
the nature of sacrifice. Sacrifice cannot be a good bargain and remain sacrifice. It is only under the deformation of capitalism that sacrifice undergoes
this dramatic transformation.

34. Karl Marx, *Grundrisse*, trans. Martin Nicolaus (New York: Penguin, 1993), 92.
35. The number of failed commodities produced each year is astonishing. Because so many different commodities surround us all the time, it is difficult
to remember those that have not caught on among consumers. With car-
bonated sodas, the various failures stand out more clearly: Pepsi Free, New
Coke, Cherry Pepsi, Vanilla Coke, and many others.
36. David Ricardo, *The Principles of Political Economy and Taxation* (Mineola,
NY: Dover, 2004), 5.
37. Deleuze and Guattari proclaim, "Every time a desire is betrayed, cursed, uprooted from its field of immanence, a priest is behind it. The priest cast the
triple curse on desire: the negative law, the extrinsic rule, and the transcendental ideal." Gilles Deleuze and Félix Guattari, *A Thousand Plateaus: Capitalism and Schizophrenia*, trans. Brian Massumi (Minneapolis: University
of Minnesota Press, 1987), 154.
38. Georges Bataille, "The Jesuve," in *Visions of Excess: Selected Writings, 1927–
1939*, trans. Allan Stoekl (Minneapolis: University of Minnesota Press, 1985), 73.
39. For Bataille's most sustained discussion of the role that sacrifice plays in
human society, see Georges Bataille, *The Accursed Share*, vol. 1, trans. Robert
Hurley (New York: Zone, 1991).

5. A GOD WE CAN BELIEVE IN

1. Spinoza's effort to maintain God as the only substance in the *Ethics* occurred
in response to this threat. This theological turn was not an acceptable solution for Church authorities, however, who essentially prevented the publication of Spinoza's masterpiece in his lifetime. The problem with Spinoza's
extension of God as the sole and unique substance is that it does not correct
the uprooting of social authority that the heliocentric theory enacts. God
does not regain a place in Spinoza's thought. But neither does Spinoza adequately come to terms with modernity's dislocation of God. It would fall to
Hegel to recognize the implications of this dislocation when he grasps that

substance is itself subject, that substance suffers from the same self-division as the subject.

2. The through line that leads from the dislocation of God to the execution of the monarch supports Albert Camus's statement in *The Rebel* that God, not Louis XVI, is the real target of the guillotine.

3. Perhaps the greatest difference between liberal and dialectical philosophers concerns the definition of freedom. For the former, freedom is simply the ability to do what one wants. For the latter, it requires a break from the substantial order that produces the subject and its desires. If I act just how the social substance ordains me to act, the dialectical thinker believes that this cannot be freedom.

4. In the Third Meditation, Descartes grants to God the attributes of an Other that he as a subject lacks. This represents a clear failure to accede to Hegel's dictum from *The Phenomenology of Spirit* that we must grasp substance as subject. For Descartes, substance is really substance—and thus a substantive Other on which one can rely. Even Descartes's lack of knowledge about God is not a barrier to this reliance. He states, "It does not matter that I do not grasp the infinite, or that there are countless additional attributes of God which I cannot in any way grasp, and perhaps cannot even reach in my thought; for it is in the nature of the infinite not to be grasped by a finite being like myself." René Descartes, *Meditations on First Philosophy*, trans. John Cottingham (Cambridge: Cambridge University Press, 1986), 32.

5. Alenka Zupančič, *Ethics of the Real: Kant, Lacan* (New York: Verso, 2000), 61.

6. Immanuel Kant, *Critique of Practical Reason*, in *Practical Philosophy*, ed. and trans. Mary J. Gregor (New York: Cambridge University Press, 1996), 190. Kantian morality not only eliminates God as a starting point, but it reverses the relationship between the good and morality. The good doesn't determine morality, but the moral law determines the good.

7. Kant sees that our role in determining the moral law constitutes us as free subjects, and he thus reverses the typical relationship between freedom and morality. It is not the moral law that depends on our freedom but our freedom that depends on the existence of the moral law. As Henry Allison puts it, "freedom is actual, or better, actualized, in the interest that we take in the moral law." Henry E. Allison, *Kant's Theory of Freedom* (Cambridge: Cambridge University Press, 1990), 248. Without the existence of the moral law, the question of our freedom would simply remain an open question, as it does for all philosophers who fail to account for the radical break that the very existence of the moral law introduces.

8. For a more thorough argument for Kant as the inventor of modern freedom, see Paul Eisenstein and Todd McGowan, *Rupture: On the Emergence of the Political* (Evanston, IL: Northwestern University Press, 2012).

9. Ludwig von Mises, *Human Action: A Treatise on Economics* (New Haven: Yale University Press, 1949), 280.

10. The defenders of capitalism almost without exception frame their defense in terms of the trade-off between freedom and equality. They sacrifice some equality for the sake of complete freedom. But this very way of conceiving the problem hides the absence of freedom in the free market.

11. Von Mises, *Human Action*, 259.

12. In her discussion of the relationship between capitalism and religious belief, Kiarina Kordela points out that the belief that capitalism demands is far more oppressive than earlier forms of belief because it is wholly unconscious and irrational, though it exists within a rational system. She says, "the epistemological fact that the Other of a secular society is not logically grounded hints not to any liberation of the subject from it. Rather, it is an indication of the nonrepresentable, subliminal, and unconscious character of the containment of the subject within the social Other. When reason and representation fail, belief takes over—belief in something irrational, not accountable by means of reason, and as such absolute." A. Kiarina Kordela, "Political Metaphysics: God in Global Capitalism (the Slave, the Masters, Lacan, and the Surplus)," *Political Theory* 27, no. 6 (1999): 790.

13. Even the greatest capitalist heretic, Karl Marx, accepts the fundamental premise of the capitalist system. Marx envisions communist society as a society of unlimited productivity, which is a reformulation of the capitalist ideal itself rather than a rejection of it. Though Marx does reject the free market, he remains within the logic of capitalism at the central point of his alternative economic conception. He fails to be heretical enough.

14. F. A. Hayek, *The Road to Serfdom* (Chicago: University of Chicago Press, 2007), 151. In addition to giving the lie to Hayek's professions of absolute devotion to freedom, his statement has the additional virtue of illustrating the heavy lifting that utility does for the great defenders of capitalism.

15. Hayek writes, "'freedom' refers solely to a relation of men to other men, and the only infringement on it is coercion by men." F. A. Hayek, *The Constitution of Liberty* (Chicago: University of Chicago Press, 2011), 60.

16. When Nietzsche proclaims the death of God in *The Gay Science*, he is simply describing the process that capitalist modernity has unleashed, not arguing for disbelief in God. We don't recognize the event and remain removed from it because we moved so quickly to the new manifestation of God, what Nietzsche would see as the Last Man, a social authority that refuses to avow its authority.

17. Baruch Spinoza, *The Ethics*, trans. Samuel Shirley (Indianapolis: Hackett, 1992), 59.

18. F. Scott Fitzgerald, *The Great Gatsby* (New York: Scribner, 2004), 167.

19. Not only do advertisements offer us relief from freedom by erecting a new figure of the Other, but they also simultaneously transform freedom into choice. This transformation removes freedom from the level of the ontological and turns it into an empirical question about particular commodities. The question of freedom is a question, as existentialists like Søren Kierkegaard and Jean-Paul Sartre understand, of the project that defines my existence. I am free to decide what project will define me, even if external forces conspire to limit my possibilities for realizing this project. This ontological freedom represents a heavy burden for the subject because no Other can define my project for me. Capitalism provides an Other who could do so, and it deflects the terrain of this freedom onto that of empirical choice. The capitalist subject does not have to confront the question of what project will define its existence. Instead, it must decide what brand of cough medicine to purchase. Anyone who has tried to purchase cough medicine will know that this decision is every bit as vexed as that of one's existential project, but one has the support of the Other when making it, a support that does not exist for one's existential project.

20. David Wilson and William Dixon, "*Das Adam Smith Problem*: A Critical Realist Perspective," *Journal of Critical Realism* 5, no. 2 (2006): 251.

21. Adam Smith, *The Theory of Moral Sentiments* (New York: Penguin, 2009), 13.

22. Samuel Fleischacker, *On Adam Smith's "Wealth of Nations": A Philosophical Companion* (Princeton: Princeton University Press, 2004), 57.

23. Though Smith could not have read Kant, the converse is not true. Kant was acquainted with and appreciated Smith's moral philosophy, even though Kant's emphasis on the moral law departs significantly from Smith's reliance on sentiment. Kantian morality is thoroughly unsentimental, which is why the question of Adolf Eichmann as a figure of Kantian moral duty could ever arise. It is clear that Eichmann fails the standards of Smith's morality of compassion, but less clear (though ultimately the case) that he fails from a Kantian moral perspective.

24. In *The Philosophy of History*, Hegel claims, "This may be called the *cunning of reason*—that it sets the passions to work for itself, while that which develops its existence through such impulsion pays the penalty, and suffers loss." G. W. F. Hegel, *The Philosophy of History*, trans. J. Sibree (New York: Dover, 1956), 33. For Smith, the pursuit of wealth creates suffering rather than joy for those engaged in it, but this activity ends up providing society with its material needs. Smith argues that it is the particular that "pays the penalty" for the sake of the general interest, which puts him at odds with capitalism's emphasis on the individual.

25. Smith, *The Theory of Moral Sentiments*, 215.

26. Adam Smith, *An Inquiry Into the Nature and Causes of the Wealth of Nations* (Hamburg: Management Laboratory Press, 2008), 345.

27. In his appendix to *The Kingdom and the Glory*, Giorgio Agamben points out the undoubtedly "biblical origin" of Smith's metaphor of the invisible hand. He then goes on to note how capitalist modernity remains within the constraints of a divine authority. Agamben writes, "when modernity abolishes the divine pole, the economy that is derived from it will not thereby have emancipated itself from its providential paradigm." Giorgio Agamben, *The Kingdom and the Glory*, trans Lorenzo Chiesa (Stanford: Stanford University Press, 2011), 285.

28. In a revelatory passage from *Seminar VI*, Lacan states, "the desire of the neurotic, I will say, is that which is born when there is no God." Jacques Lacan, *Le Séminaire, livre VI: Le désir et son interprétation, 1958–1959*, ed. Jacques-Alain Miller (Paris: Martinière, 2013), 541. Lacan identifies the emergence of neurosis with the death of God because neurosis relies on a psychic investment in the existence of an Other that evidently doesn't exist. Prior to the death of God, the Other did really appear to exist, which obviated the possibility of neurosis. This is why psychoanalysis did not form until after the development of capitalism and its installation of a new form of the Other.

29. Karen Horney, *The Neurotic Personality of Our Time* (New York: Norton, 1937), 188.

30. The idea of an unknowing Other becomes thinkable for the first time in the capitalist epoch, but this provides the possibility for rethinking the concept of God itself in these terms. Rather than an omniscient God, we should posit an unknowing God. This is the conception of God developed by Richard Boothby (Loyola University, Maryland). According to Boothby, it is only by reconceiving God as unknowing and not by rejecting the God hypothesis altogether that we can see the possibility of human freedom. Boothby accomplishes this through an astonishing interpretation of Hegel's philosophy, where Boothby identifies the first philosophical formulation of the figure of the unknowing God. See Richard Boothby, "Hegel with Lacan: On the Other in Question," unpublished MS.

31. Jacques Lacan, *Le Séminaire XII: Problèmes cruciaux pour la psychanalyse, 1964–1965*, unpublished seminar, session of June 16, 1965.

6. A MORE TOLERABLE INFINITY

1. Georg Lukács, *The Young Hegel: Studies in the Relations Between Dialectics and Economics*, trans. Rodney Livingstone (Cambridge: MIT Press, 1976), 565.

2. Lukács's investment in Hegel's dialectics would force his retraction, under Stalinist pressure, of his early thought as too idealist. Nonetheless, it is only the early Lukács, the Hegelian Lukács, that retains today any theoretical importance.

3. The translation of *die schlechte Unendlichkeit* as "spurious infinite" for decades chagrined Hegel scholars. The implication of the term *spurious infinite* is that this form of infinity is not infinite at all, whereas Hegel's point is that it is in fact infinite, but bad insofar as it remains dependent on its other in a way that it cannot avow.

4. As W. T. Stace puts it in his classic commentary on Hegel, "True infinity is the self-limited." W. T. Stace, *The Philosophy of Hegel* (New York: Dover, 1955), 146.

5. G. W. F. Hegel, *The Science of Logic,* trans. George di Giovanni (Cambridge: Cambridge University Press, 2010), 119.

6. Of course, many people acknowledge the possibility of the eventual heat death of the universe but remain capitalist subjects insofar as they engage in a fetishistic disavowal of it. They know it will come, but they act as if they don't know.

7. Nicholas Georgescu-Roegen, *The Entropy Law and the Economic Process* (Cambridge: Harvard University Press, 1971), 18. Georgescu-Roegen speculates, on the basis of the Entropy Law, that the destiny of humanity will reach its inevitable conclusion sooner rather than later. The problem is not just the eventual exhaustion of all energy, but the rapidity with which the capitalist system runs through what Georgescu-Roegen calls the human "dowry" of energy by transforming it into waste.

8. F. A. Hayek, *The Road to Serfdom* (Chicago: University of Chicago Press, 2007), 128–29.

9. Niall Ferguson, *The Ascent of Money: A Financial History of the World* (New York: Penguin, 2008), 358.

10. Angus Maddison, *The World Economy: A Millennial Perspective* (Paris: Development Centre of the Organisation for Economic Co-operation and Development, 2001), 17. See also Angus Maddison, *Dynamic Forces in Capitalist Development: A Long-Run Comparative View* (Oxford: Oxford University Press, 1991).

11. The great exponent of the fear of surplus population is, of course, Thomas Robert Malthus, who is also a fervent believer in capitalism. Malthus reconciles these contradictory positions by blaming the lower classes, not the laws of capitalism, for the problems of overpopulation. At the key moment in his thought, he turns from an economist into a moralist and thereby misses what might have been a groundbreaking insight into the relationship between capitalism and population. This turn also earned him the enmity of Marx.

12. David Harvey explains the necessity of expansion as a product of the competitive nature of the capitalist economy. If one capitalist doesn't reinvest capital and expand, another will, and this will eliminate the former qua capitalist. There is no such thing as a static capitalist. Harvey says, "If I, as a

capitalist, do not reinvest in expansion and a rival does, then after a while I am likely to be driven out of business. I need to protect and expand my market share. I have to reinvest to stay a capitalist." David Harvey, *The Enigma of Capital and the Crisis of Capitalism* (Oxford: Oxford University Press, 2011), 43.

13. Even if the earth's population begins to decrease in the future (as current prediction models suggest), this will not spell the death of the capitalist system, but it will mark a radical change. Though capitalism feeds off the expansion of population, it doesn't require it. One can envision a form of capitalism that operates by vastly expanding the number of necessary commodities to compensate for a diminution of laborers and consumers.

14. Many critics of the capitalist system point to the statement of Gordon Gekko (Michael Douglas) in Oliver's Stone's *Wall Street* (1987), "Greed . . . is good," as evidence of the immorality of unrestrained capitalism. In addition to the difficulty that the film presents Gekko as only an isolated immoral capitalist and not as a capitalist as such, the problem with this indictment is that Gekko is correct. Within the capitalist system, greed is good and contributes to the expansion of productivity. But greed undermines itself. That is, the greedy capitalist fails to see how greed constructs the very obstacles that it tries to eliminate.

15. Blaise Pascal, *Pensées*, ed. and trans. Roger Ariew (Indianapolis: Hackett, 2005), 16.

16. Alfred Marshall, *Principles of Economics*, 8th ed. (London: Macmillan, 1961), 93. In order for the bad infinite to guide capitalist production, this production must constantly encounter limits that it can overcome.

17. Ibid., 223.

18. Adam Smith, *An Inquiry into the Nature and Causes of the Wealth of Nations* (Hamburg: Management Laboratory Press, 2008), 412.

19. This is even true of many on the left. The critique of capitalism that Thomas Piketty announces in *Capital in the Twenty-First Century* takes Smith's assumption of infinite movement forward for granted. He criticizes capitalism as a system because it doesn't have enough growth, because the rate of return on investments in capital outpaces growth. This dynamic enriches those who have capital to invest at the expense of those—such as the working class—who must depend on their wages for income. Piketty's solution for fixing this problem of allotment of wealth involves limiting returns through taxes in order to give growth a boost. He doesn't evince any skepticism about the prospect of infinite growth. Piketty doesn't see the divergence between return and growth as an anomaly in the capitalist system but rather as its standard operating procedure. Inequality is the necessary outcome of capitalist relations of production. He says, "the fundamental $r > g$ inequality, the main force of divergence in my theory, has nothing to do with any

market imperfection. Quite the contrary: the more perfect the capital market (in the economist's sense), the more likely r is to be greater than g." Thomas Piketty, *Capital in the Twenty-First Century,* trans. Arthur Goldhammer (Cambridge: Harvard University Press, 2014), 27.

20. The task for the behavioralist is, as Dan Ariely puts it, to provide "tools, methods, and policies that can help all of us make better decisions and as a consequence achieve what we desire." Dan Ariely, *Predictably Irrational: The Hidden Forces That Shapes Our Decisions* (New York: HarperCollins, 2008), 241.

21. The failure of behavioral economics to grasp that subjects might find satisfaction in loss rather than mistakenly opt for it manifests itself in Daniel Kahneman's *Thinking Fast and Slow.* Kahneman recognizes points at which people ensure their own defeat, but such acts must be anomalous for him. He writes, "people who face very bad options take desperate gambles, accepting a high probability of making things worse in exchange for a small hope of avoiding a large loss. Risk taking of this kind often turns manageable failures into disasters. The thought of accepting the large sure loss is too painful, and the hope of complete relief too enticing, to make the sensible decision that it is time to cut one's losses. This is where businesses that are losing ground to a superior technology waste their remaining assets in futile attempts to catch up. Because defeat is so difficult to accept, the losing side in wars often fights long past the point at which the victory of the other side is certain, and only a matter of time." Daniel Kahneman, *Thinking Fast and Slow* (New York: Farrar, Straus and Giroux, 2011), 318–19. One might respond to Kahneman that the losing side often fights when defeat is certain because they find satisfaction in the defeat itself. But such an understanding is impossible for the behavioral economist, who, despite modifications, believes in the pursuit of the good.

22. Bruno S. Frey, *Happiness: A Revolution in Economics* (Cambridge: MIT Press, 2008), 3.

23. A placard on the wall of the gym where my high school football team trained announced, "The biggest room in the world is the room for improvement." This little bit of propaganda could nicely serve as a mantra for capitalism as such.

24. The moments in *Mad Men* when we see Don attain some genuine satisfaction occur when he directly courts failure or embraces his own status as an outsider in relation to the capitalist system. Perhaps the high point of the series in this regard takes place in the final episode of the sixth season when Don unconsciously sabotages a pitch to Hershey's Chocolate and then takes his children to see the dilapidated whorehouse in which he grew up, a childhood that he had previously hidden from them. Unfortunately for Don, the series concludes not with his own satisfaction in loss but with him serving up satisfaction for the sake of advertising Coca-Cola.

25. Rachel Carson, *Silent Spring* (Greenwich, CT: Fawcett, 1962), 129.

26. They proclaim, "A new politics requires a new mood, one appropriate for the world we hope to create. It should be a mood of gratitude, joy, and pride, not sadness, fear, and regret." Ted Nordhaus and Michael Shellenberger, *Break Through: From the Death of Environmentalism to the Politics of Possibility* (Boston: Houghton Mifflin, 2007), 153.

27. When Hegel conceives of nature as the self-externalization of spirit, this is his way of articulating nature as spirit's inherent and yet contingent obstacle. In contrast to the caricature often used to describe his *Philosophy of Nature,* Hegel is in fact perfectly ready to admit natural contingency into his understanding of nature, and he attacks those who insist on imposing a rigid system on the natural world.

28. Michael Sandel, *What Money Can't Buy: The Moral Limits of Markets* (New York: Farrar, Straus and Giroux, 2012), 28.

29. Anna Kornbluh (University of Illinois, Chicago), "Do Not Give Ground on Infinity," unpublished MS.

30. The sole virtue of the misguided *Prometheus* (Ridley Scott, 2012), other than the stunning scene of a self-abortion, is that it shows how far a wealthy capitalist subject will go to extend his expiring life. Peter Weyland (Guy Pearce) finances a deep-space voyage on the basis of a speculative hypothesis about the origin of life in order to discover the source of terrestrial life, and he hopes that this will unlock the secret to extending his own life. But the happy result is that the discovery only hastens his death.

31. As Heidegger puts it, "Dying is something that every Dasein itself must take upon itself at the time." Martin Heidegger, *Being and Time*, trans. John Macquarrie and Edward Robinson (San Francisco: HarperCollins, 1962), 284.

32. Søren Kierkegaard, *The Sickness Unto Death: A Christian Psychological Exposition for Upbuilding and Awakening,* trans. Howard V. Hong and Edna H. Hong (Princeton: Princeton University Press, 1980), 18.

33. Despite his clear debt to Heidegger, one might convincingly make the argument that Jean-Paul Sartre in the greater philosopher because he turns away from death as the ultimate existential problem and focuses instead on significance. Our real challenge, as Sartre sees it, involves creating a significance for our existence that would enable us to act. Authentic being toward death, Heidegger's ideal, fails to accomplish this.

34. Karl Marx, *Capital: A Critique of Political Economy,* vol. 3, trans. David Fernbach (New York: Penguin, 1981), 358.

35. Ibid., 358–59.

36. The focus on the natural world as a limit stems from its intractable status. The limits that labor and capital represent to production are fungible, but the natural world is not. This is what John Stuart Mill correctly grasps in his theorization of political economy. Mill writes, "The limitation to production,

not consisting in any necessary limit to the increase of the other two elements, labor and capital, must turn upon the properties of the only element which is inherently, and in itself, limited in quantity." John Stuart Mill, *Principles of Political Economy with Some of Their Applications to Social Philosophy*, 2 vols. (New York: Appleton, 1872), 1:228.

37. Karl Marx and Frederick Engels, *The German Ideology* (Moscow: Progress, 1976), 53. This vision of the communist future provides the unacknowledged basis for Gilles Deleuze and Félix Guattari's anticapitalist thought in *Anti-Oedipus* and *A Thousand Plateaus*. Their diatribe against fixed identity and encomium to deterritorialization is an elaboration of the future proclaimed here by Marx and Engels.

7. THE ENDS OF CAPITALISM

1. Joyce Appleby, *The Relentless Revolution: A History of Capitalism* (New York: Norton, 2010), 119.

2. John Stuart Mill, *Utilitarianism*, in *Utilitarianism and On Liberty* (Malden, MA: Blackwell, 2003), 182.

3. Just as utilitarian ethics is isomorphic with the capitalist structure, Kantian ethics is implicitly anticapitalist. In the second formulation of the categorical imperative, Kant rejects treating others as a "mere means" rather than as ends in themselves. For the capitalist, everything and everyone are means to the end of more productivity and more accumulation.

4. The introduction of a newer and better model is not the only way that dissatisfaction subtends consumption. It also manifests itself in the declining price of the product. One waits to buy the product at the best price, but then the price inevitably drops after one has purchased the commodity. Though simply a structural effect of the capitalist system, the dynamic of the dropping price has the effect of bonding the subject to the process of consumption through the dissatisfaction that it creates.

5. It is not difficult to imagine pushing workers to the extreme as an ethical duty. The capitalist does this on behalf of social productivity, which counts more than the discomfort of a few workers and may ultimately redeem this discomfort. One might even imagine a capitalist version of Maurice Merleau-Ponty's *Humanism and Terror*, which functioned as an apology for Stalinism on the basis of the future it would make possible.

6. *Modern Times* echoes the critique of industry's indifference to the worker formulated in René Clair's *À Nous la liberté* (1931). It echoes the earlier film to such an extent that the producers responsible for *À Nous la liberté* sued Chaplin for plagiarism. It was only the intervention of Clair, out of affection for Chaplin and appreciation for his art, that brought the lawsuit to an end.

7. Capitalists have historically resorted to extreme methods—Pinkerton detectives, legal machinations, and even open displays of violence—to put an end to strikes because they recognize implicitly that the strike represents a challenge to the ideal of productivity that guides the capitalist system. The strike is an existential threat to capitalism.

8. Aristotle, *Physics*, trans. R. P. Hardi and R. K. Gaye, in *The Complete Works of Aristotle*, ed. Jonathan Barnes, 2 vols. (Princeton: Princeton University Press, 1984), 1:333.

9. The connection between the idea of the good and the valuation of the final cause is decisive in Aristotle's thought. If one begins with the belief that subjects pursue some good and that this is the motivating factor in all their actions, one necessarily arrives at a conception of the final cause. In every case, some specific good is the final cause on behalf of which subjects act. It is only by abandoning the idea of the good, which capitalism doesn't do, that we can free ourselves definitively from thinking in terms of final causes.

10. Modern science's complete dismissal of the final cause reveals the incompatibility of science and traditional religious belief. The only way to sustain belief and remain a follower of modern science is to adopt Kierkegaard's approach and accept that God manifests itself in the world only in counterintuitive ways and disruptions rather than in the form of final causes. That is, science leaves us with the choice of nonbelief or fideism.

11. When Thomas Nagel tries to revive teleology in modern philosophy, he does so with the express intent of counteracting scientific materialism, even though his teleology attempts to dispense with the divine. For this creative but ultimately failed effort to revive the final cause, see Thomas Nagel, *Mind and Cosmos: Why the Materialist Neo-Darwinian Conception of Nature Is Almost Certainly False* (Oxford: Oxford University Press, 2012).

12. Insofar as we are capitalist subjects invested in productivity, Bruno Latour is correct to claim, as the title of his famous book says, *We Have Never Been Modern*. Of course, this is not Latour's point at all. He wants instead to confound modernity's clean divisions, such as that between subject and object, culture and nature. See Bruno Latour, *We Have Never Been Modern*, trans. Catherine Porter (Cambridge:Harvard University Press, 1993).

13. Ludwig von Mises, *Human Action: A Treatise on Economics* (New Haven: Yale University Press, 1949), 489.

14. The great filmic manifestation of this logic of the final cause in capitalism occurs in *Glengarry Glen Ross* (James Foley, 1992). This film recounts the travails of four salespeople tasked with peddling worthless real estate as if it were an attractive investment. Early in the film, a representative from the main office, Blake (Alec Baldwin), arrives to gives the floundering sales agents a pep talk, in which he upbraids them with great viciousness and with

a pure appeal to the final cause that disregards everything else. He says, "I made $970,000 last year. How much you make? You see pal, that's who I am, and you're nothing. Nice guy? I don't give a shit. Good father? Fuck you! Go home and play with your kids. You wanna work here—close!"

15. It is not accidental that Spinoza functions as the philosophical point of departure for many of the most vehement critics of contemporary capitalism. But the key to Spinoza's value does not lie in his refusal of all negativity, as Marxists like Antonio Negri and Michael Hardt believe, but in his absolute rejection of the final cause, which is a pillar of capitalism's appeal.

16. Giorgio Agamben, "On Potentiality," in *Potentialities*, trans. Daniel Heller-Roazen (Stanford: Stanford University Press, 1999), 182.

17. Agamben's emphasis on impotentiality reveals his proximity to psychoanalysis, despite his refusal to avow this proximity. Perhaps we could risk the thesis that Agamben is too close to psychoanalysis to recognize the resemblance.

18. For Arendt's critique, see Hannah Arendt, *The Human Condition*, 2d ed. (Chicago: University of Chicago Press, 1998). The link between Agamben's critique of capitalism and Arendt's is evident, though Agamben mentions Arendt's critique only in his discussion of the modern reduction of politics to bare life in *Homo Sacer*, not in his description of potentiality and impotentiality.

19. Contemporary theorists of biopower tend to repeat Arendt's error when they reduce existence to the perpetuation of life. Power over the body is always at the same time a provocation for the desiring subject. No social authority cares about the body. It is desire that counts.

20. Those who first started to wear baggy pants weren't trying to begin a fashion trend, which is why they were able to do so. It is emblematic of a paranoid outlook to believe that someone can consciously begin a fashion trend. The trend commences not with an individual decision but with the embrace of a particular style by the anonymous social authority that has no concrete existence.

21. G. W. F. Hegel, *Lectures on the Philosophy of World History*, vol. 1: *Manuscripts of the Introduction and Lectures of 1822–23*, eds. and trans. Robert F. Brown and Peter C. Hodgson (Oxford: Clarendon, 2011), 418. Just to be clear, if he had to vote, Hegel would certainly have voted to exculpate Socrates, but only because he is a modern, a devotee of the freedom of the subject.

22. Alain Badiou, for instance, considers May 1968 the most recent candidate for the status of a political event. Though its status remains up in the air, the responsibility for constituting it as an event falls to those who would be faithful to it. Through fidelity to the rupture of May 1968, subjects will retroactively give it the status of a political event in Badiou's way of thinking.

23. This is, of course, the slogan of LSD proponent Timothy Leary.

24. The use of the limp body is also a common strategy of young children who want to resist the regime of productivity—going to grandma's house, for instance—that parents impose on them. My twins utilized this technique of nonproductivity so often that we began to label it, "Going Savio." This label did not lessen the frustration that the technique created, a frustration that bespeaks its effectiveness.

25. Luc Boltanski and Eve Chiapello, *The New Spirit of Capitalism*, trans. Gregory Elliott (London: Verso, 2005), 168.

26. Simon Critchley advocates an active refusal to take up the question of ruling and to flee from state power. This distancing lies at the heart of his definition of politics. In his most significant book (which includes "Politics of Resistance" in the subtitle), he claims, "politics is the praxis of taking up distance with regard to the state, working independently of the state, working in a situation." Simon Critchley, *Infinitely Demanding: Ethics of Commitment, Politics of Resistance* (London: Verso, 2007), 112. Critchey's insistence on resistance deliberates avoids the question of what type of state one will resist. No matter how just the state, resistance will always be in order for Critchley, which conveniently allows him to rely on someone else to make the decision that founds the state.

27. In *The Century*, Badiou notes, "what fascinated the militants of the twentieth century was the real. In this century there is a veritable exaltation of the real, even in its horror." Alain Badiou, *The Century*, trans. Alberto Toscano (Malden, MA: Polity, 2007), 19.

28. G. W. F. Hegel, *Elements of the Philosophy of Right*, ed. Allen W. Wood, trans. H. B. Nisbet (Cambridge: Cambridge University Press, 1991), 21–22.

8. EXCHANGING LOVE FOR ROMANCE

1. The ubiquity of mirrors at the gym does not speak simply to the narcissistic status of bodily fitness but to the transformation of the participant into a commodity. While working out and after doing so, one looks at oneself in the mirror from the perspective of the admiring other, as potentially lovable.

2. Even fast food restaurants like McDonalds use the prospect of love as a way to advertise a product as unromantic as Chicken McNuggets. There is no commodity that cannot overlap with the fantasy of love.

3. It is possible, of course, to imagine capitalism without the continued existence of romantic love in its present form, but not without some form of it. Romantic love is the sine qua non of the capitalist universe because it provides for us an idealized version of the commodity through which we learn how to evaluate every other commodity.

4. One should not somehow feel exempt from the capitalist ideology of love if one has managed to avoid the use of dating services. The dating service simply lays bare the logic that undergirds romantic relations as such in the capitalist universe, and its political value consists in fully exposing the logic that would otherwise remain partially obscured. It is not the users of dating services who should feel guilty, but those of us who have avoided them in order to guard the illusion of purity in romance. We are the ones with the real blood on our hands.

5. Joan Copjec, *Imagine There's No Woman: Ethics and Sublimation* (Cambridge: MIT Press, 2002), 79.

6. The fact that Plato gives a compelling speech about love to Aristophanes also complicates any interpretation of the dialogue since Aristophanes publicly mocked Socrates in his comedy *The Clouds*. One might expect Plato to avenge himself on Aristophanes by attributing a ridiculous theory to him, but Plato refuses to do so. Even if Plato doesn't identify himself with the conception of love that Aristophanes proffers, and even if it has a fanciful quality to it, no one can miss its metaphorical resonance with the experience of love.

7. The purity of Socrates famously manifests itself in his relationship to alcohol. As Alcibiades points out, "though he didn't much want to drink, when he had to, he could drink the best of us under the table. Still, and most amazingly, no one ever saw him drunk." Plato, *Symposium*, trans. Alexander Nehemas and Paul Woodruff, in *Plato: Complete Works*, ed. John M. Cooper (Indianapolis: Hackett, 1997), 501. Socrates' inability to get drunk parallels his inability to love insofar as both involve giving oneself up to the other.

8. Ibid., 498.

9. Of course, no subject can attain purity, but Socrates is a character created by Plato, not an actual subject.

10. Juan Pablo Lucchelli, *Métaphores de l'amour* (Rennes: Presses Universitaires de Rennes, 2012), 57.

11. Jean-Paul Sartre, *Being and Nothingness*, trans. Hazel E. Barnes (New York: Washington Square Press, 1956), 490.

12. Though Sartre is one of the great anticapitalist thinkers in modernity, his refusal of the unconscious constantly undermines his capacity to think outside capitalism's own terrain. Love represents an exemplary case of this, which Sartre's own life bore out. He treated lovers as commodities to be acquired, and when they no longer provided satisfaction, he moved on to the next one. His failed theory of necessary and contingent love marks an attempt to separate these acts from the commodity logic that underwrites them.

13. The apparent exception here occurs in the film *Lars and the Real Girl* (Craig Gillespie, 2007), in which Lars (Ryan Gosling) does seem to fall in love with

a blow-up doll. Though other characters in the film play along with Lars and treat the blow-up doll as a real love object, in the end Lars himself must abandon this object because of its evident inadequacy. The blow-up doll is too perfect to be loved.

14. Denis de Rougement, *Love in the Western World*, trans. Montgomery Belgion (New York: Harcourt Brace, 1940), 45. Perhaps the most important insight in Rougemont's work is his understanding that love clearly predates capitalism. Though he never mentions capitalism in so many words, Rougement begins the history of love well before its advent, even as he does show how capitalist modernity alters it.

15. The pathos of this attitude becomes painfully evident at the conclusion of Patricia Highsmith's masterpiece *The Cry of the Owl*. The novel ends with the character Greg guilty of murder and perhaps facing the death penalty, but as he explains himself to the police, he insists to them that he had sex on two occasions with the married Nickie, even though this does nothing to exculpate him. Greg wears his sexual conquests of Nickie like a badge of honor. They indicate to him that he has really accumulated a satisfying object, though the disinterest of the police exposes the folly of this line of thought.

16. Jacques Lacan, *Le Séminaire, livre XVI: d'un Autre à l'autre, 1968–1969*, ed. Jacques-Alain Miller (Paris: Seuil, 2006), 232.

17. Jacques Lacan, *Le Séminaire, livre VIII: le transfert, 1960–1961*, ed. Jacques-Alain Miller (Paris: Seuil, 2001), 216.

18. In his *Seminar XII*, Lacan provides the most refined version of what would become his classic definition of authentic love (which appears in a slightly different form in *Seminar IV*). He says, "Love is giving what one doesn't have to someone who doesn't want it." Jacques Lacan, *Le Séminaire XII: Problèmes cruciaux pour la psychanalyse*, unpublished seminar, session of March 17, 1965.

19. The first clue that one is falling out of love is that the negative quality of the beloved regains its negative valence. This occurred to me when I began to find a distinctive mark on my romantic partner's face repulsive, whereas before I had always viewed it as a sign of her singularity. Unfortunately, it required two years for this repulsion to manifest itself in the end of the relationship.

20. Alain Badiou (with Nicolas Truog), *Éloge de l'amour* (Paris: Flammarion, 2009), 15–16. See also Alain Badiou, *Being and Event*, trans. Oliver Feltham (New York: Continuum, 2005).

21. I once received a poem from a paramour on Valentine's Day that captures this idea perfectly. It read, "It may be a capitalist plot / But I really like you a lot / So I'm sending you this Valentine's Day card / Whether you like it or not." The poem did not change my belief in the ideological nature of the

holiday, but it did serve as a reminder that a capitalist plot is never just a capitalist plot. Every such plot must have a kernel of authenticity in order to be effective.

22. In his *Seminar V*, Lacan describes the process of substitution of a personal authority for a social one. He says, "Since everything depends on the Other, the solution is to have an Other all to oneself. This is what one calls love. In the dialectic of desire, it is a question of having an Other to oneself." Jacques Lacan, *Le Séminaire, livre V: les formations de l'inconscient, 1957–1958*, ed. Jacques-Alain Miller (Paris: Seuil, 1998), 133.

23. One of the weaknesses of George Orwell's *1984* lies in Orwell's inability to imagine love functioning as an ideology (or as romance). But this is also a strength of the novel because it leads Orwell to emphasize the disruptiveness of love for a seemingly omnipotent power structure. The love between Winston and Julia represents a genuine threat. In order to become a proper subject of the power structure again, Winston must renounce Julia and his love for her.

24. Advancing telephone technology makes it increasingly difficult to hide multiple calls because most phones now register incoming calls. This means that one will know how many times a lover has tried to call within a given time. Once a beloved finds out that a lover has called fifty times in the last hour, the lover will most likely fall from grace or receive a visit from the police. The result is that this form of trauma associated with love—the call without any response—will likely become less frequent.

25. Because of its straightforward celebration of complementarity, one of the great ideological moments in the history of cinema occurs at the end of Cameron Crowe's *Jerry Maguire* (1996), when Jerry (Tom Cruise) tells Dorothy Boyd (Renée Zellweger), "You complete me."

26. Romantic comedies almost always focus on characters with an adequate amount of wealth, so that even when they find themselves unemployed, like Kathleen Kelly (Meg Ryan) in Nora Ephron's *You've Got Mail* (1998), they never despair about how they will pay the rent.

27. The other genre that often resorts to the montage sequence, the sports film, does so for a similar reason. The montage in the sports film is almost inevitably a training montage—depicting but compressing the labor required for the final victory. The specific function of this montage is to hide labor itself in order to create the impression that we can have the commodity (a victory) without the labor necessary to produce it. One of the virtues of the apparently wholly ideological *Miracle* (Gavin O'Connor, 2004), a film celebrating the Olympic triumph of the 1980 United States hockey team, is its commitment to displaying as fully as possible the labor that makes the triumph possible.

28. When discussing the romantic comedy as a genre in a film class, a student claimed that the films compress the time of falling in love because this is

the most boring time in a relationship. This response itself—and its obvious falsity—testifies to the effectiveness of capitalism's replacement of love with romance.

29. Capitalist society not only transforms romantic love (or eros) into romance, but it always does the same with Christian love (or agape). Christ welcomes the love of followers, but his love, like that of a beloved, turns back to the follower in a traumatizing way. Christ's response to love never allows the subject to remain in the safety of a social identity but demands that the subject abandon this identity for the sake of Christ. For the faithful, Christ must occupy the place of the Other and become the reference point for the organization of the subject's being. Christians cannot just have their Christian love be a part of their identity. It must encompass that identity entirely, a fact illustrated powerfully throughout the Gospels. To be in Christian love, as Christ shows in his response to the rich man who wants to know what he must do to win eternal life, is to abandon all our former pleasures in the world. To want love without this devastation is not to want love at all, but to prefer romance. Though we might chuckle at the prospect of a romance with Christ, this is what the capitalist version of Christianity offers. Christian love devastates the beloved and takes from her or him what is most valuable. It is not a commodity that one can acquire. But under capitalism, Christianity becomes a romance comedy that ends with the discovery of one's soul mate in Christ.

9. ABUNDANCE AND SCARCITY

1. Nicholas Xenos contends that "the hunters have very few needs, and those that they have are satisfied with relative ease." Nicholas Xenos, *Scarcity and Modernity* (New York: Routledge, 1989), 2–3. Xenos contends that scarcity is an invention of the capitalist world, which employs it as an ideological justification for capitalist relations of production.

2. One of the great social achievements of capitalism is its elimination of direct physical violence as ubiquitous in the social order. Though capitalism perpetuates horrible violence in the general form of the oppression of labor and the specific form of, say, mining disasters, it largely eliminates direct expropriation by one person of what another has. The system itself does the dirty work, for the most part.

3. Even though he is an evolutionary psychologist rather than a capitalist economist, Steven Pinker revealed his status as an implicit defender of the capitalist system during a talk at the University of Vermont entitled "War and Peace: A History of Violence" (October 10, 2013). During the question and answer period, Pinker claimed, in response to a question about capitalism creating an increasing amount of poverty, that poverty was simply the nat-

ural state of the world. The assumption of a basic scarcity is the fundamental capitalist assumption, and it has no empirical, let alone ontological, justification. When one makes this assumption, one lays one's cards on the table, and the audible gasps from the audience testified implicitly to the revelation that occurred.

4. David Ricardo, *The Principles of Political Economy and Taxation* (Mineola, NY: Dover, 2004), 75.

5. In *The Order of Things*, Michel Foucault theorizes scarcity not as a necessary presupposition of capitalism itself but the result of the development of economics in the nineteenth century. As he says, "What makes economics possible, and necessary, then, is a perpetual and fundamental situation of scarcity." Michel Foucault, *The Order of Things: An Archaeology of the Human Sciences* (New York: Random House, 1971), 256–57. Even in Foucault's analysis, however, scarcity has a place within thought from the moment of capitalism's emergence, which it didn't actually have. It falls to Ricardo to give it the priority that it comes to have in what Foucault calls the modern episteme.

6. It would be nice if its association with the assumption of natural scarcity led to economics being known as the "dismal science." But the pejorative appellation, invented by Thomas Carlyle, actually stems from Carlyle's disappointment that economics—what Carlyle calls the logic of supply and demand, since the label "economics" didn't exist yet—eliminated the justification for the forced labor of slavery. Thus, considering its origins, economists should wear the name "dismal science" like a badge of honor.

7. Lionel Robbins, *An Essay on the Nature and Significance of Economic Science*, 3d ed. (New York: New York University Press, 1984), 15. Robbins goes on to offer a succinct definition of economics as the science that deals with how humans cope with the scarcity of means. He claims that it addresses "the forms assumed by human behaviour in disposing of scarce means." Ibid.

8. Léon Walras points out the link between value in the capitalist system and scarcity. He notes, "any value in exchange, once established, partakes of the character of a natural phenomenon, natural in its origins, natural in its manifestations and natural in essence. If wheat and silver have *any value at all*, it is because they are scarce, that is, useful and limited in quantity—both of these conditions being natural." Léon Walras, *Elements of Pure Economics, or the Theory of Social Wealth*, trans. William Jaffé (London: George Allen and Unwin, 1954), 69.

9. Marx, of course, also imagines a future free of scarcity, but it is not a future far away, as it is for the defenders of capitalism. For Marx, capitalism is at once the condition of possibility for the elimination of scarcity and the barrier to that elimination. We needed capitalism at a certain historical moment, but at another it constrains our capacity for abundance. Marx overcomes the contradiction by temporalizing it.

10. Dierdre N. McCloskey, *The Bourgeois Virtues: Ethics for an Age of Commerce* (Chicago: University of Chicago Press, 2006), 125.

11. Ibid., 53.

12. Ibid.

13. It is possible that early humans left the abundance of hunting and gathering for the scarcity of agriculture (which would ultimately lead to the development of capitalism) because they wanted to introduce scarcity into their existence. Historians of this period see no clear evolutionary advantage in the agricultural lifestyle and hence question why humans opted for it. But its advantage may have been its absence of abundance.

14. Freud accepted the seduction theory because he remained too attached to the idea of the living being as the basis of subjectivity rather than the psyche. The living being requires others to encounter excessive stimulation, whereas the psyche finds this excess already within itself.

15. This is not just capitalist ideology, but what is ideological is the idea that society couldn't exist at all without the societal glue of scarcity. In a society without scarcity, the social bond would undergo a profound transformation, but it wouldn't disappear altogether.

16. The vagueness of the fantasy of abundance is not confined to the Qur'an. The same vagueness occurs in Judaism, Christianity, and Marxism. In each case, the vision of the future world of abundance never includes more than a sentence or two of description, just like romantic comedies that only briefly hint at life after marriage. Buddhism seems to be the exceptional religion in this regard. It avoids the promise of abundance and offers a pure scarcity or nothingness instead. But this is a sleight of hand: Buddhist scarcity is just the form of appearance of pure abundance and thus also cannot be adequately described.

17. Juan-David Nasio, *Le Fantasme: le plasir de lire Lacan* (Paris: Payot, 2005), 13.

18. Adam Smith, *The Theory of Moral Sentiments* (New York: Penguin, 2009), 214.

19. Ibid.

20. Like Marx, Lenin spends almost none of his theoretical time on the abundant future but trains his eye completely on the prevailing scarcity. Through this emphasis, Lenin shows that he understands where our satisfaction actually lies—not in the abundance of the future but in today's struggle against scarcity, even when that struggle aims at an abundant future.

21. A powerful critique of a society based of the ideal of pure abundance occurs in an episode from the original *Star Trek* series entitled "This Side of Paradise." In the episode, the *Enterprise* arrives at a colony where everyone is healthy and happy, and the colony produces enough to meet its needs without any disharmony among its members. The catch is that this paradise is the result of spores that have invaded the bodies of the colonists and

completely eliminated their desire. In order to find pure utopia satisfying, the series implies, one must cease to be a desiring subject. Or happiness comes at the expense of enjoyment.

22. The definitive account of the internal failure of the nineteenth-century utopian project is Nathaniel Hawthorne's *The Blithedale Romance*, a novel that far outstrips in importance his much more well-known *The Scarlet Letter*. *The Blithedale Romance* shows how the utopian commune modeled on the actually existing Brook Farm led directly to the self-destructive production of lack even among the most enlightened subjects.

23. Paul Krugman, *Peddling Prosperity: Economic Sense and Nonsense in the Age of Diminished Expectations* (New York: Norton, 1994), 26. The exception, for Krugman, is John Maynard Keynes, who was the first economist to propose a theory of the business cycle that both made sense of it and offered a path toward mitigating its damage.

24. Marxist David Harvey largely avoids this error. See, for instance, David Harvey, *Seventeen Contradictions and the End of Capital* (London: Profile, 2014).

25. One such effort at rethinking is Ernest Mandel's *Long Waves of Capitalist Development*, where Mandel translates the concept of the business cycle into that of waves of capitalist development that crest at a decreasing point, thereby leading gradually to the inevitable collapse of the capitalist system. Mandel preserved the Marxist teleology while integrating capitalism's capacity for recovery from the business cycle's downturn.

26. John Maynard Keynes, *The General Theory of Employment, Interest, and Money* (New York: Harcourt, 1964), 162. Keynes likely takes the term *animal spirits* from David Hume, though Descartes also employs it.

27. Later in *The General Theory of Employment, Interest, and Money*, Keynes chalks up the temporary decline in the animal spirits to the human tendency to save instead of invest. But this is a bizarre explanation from someone who posits the existence of animal spirits, which suggest a capacity for overcoming this tendency. Keynes claims, "there has been a chronic tendency throughout human history for the propensity to save to be stronger than the inducement to invest. The weakness of the inducement to invest has been at all times the key to the economic problem." Ibid., 348–49.

28. Psychoanalysis emerges in response to the subject's experience of abundance, not its encounter with scarcity. This is one reason why patients tend to be well-off rather than impoverished. If one's problem is scarcity or the absence of the object, psychoanalysis can provide no assistance, since it insists that the object is necessarily lost.

29. The entrance into signification renders the human animal a subject of excess because signification itself is excessive. Attempts to explain signification in terms of evolutionary adaptation fail to take this excessiveness of the

signifier into account. Even if language initially promised a better adaptation, it breaks this promise through the excessive suffering that it produces.

30. Ernest Hemingway, *The Sun Also Rises* (New York: Scribner, 2003), 251.

31. The clear decline in Hemingway's fiction has a direct link to his relationship to ontological scarcity. In the novels after *A Farewell to Arms*, characters begin to acquire the capacity to endure this scarcity and even to shine in the face of it. But this endurance only becomes possible with the conversion of ontological scarcity to a mere empirical scarcity. One the Hemingway hero arrives on the scene, ontological scarcity exits, and Hemingway's fiction pays the price.

32. Though time seems to torture Quentin throughout this section of the novel, his obsession with time is actually an attempt to produce scarcity out of abundance. A temporal world is a world where he can dream of one day escaping Caddy's overpresence, which he does when he kills himself. The Quentin section of Faulkner's novel reveals that temporality or scarcity is not our ultimate ontological problem. Abundance is far more vexing.

33. Molly Rothenberg, *The Excessive Subject: A New Theory of Social Change* (Malden, MA: Polity, 2010), 229.

34. Throughout this chapter, I am indebted to Bea Bookchin (University of Vermont) for her thoughts on a postscarcity economy.

10. THE MARKET'S FETISHISTIC SUBLIME

1. In *Seminar VII*, Jacques Lacan offers his classic definition of sublimation. He states, "the most general formula that I can give you of sublimation is the following: it raises an object . . . to the dignity of the Thing." Jacques Lacan, *The Seminar of Jacques Lacan, Book VII: The Ethics of Psychoanalysis, 1959–1960*, ed. Jacques-Alain Miller, trans. Dennis Porter (New York: Norton, 1992), 112.

2. Althusser claims, "In 1845, Marx broke radically with every theory that based history and politics on an essence of man." Louis Althusser, *For Marx*, trans. Ben Brewster (London: Verso, 1969), 227. For Althusser's student, Étienne Balibar, Marx doesn't just break from humanism in 1845 but also from philosophy as such. In *The Philosophy of Marx*, he argues, "The 'Theses on Feuerbach' hence demand a definitive exit (*Ausgang*) from philosophy, as the only means of realizing what has always been its loftiest ambition: emancipation, liberation." Étienne Balibar, *The Philosophy of Marx* (New York: Verso, 1995), 17.

3. Karl Marx and Frederick Engels, *The Communist Manifesto: A Modern Edition*, trans. Samuel Moore (New York: Verso, 1998), 38–39.

4. As Marx puts it in the *Grundrisse*, "There are no absolute values, since, for money, value as such is relative. There is nothing inalienable, since everything is alienable for money. There is no higher or holier, since everything

appropriable by money." Karl Marx, *Grundrisse,* trans. Martin Nicolaus (New York: Penguin, 1993), 839.

5. Karl Marx, *Capital: A Critique of Political Economy,* vol. 1, trans. Ben Fowkes (New York: Penguin, 1976), 163. This analysis of the fetishism of commodities has had a philosophical fecundity that no other part of Marx's thought has experienced. It led directly to Georg Lukács's theorizing of reification and the development of the Frankfurt School that came out of this theorizing.

6. Marx's analysis of the fetishism of the commodity and its immanent tran-scendence is unthinkable outside the background of Hegel's philosophy. Though Spinoza constructs a philosophy of complete immanence, Hegel is the philosopher to grasp transcendence existing only within immanence (though Kant first suggests this possibility). With this philosophical formu-lation, Hegel anticipates and makes possible Marx's theorization of com-modity fetishism. According to Marx, commodification creates transcendence in a wholly immanent universe, and this is the source of sublimity.

7. Immanuel Kant, *Critique of the Power of Judgment,* trans. Paul Guyer and Eric Matthews (Cambridge: Cambridge University Press, 2000), 145.

8. Ayn Rand and her acolytes represent possible exceptions to this rule. It doesn't require a great leap to imagine her mounting the barricades under the flag of capitalism itself.

9. It is tempted to envision the collector as a challenge to the capitalist ethos because the collector assembles what has no use. But the apotheosis of the collector fails to recognize that capitalism itself is nothing but the accumu-lation of the useless in the form of the commodity. We completely fail to understand the commodity if we attach utility to its value.

10. Deirdre N. McCloskey, *The Bourgeois Virtues: Ethics for an Age of Commerce* (Chicago: University of Chicago Press, 2006), 53.

11. This is true for Kant's sublime as well. If we saw the stars as they formed, they would lose their sublime status, which emerges out of our temporal and spatial distance from them.

12. The frustration that every consumer experiences when dealing with exces-sive packaging is akin to the frustration that one experiences during a dif-ficult trek to a holy site. The transcendence is inextricable from the lack of easy access.

13. Depression is not the result of failing to obtain what we want but of recog-nizing that even what we want will not provide the satisfaction that we can imagine. This is why depression is so widespread within capitalism, which relies on the exact structure that produces depression—an image of satis-faction that no experience can ever approximate.

14. I myself have been guilty of this series of purchases for a single film in one instance, but I never watched any of the versions because my initial theatri-cal experience of the film was too traumatic and memorable to repeat.

15. Georg Simmel, *The Philosophy of Money*, 2d ed., trans. Tom Bottomore and David Frisby (New York: Routledge, 1990), 66.

16. The emphasis that marginal utility theory places on the consumer's anticipated satisfaction rather than the consumer's actual satisfaction shows again that the defenders of capitalism expose its psychic appeal much better than its critics. Even this simple observation explains why consumers invest themselves in what actually fails to satisfy them.

17. Carl Menger, *Principles of Economics*, trans. James Dingwall and Bert F. Hoselitz (New York: New York University Press, 1981), 240–41.

18. Immanuel Kant, *Critique of Practical Reason*, in *Practical Philosophy*, ed. and trans. Mary J. Gregor (New York: Cambridge University Press, 1996), 269.

19. According to Walter Davis, this moment, not the abandonment of things in themselves in the first *Critique*, represents Kant's turn toward a lamentable subjectivism. Rather than experiencing the sublimity inhering in the subject's distance from the external world, Kant translates this distance into the subject's internal distance from itself. See Walter A. Davis, *Deracination: Historicity, Hiroshima, and the Tragic Imperative* (Albany: SUNY Press, 2001).

20. For the first theorist who recognizes Hegel as the great critic of capitalist society, see Gillian Rose, *Hegel Contra Sociology* (Atlantic Highlands, NJ: Humanities, 1981).

21. G. W. F. Hegel, *The Phenomenology of Spirit*, trans. A. V. Miller (Oxford: Oxford University Press, 1977), 377.

22. At first glance, Friedman's analysis of capitalist morality seems completely convincing. The idea that one must pay a price for one's prejudices is clearly in evidence when one contemplates a diner that refuses to serve black customers and thus cuts into its possible market. But the problem is that Friedman assumes a neutral starting point for the social order, a social order initially free of any prejudice. At many points throughout the history of capitalism, the refusal to serve a certain clientele did not harm a proprietor's bottom line but rather enhanced it. If one does business in a racist society, then the system penalizes the proprietor for a lack of racism, not a surfeit of it. Friedman fails to see this because an impossible neutrality functions as his system's one a priori category.

23. There are those who do take up the case for the lumpenproletariat and their revolutionary potential. Though much more a Marxist than Said, Frantz Fanon adopts this position. He believes that in the colonial situation capitalist has already bought off the industrial proletariat, but the lumpenproletariat sustain a revolutionary spirit. See Frantz Fanon, *The Wretched of the Earth*, trans. Richard Philcox (New York: Grove, 2004). The great filmic representation of the revolutionary potential of the lumpenproletariat occurs at the conclusion of Ousmane Sembène's *Xala* (1975), where a group of outcasts join together and cover the naked torso of a bourgeois leader with their

spit. This is their response to his betrayal of the country and the revolution to the capitalists from the colonizing power France.

24. In his subsequent *Culture and Imperialism,* the role of capitalism in Said's account becomes more pronounced, though he still does not mention the relationship between the commodity structure and the exotic other. See Edward Said, *Culture and Imperialism* (New York: Vintage, 1993).

25. In this sense, orientalism represents a translation of Foucault's thought to the relation between West and East. Western writers have assembled knowledge about the East with the ultimate aim of obtaining power over this otherness, just like the medical system gains power over bodies by cutting them up and acquiring knowledge about their functioning.

26. Edward Said, *Orientalism* (New York: Vintage, 1978), 222. What separates Hegel from all orientalism, despite denigrating comments about the East, is his refusal to grant any knowledge of the mystery of otherness to the others themselves. The mystery of the Orient, in other words, confounds those in the Orient just as much as it does Westerners. For Hegel, there is no subject supposed to know, as there is for the orientalist, who believes that oriental subjects have access to a secret knowledge and thus do not suffer from the unconscious in the way that Westerners do.

27. Peter Brunette, "Sophia Coppola's Overly Subtle *Lost in Translation,*" Indiewire, www.indiewire.com/movies/movies_030917lost.html.

28. For a more exhaustive (and perhaps exhausting) interpretation of *Lost in Translation,* see Todd McGowan, "There is Nothing Lost in Translation," *Quarterly Review of Film and Video* 24, no. 1 (2006): 53–64.

29. Joseph A. Schumpeter, *Capitalism, Socialism, and Democracy* (New York: Harper, 2008), 137.

30. The position of complete secularity is that of philosophical pragmatism, and this pragmatism is fully compatible with the functioning of capitalism. It suffices to open any book by Richard Rorty to see the ease with which pragmatism accepts capitalism's primary assumptions.

CONCLUSION: ENJOY, DON'T ACCUMULATE

1. Karl Marx, *Capital: A Critique of Political Economy,* vol. 1, trans. Ben Fowkes (New York: Penguin, 1976), 742.

2. The fundamental idea of psychoanalysis lies in the opposite direction from that of capitalism. For psychoanalysis, "Too much is not enough." That is to say, every excessive accumulation results in an unavoidable confrontation with lack, and it is this confrontation that sends the capitalist subject into psychoanalysis.

3. Karl Marx, *Capital: A Critique of Political Economy,* vol. 2, trans. David Fernbach (New York: Penguin, 1978), 199.

Index

Nixon, Richard, 83–84
No Exit. See Sartre, Jean-Paul
Nordhaus, Ted, 147–48, 271*n*26
Notting Hill. See Michell, Roger

Obama, Barack, 58, 252*n*2, 253*n*11, 261*n*24
Objectivism, 75
Object relations psychoanalysis, 27–28
Obsession, 16–17
Occupy movement, 84, 258*n*18
O'Connor, Gavin, *Miracle*, 278*n*27
One Hundred Years of Solitude. See
	Márquez, Gabriel García
Onfray, Michel, 5
Orientalism, 231–35, 286*n*25, 286*n*26
Orwell, George, *1984*, 278*n*23
Owen, Robert, 13, 205

Pascal, Blaise, 143
Peckinpah, Sam, *The Getaway*, 171
Piketty, Thomas, 269–70*n*19
Pinker, Steven, 279–80*n*3
Plato, 116, 181–84, 245*n*1, 276*n*6, 276*n*7,
	276*n*9
Polgreen, Lydia, 261*n*17
Pornography, 171
Postscarcity, 200, 211, 214
Potentiality, 166–67, 274*n*18
Power, 10, 232, 274*n*19
Pretty Woman. See Marshall, Garry
Private language, 52–53
Proletariat, 7–8, 210, 285–86*n*23
Prometheus. See Scott, Ridley
Promise, 11–16, 33, 38, 48, 199, 223–25,
	231, 235–38, 244, 246*n*15
Psycho. See Hitchcock, Alfred
Ptolemy, 115
Putnam, Robert, 60
Les quatre cents coups. See Truffaut,
	François

Qur'an, 203, 281*n*16

Rancière, Jacques, 55, 71, 76, 252*n*6
Rand, Ayn, 76–77, 87, 118, 256*n*6,
	256–57*n*8, 284*n*8
Atlas Shrugged, 74–75

Rational Choice theory, 56–57, 144–45
Rear Window. See Hitchcock, Alfred
Refn, Nicolas Winding, *Drive*, 79–81,
	258*n*16
Reich, Wilhelm, 7–11, 246*n*9, 246*n*10
Renaud, Chris, *The Lorax*, 95
Renton, David, 101
Repression, 5–18, 239, 243, 246*n*13
Revolution, 9, 12–16, 40, 50, 70–71, 77,
	153–56, 172, 214, 229–30, 235
Ricardo, David, 95, 108–10, 198–99, 222
Robbins, Lionel, 96, 198–99, 262*n*33,
	280*n*7
Robson, Mark, *Earthquake*, 139
Roberts, Julia, 193–94
Romeo and Juliet. See Shakespeare,
	William
Roosevelt, Franklin, 58, 83, 252*n*2, 262*n*31
Rorty, Richard, 286*n*30
Rose, Gillian, 285*n*20
Rothenberg, Molly, 214, 255*n*22
Rougement, Denis de, 186, 277*n*14
Rousseau, Jean-Jacques, 51, 54, 69
Russian Revolution, 70–71

Said, Edward, 231–32, 286*n*224,
	285–86*n*23
Sandel, Michael, 148–50
Sarkozy, Nicolas, 76
Sartre, Jean-Paul, 123, 184, 266*n*19, 271*n*33,
	276*n*12; *No Exit (Huis clos)*, 212
Satz, Debra, 148–49
Saussure, Ferdinand de, 24–25, 248*n*7,
	248*n*9
Savio, Mario, 170
Scalia, Antonin, 261*n*24
The Scarlet Letter. See Hawthorne,
	Nathaniel
Schelling, F. W. J., 248*n*7
Schumpeter, Joseph, 90–91, 236, 259*n*2
Scott, Ridley, *Prometheus*, 271*n*30
Second Law of Thermodynamics, 93, 138
Seddon, David, 101
Sembène, Ousmane, *Xala*, 285–86*n*23
September 11, 2001, 44, 236
Sexual liberation, 7–10, 171
Shellenberger, Michael, 147–48, 271*n*26

CPSIA information can be obtained
at www.ICGtesting.com
Printed in the USA
LVHW110021190319
611031LV00005BA/59/P